# Diverse Voices

# Diverse Voices

## Essays on Twentieth-Century Women Writers in English

*Edited by*
**Harriet Devine Jump**

*With a Foreword by*
**Julia Briggs**

St. Martin's Press
New York

First published in the United States of America in 1991

Printed in Great Britain

ISBN 0-312-06189-7

---

*Library of Congress Cataloging-in-Publication Data*

---

Diverse voices : essays on twentieth-century women writers in English
/edited by Harriet Devine Jump : with a foreword by Julia Briggs.
  p.  cm.
  ISBN 0-312-06189-7
  1. American literature-Women authors-History and criticism.
  2. Women and literature-United States-History-20th century.
  3. Women and literature-Great Britain-History-20th century.
  4. American literature-20th century-History and criticism.
  5. English literature-Women authors-History and criticism.
  6. English literature-20th century-History and criticism.
  I. Jump, Harriet Devine
  PS228.W65D8  1991
  820.9'9287-dc20                              91-2001
                                                  CIP

# Contents

*v*

# Foreword

## Julia Briggs

As for the women, who did not
want to be involved, they are involved.

Margaret Atwood's deceptively simple statement relates
the lives of women to the conditions in which they live,
whether they choose to become 'involved', as feminists,
in attempting to change those conditions or whether
they merely live under them in conscious or unconscious
acquiescence. The question of 'involvement' and the
forms it takes remains a central issue for feminist critics
who are engaged in bringing together their academic
work (traditionally supposed to be 'objective', detached
from the world of personal feeling) and their political
commitments as feminists. Political motivations
pursued within the world of academic work have often
been regarded as suspect and feminist criticism has been
drawn towards more impersonal and abstract methods of
description, finding in deconstructive and psycho-
analytical models a set of potentially neutralising yet
adequately complex terms to describe what is hidden in
the power relations between men and women, concealed
within man-made language and women's writing. Yet

the actuality or particularity of women's lives remains the starting point for women writers and critics and though we may be intellectually troubled by an over-simplification inherent in the concept of that actuality our experiences still remain the primary ground for our 'involvement'. The⁻personal and the political cannot ultimately be separated.

Which is one way of describing the origin of this book: most of these essays began as lectures for the women's writing course, an option within the English degree at Oxford University. Apart from myself, nearly all who gave them were graduate students, involved in research but without teaching positions, and we were all conscious that, though most colleges were now mixed, the university as a whole had not entirely awakened from its monastic past. While women were no longer literally marginalised, confined to the women's colleges that edged the town like fringe upon a petticoat, they were still figuratively so, studying within an institution whose values and outlook had been largely determined by men. The aim of this particular lecture course was to throw open some windows, to widen our audience's tastes by introducing them to women writers they might not otherwise come across in the course of their studies, writers whose countries, histories, attitudes might well be unfamiliar. Though feminists, we ourselves came from different backgrounds both geographically (including America, Canada and Australia) and intellectually, and this produced an exhilarating plurality.

The lecture course itself was an alternative event, not only to the generally male-authored English degree but also to our own women's writing course, which had started out in such anxiety to be accepted that it had laid down its own brief canon of authors, initially intended only as a guide line for our earliest students, but rapidly becoming prospective. Thus we regularly lectured on Mary Wollstonecraft, Charlotte Brontë, Emily Dickinson, George Eliot, Virginia Woolf and Sylvia Plath (in an effort to deal even-handedly with England and America, nineteenth and twentieth centuries, novelists and poets), but a second series evolved in which we tried out our pet enthusiasms, whether these were the subjects of our research or simply writers who had meant a lot to us and whom we wanted to share with others. Since we first gave these lectures, the course has been altered in response to changing directions within the subject. Now it begins in the Middle Ages, and this year's lectures took in Dame Julian and Margery Kempe, Mary Wroth and Margaret Cavendish.

Of the nine essays in this book five are concerned with American writers of whom two were expatriates and two were associated with particular regions (Nebraska and the South) while the others are black American poets, with their own particular sense of where their roots lie. The rest are from Canada, Australia, Africa and Ireland and for all of them in different ways the demands of the mother tongue and the motherland are among the central problems encountered in writing from within a patriarchy which alienates women by disinheriting them from both, so that they feel, with Virginia Woolf, that they 'have no country', that they are exiles whether in fact or merely in spirit. Departed imperialisms, in particular, leave in their wake a sense of displacement, of lost roots, which affects the powerless most, and something of this loss is to be heard in the voices of women poets from Ireland and Africa. But all women writers in a society that sees them as 'other' must find or create for themselves a position as subject from which they can begin the long struggle to wrest the male-determined language to their own ends. The diverse ways in which different women writers have addressed language, selfhood and society provide the unifying themes of this book, and though they tackle these themes from a wide variety of angles, subversion, resistance or alienation are always present in some form or another.

It is fitting that the volume should open with Clare

Brant's discussion of Gertrude Stein because, as she demonstrates, Stein's overriding concern was to subvert the way in which language had traditionally functioned. The need for women writers to re-appropriate or remake man-made language is never less than an urgent concern, as French feminists have been quick to recognise, calling for an *écriture feminine*, a concept that Stein in some respects anticipated. Stein could not accept the patriarchal structuring of language and representation ('phallogocentrism') that set out to achieve some predetermined and limited goal and exploited the author's power to limit or determine meaning through the use of a fixed viewpoint, a single perspective, a rigid syntax. The resulting modernist texts are notoriously difficult to read because they rejoice in their own openness, uncertainty and multiplicity. Stein recognised that 'as long as patriarchy controls representation, to be intelligible in conventional ways is to participate in a struggle loaded against women'. Her radical solutions often travelled further than many of her readers could follow, but in her later work she uses language more familiarly and less demandingly, writing about herself in the ironically titled *The Autobiography of Alice B. Toklas,* and on behalf of a feminist cause in her play about the American suffrage worker Susan B. Anthony; here she is more explicitly and politically feminist, adapting traditional language to assail traditional inequalities.

Stein's radical solutions to the problem of man-made language might be connected persuasively with the extent of her alienation – she was Jewish, expatriate and lesbian, although Paris between the wars offered an inner circle of just such outsiders as herself. But, as this essay points out, readers are often only too willing to turn to Stein's biography as a way of avoiding the uncompromising difference of much of her writing, or in order to find reassurance in the comfortable persona that Stein created in her autobiographies. As a result the relation between biography and critical writing on Stein remains uneasy, though this particular unease is by no means confined to Stein. The question of the relationship between the writer and her biography turns out to be the most difficult of all, since the feminine as subject can never be less than problematic; furthermore the writing self is not a person with known boundaries but a fragile, continuously shifting and even disintegrating construct and the character of her writing is determined as much by the male-created language she uses, the male-authored books she has read and the male-dominated age she lives in as by her female body or her personal circumstances. How is she to find the authority of a writer while remaining a woman? It is precisely in the area of her daily experiences, her 'life', that she encounters these undermining influences, however difficult it is for her or for anyone else to reconstruct her experiences of her life adequately. The project of feminism itself is grounded in the felt difference between the lives of men and women and the numerous experiences within language, literature and history that bring difference home to us. The difficulties that women writers encounter in their lives, the nature of their lived experiences, has a determining if not a direct influence on their writing. How or whether we choose to theorise these difficulties may vary; what we cannot do is ignore them altogether.

The next two essays offer contrasting studies in interpretation: my account of Willa Cather is deliberately limited to the terms in which she presented herself to her readers, bringing out the uneasy dialectic in her work between domesticity and creativity, the role of the mother and the role of the artist, between the self and the family, the provincial home town and the wider world, oppositions that are dramatised, but only artificially resolved. Cather, like Eudora Welty and Christina Stead (discussed later in this book), was not personally sympathetic to feminist political programmes or to women's schemes for self-betterment, even though some (by no means all) of her writing draws women on a heroic scale. Though Cather creates occasional moments of reconciliation, there remain central inconsistencies, gaps in explanation, so that art figures in her work as not speaking itself or as logically unnecessary. Such self-contradiction was perhaps inevitable: to be a woman writer celebrating and criticising America in the early years of this century was in itself to break unspoken rules; Cather had absorbed enough of these to be deeply ill at ease with her chosen role.

While my account opens up Cather's inconsistencies, it makes no attempt to deconstruct them. Dianne Chisholm's account of HD, by contrast, starts with the existing biographies and shows why the equation of the artist with her work necessarily involves simplification and distortion, since the writing self is not a 'given' but a 'found'. In this account, HD's writings become a particularly telling example of the woman writer's search for a way of expressing herself, moving through the self-effacing and gender-suppressing mode of her own adopted signature HD and of Imagism itself to an active quest, not so much for her self as for her inner 'other' in autobiography, or as it is here termed, '*autre*biography'. Working with Freud familiarised HD with the notion of the uncanny subject, the concealed self, revealed in a cryptic or occult language or through depersonalising myth. HD's later work describes both the sense of self-loss inherent in being a woman and thus excluded from the system of male meanings, and then the wonder of self-discovery through a series of creative self-definitions in which both loss and self-discovery become part of a wider feminine myth that can be expressed in terms of Helen of Troy or the Virgin Mary. For HD the act of writing becomes, it is suggested, the recovery of the unknown 'other', deep within the self.

Willa Cather was a woman trying to insert herself inconspicuously into a masculine tradition of writing, but Gertrude Stein and HD were modernists, their resistance to traditional language and form driving them on to conduct radical experiments in prose and verse which demand (and here receive) an appropriately sophisticated analysis. Margaret Atwood presents no such obvious obstacles to the reader, but like the other contemporary writers here discussed she is sharply aware of the issues raised by the feminist movement that grew up during the 1960s, and has some serious reservations about its presentation of women as victims when they so often participate in their own victimisation, or else victimise one another. Harriet Jump's essay defines Atwood's attitudes by drawing on her poems and essays, many of which are explicitly concerned with women's oppression, while acknowledging that there are more and less positive ways of responding to the problem. Her own preferred solution is to make use of the activity implied in creativity: in a threatening situation she will talk or write herself out of it. Writing as resistance provides the central theme of *The Handmaid's Tale*, a dystopia set in a hair-raisingly fundamentalist regime in which women are actively colluding in their own oppression. The story is a narrative of progressive politicisation, in which the heroine's experiences awake her to radical awareness and radical action, her most significant act of rebellion being the actual writing of the book itself. Atwood's most recent novel, *Cat's Eye*, is about the cruelty of women to women, but also about the possibility of forgiveness and the refusal of victim status.

The triumphant rejection of victim status is at once more difficult and more energetically won by the black women poets celebrated in Helen Kidd's essay. In order to communicate some sense of the variety and singularity of their achievement she has selected five – June Jordan, Maya Angelou, Alice Walker, Ntozake Shange and Audre Lorde – who between them represent a variety of responses while drawing on common traditions of black music, song and preaching. June Jordan's 'Poem

about My Rights' firmly repudiates the acts of de-
gradation that she has endured as a black woman:

> *I am not wrong: Wrong is not my name*
> My name is my own my own my own
> and I can't tell you who the hell set things up like this

The act of rape lies at the centre of this poem, an act
involving not merely the careless effacement of her
identity but the transference of guilt onto the victim: 'I
am the history of the rejection of who I am'. Rape is seen
as a parallel to the contemptuous invasion and enslave-
ment of black nation by white and so the poem draws in
the dark history of white imperialism, made painfully
immediate in the recent wars in Africa, 'the monster
jackboot ejaculation on Blackland'. The analogies
between rape and imperialism are a recurrent theme in
the work of those women writers and critics who have
been exposed to either, and they are caught up again and
carefully redefined in Clare Wills's essay at the end of the
book.

Yet despite her damning analysis of the workings of
gender and political oppression, elsewhere June Jordan
celebrates her own sexuality, and several of the other
poets in this essay are concerned to 'write the body' and
its desires in very direct ways: 'Does my sexiness upset
you?' challenges Maya Angelou, while Ntozake Shange's
'lady in blue' rejects the white fear of feeling, the
tendency to 'make every thin dry and abstract wit no
rhythm', admitting instead that

> thinkin wont do me a bit of
> good tonite / I need to be loved . . .

Women's need for men is one of the most complicating
and potentially compromising of elements within feminism, since it is in danger of inviting the very exploitation it seeks to avoid; the only escape seems to be into

separatism. Black women writers have been particularly affirmative, in this area as in others, celebrating women's desires both for women and men with an uninhibited joy and openness that is neither coldly ideological nor lacking in self-interrogation.

The Australian novelist Christina Stead described the love of a man as 'one of the best and most momentous things in life'. Stead recognised, rather as Willa Cather had done, the forces that hold women back in terms of home, family, and in her particular case, her father and she fled from these into the life of an expatriate, wandering between Europe, England and America and adopting a leftist politics. In this way, as Kate Lilley demonstrates, she used her exile to displace her sense of inner alienation or enstrangement, grounding it in nationality rather than in gender. She saw escaping from father and Australia as a voyage of self-discovery, freeing her from the net of restraints and expectations and releasing her to find fulfilment in love and writing. Abroad she could be an acknowledged alien, at once responsive to and critical of the world around her, adaptable and mobile within it. Her fiction is focused on the lives of women and her settings derived from her own experiences, but the final goal of self-determination implicit in flight and exile can only be envisaged within a loving and supportive relationship: the bad father is exchanged for a benevolent father-figure, but the patriarch is not entirely outgrown.

Teresa in Stead's *For Love Alone* 'found nothing in the few works of women she could find that was what they must have felt'. Like Stead, the Southern writer Eudora Welty firmly dissociated herself from what she dismissed as 'feminine repartee', preferring to regard writing as an activity 'outside sex', yet as Diane Roberts points out her fiction returns almost compulsively to episodes of rape, the most obvious and violent form of expression that male power can take. In analysing her treatment of this subject, Roberts sees Welty as caught between an anxiety to play down its effects, since the overvaluation of virginity is an aspect of Southern patriarchy that she dislikes, and a recognition that it can lead to a debilitating loss of self. In her fairy-tale treatment of American settlement, *The Robber Bridegroom*, the rapes of the Indian girl and of Rosamond can be associated with acts of territorial conquest and subsequent seizure, but the narrative itself remains enigmatic or perhaps merely follows in the bloody footsteps of history: the Indian girl dies while Rosamond marries her rapist. Welty's heroines, including Rosamond herself, enact resistance but remain trapped in a world of aggressive masculine power.

The last two essays in the collection take up the question of the relationship between the personal and political in women's writing from Africa and Ireland. Caroline Rooney provides an introduction to the writings of the South African Coloured writer Bessie Head and the Ghanaian Ama Ata Aidoo. At the outset, she warns us that their inclusion raises in a particularly delicate form the question that runs through the whole volume, as to what 'feminism' is and whether it is appropriate or appropriating for us to apply it to women writers working within a culture and social structure so different from ours, except in so far as we have succeeded in imposing ours upon theirs. In the careful readings that follow, Rooney suggests ways in which western critics may easily misread African writing, failing to recognise that its sustaining values may be other than those we recognise, that for example the meanings both of love and politics in Head's novel *Maru* may be subtly different from what we suppose them to be. Similarly, Aidoo's texts work to revalue feelings of familial or community relations which are alien to us and these are often invested in women in particular as preservers of their culture from the inroads made both by colonialism and in its wake. African women's writing cannot simply be assimilated into our own forms of feminism since it confronts different problems; it is often concerned to reconsider, even revalue social stabilities that have been interrupted or destroyed by western culture. African women writers are very much alive to the potential conflict between the traditional and the possible roles that women can play within a society that is itself in transition.

Ireland, like Africa, is recovering slowly from a long possession and, as Clair Wills tellingly demonstrates, its women poets are engaged in a search for strategies to relocate themselves within the history and community that are theirs. Dispossessed of both cultural and national identity, they must try to find voices for themselves in a country dominated by an exceptionally masculine poetics, in which the myths of womanhood have continually asserted and idealised the passive and asexual states of virginity and maternity and in which Ireland herself has consistently been figured as a mother, a trope relating sexual to political submissiveness. Eavan Boland has described her project to write herself into the Irish poetic tradition by using the 'truths of womanhood' to throw light on 'the defeats of a nation'. A complicating factor here is that women's social and cultural confinement to a private and personal world has to some extent been statutorily imposed in Ireland, so that Boland has had to resist women's traditional association with narrowly personal or private worlds such as the 'truths of womanhood' might imply. Both Boland and the Belfast poet Medbh McGuckian have sought to widen poetic horizons by strenuously rewriting familiar Irish myths so as to correct what they see as elements of falsification or distortion. Boland has attempted to do this by writing in what had been left out of history and culture; McGuckian's method has been to destabilise existing myths of women, emphasising her dispossession of marginalisation. Both assert their hope of speaking for the community of Irish women even as they seek to redraw the cultural maps of their time.

Though this book has many shared themes, it has no unifying method and individual contributors have approached their very disparate subjects using whatever style they found most sympathetic to their project: just as individual women writers were shaped by their specific cultural determinants, so one critical method may seem more useful than another in working on them. As a result some essays make a complex and subtle use of contemporary feminist theory while others resort to more traditional approaches, assuming an un-problematic relation between the writer's expressed aims, her fictions and perhaps her life. Most of those who draw on theory turn back from time to time to refer to the 'facts' of biography, when and if these seem appropriate. We do not seek to establish a hierarchy among these methods, but rather hope that different critical approaches, like different perceptions of femin-ism itself, will generate that productive and friendly disagreement which we like to think of as characteristic of the state of feminist criticism today.

Julia Briggs
Hertford College, Oxford

# Acknowledgements

I wish on behalf of all of us to acknowledge our debt to the lectures of the women's writing course at the University of Oxford, where most of these essays originated. We are also indebted to our colleagues and our students for their support in establishing this course within the syllabus of the English Faculty. In this connection we look to the founders; in particular our gratitude must be extended to Professor Marilyn Butler who, although not represented directly in this book, none the less in many ways presides over its pages.

Grateful acknowledgement is given to the following copyright holders and publishers for granting permission to reprint material in copyright:

Lines from 'For Each of You' from *Chosen Poems: Old and New* by Audre Lorde, W. W. Norton & Company Inc., 1982 and from 'A Woman Speaks' from *The Black Unicorn*, W. W. Norton & Company Inc., 1978. Reprinted by permission of the publisher.

Lines from 'Hymn', from 'African Images' and from 'Love' from the book *Once* by Alice Walker, Women's Press, 1986, and Harcourt Brace Jovanovich. Reprinted by permission of the publishers.

Lines from 'Still I Rise' from *And Still I Rise* by Maya Angelou, copyright © Maya Angelou, 1978, Virago Press, 1986 and Random House, Inc. Reprinted by permission of the publishers.

Extracts from *Nappy Edges* by Ntozake Shange, Eyre Methuen Ltd., 1987, copyright © 1978 by Ntozake Shange. Reprinted by permission from St. Martin's Press, Inc., New York. From *for coloured girls who have considered suicide when the rainbow is enuf* by Ntozake Shange, Eyre Methuen Ltd., 1978 and Macmillan Publishing Company, New York, 1975, copyright © by Ntozake Shange. Reprinted by permission of the publishers and of Russell & Volkening as agents for the author.

Extracts from 'For the Sake of People's Poetry: Walt Whitman and the rest of us' in *On Call: Political Essays*, by June Jordan, Pluto Press, Boston, 1986; 'Alla Tha's All Right, but', from *Lyrical Campaigns: Selected Poems*, by June Jordan, Virago Press, London, 1989; 'Poem No. 2 for Inaugural Rose', 'Poem for Nana', and 'Poem about my Rights' from *Passion*, by June Jordan, Beacon Press, Boston, 1980.

While every attempt has been made where appropriate to trace the copyright holders of the above material, the editor and publishers would be pleased to hear from any interested parties.

# Notes on Contributors

*Clare Brant* was Junior Research Fellow of St Hugh's College, Oxford and is now Fellow of Jesus College, Cambridge. She works on eighteenth-century letters and eighteenth-century women's writing.

*Julia Briggs* has written on renaissance literature, ghost stories and children's books and is the author of a biography of E. Nesbit. She is currently editing Virginia Woolf and working on a book on Shakespeare for Harvester Wheatsheaf's *Feminist Re-readings* series. She is Fellow and Tutor in English at Hertford College, Oxford and, with Marilyn Butler, was co-founder of the women's writing course at Oxford.

*Dianne Chisholm* was awarded a D.Phil. from Oxford, and is author of the forthcoming study of *H.D.'s Freudian Poetics: Psychoanalysis in Translation* (Cornell University Press). She is an advisory co-editor on *Feminism and Psychoanalysis: A Critical Dictionary*, to be published by Blackwell, and a contributor to the forthcoming *Feminist Companion to English Literature* and the *Dictionary of Contemporary Critical Terms*, to be published by Yale and Toronto University Presses. She has published a number of articles and reviews, and is Professor of English at the University of Alberta.

*Harriet Devine Jump* has published articles on Wordsworth, Coleridge, Akenside and Mary Wollstonecraft and is currently writing a book on Mary Wollstonecraft for Harvester Wheatsheaf's *Key Critics* series. She has held lecturerships in Oxford at Lincoln, St Hilda's and Somerville Colleges and is now Lecturer in English at Edge Hill College, Lancashire.

*Helen Kidd* is co-editor of *New Poetry from Oxford*. Currently writing a thesis on contemporary women poets in Britain and Ireland, she is also co-editing an anthology of women's love poetry from earliest times to the present day, to be published by Virago, and is a part-time lecturer at Oxford Polytechnic. She has had poetry published in magazines and anthologies, and runs creative writing workshops.

*Kate Lilley* took her first degree at the University of Sydney and was awarded a PhD by University College, London for a thesis on 'Masculine Elegy'. She was Junior Research Fellow of St Hilda's College, Oxford, and is now Lecturer in English at the University of Sydney. She works on gender, genre and feminist theory, with reference to early modern and twentieth-century literature, and has published poetry widely in Australia.

*Diane Roberts* was awarded a D.Phil from Oxford for a thesis on women in the novels of William Faulkner. She was a lecturer at Brasenose College, Oxford, and is now Assistant Professor of English at the University of Alabama. She is currently working on a book about women and race, *The Myth of Aunt Jemima*, to be published by Routledge.

*Caroline Rooney* was born in Zimbabwe. She did post-graduate research in Oxford and has been awarded a D.Phil. for a thesis on 'The Androgyne and the Double in Literature'. She is still based in Oxford where she researches and teaches African literature.

*Clair Wills* was Junior Research Fellow of Queen's College, Oxford and is now Lecturer in the Department of Literature, University of Essex. She has written extensively on feminist theory and Irish literature.

# Chronological Table of Works

*(listed in order of composition)*

## Gertrude Stein

*Born Pennsylvania, USA, 1894*
*Died Neuilly, France, 1946*

| | |
|---|---|
| 1904–5 | *Three Lives* |
| 1906–8 | *The Making of Americans* |
| 1908–12 | *Gertrude Stein and her Brother** |
| 1911 | *Tender Buttons* |
| 1908–20 | *Geography and Plays* |
| 1909–33 | *Portraits and Prayers* |
| 1913–30 | *Operas and Plays* |
| 1913–27 | *Bee Time Vine and Other Pieces** |
| 1915–40 | *Alphabets and Birthdays** |
| 1917–46 | *Last Operas and Plays** |
| 1920–26 | *A Novel of Thank You** |
| 1926 | *Composition as Explanation* |
| 1927 | *Lucy Church Amiably* |
| 1928–30 | *How to Write* |
| 1932 | *The Autobiography of Alice B. Toklas* |
| 1934 | *Lectures in America* |
| 1936 | *Everybody's Autobiography* |
| 1938 | *Picasso* |
| 1939 | *Paris France* |
| 1940 | *Ida, A Novel* |
| 1942–4 | *Wars I Have Seen* |
| 1945 | *Brewsie and Willie* |

*Work or collection of works published posthumously.

# 1

# Gertrude Stein

## 'Some Could Be Different Ones'

## *Clare Brant*

Gertrude Stein reckoned she was the most exciting writer of the twentieth century. As she put it in *The Auto-biography of Alice B. Toklas*, 'She realizes that in English literature in her time she is the only one. She has always known it and now she says it.'[1] Unabashedly she declared 'I am a genius'.

Stein's claims can be accounted for as the self-affirma-tion of a writer struggling to be taken seriously by a sometimes hopelessly prejudiced audience, and they are perhaps claims excessive only in the degree to which she was excessively unread, misread, satirised, parodied and dismissed. Even when allotted a place in the avant-garde, many readers and reviewers persisted in mocking her as unintelligible and fraudulent: as one put it, 'the mama of dada is going gaga'.[2] However wittily this expresses widespread bafflement, the coincidence of craziness with childishness, whether of infantile senility or inarticulate maternity, takes on extra resonance if the writer so designated is a woman. Women, it would seem, cannot be tolerated as productive *enfants terribles* in literature because patriarchy finds the combination of woman with child too excluding of itself, or because its construction of the child (especially in this period) is predicated on masculinity in miniature – as Freud put it, 'His Majesty the child' – and hence incompatible with the feminine.

Critics sympathetic to Stein have also acknowledged how difficult her work seems. In 1914 H. L. Mencken observed, 'It is the great achievement of Miss Stein that she has made English easier to write and harder to read.'[3] But feminism and deconstruction together offer ways of reading Stein which recover the radical and exhilarating nature of her project.

Feminist theory relates Stein's extraordinary workings of language to a realm which challenges patriarchal systems of signification – the pre-symbolic or semiotic, associated by Kristeva with the phase of unity and communion experienced by a child before it is split from its mother and learns the phallogocentric language of divisions, orderings and hierarchies. Seen in this light, Stein's writing takes us close to the new language demanded by Cixous and Irigaray, one which has shed the old accretions of values, controls and suppressions sanctioned by patriarchy to celebrate instead plenitude, pluralism, playfulness. Critics who perceive such deconstructive movement in Stein's writing but overlook the implications of her gender and sexual orientation limit her subversion thereby; likewise, feminists who read Stein looking only for valorised images of women or themes and subjects which openly resist patriarchy will be disappointed. Stein's rebellion is not against what is said but against the whole set of linguistic structures which determine what can be said.

Stein was born in Baltimore in 1874, the youngest child of German immigrant parents who planned a family of five children. Gertrude was the seventh; had two not died at birth, she and her elder brother Leo would not have existed. Her father was a merchant whose steady prosperity ensured that the children had a comfortable upbringing, with a trip to Europe and a spell in San Francisco where another part of the family was settled. When Leo went to Harvard, Gertrude went to study at nearby Radcliffe where she encountered William James, philosopher brother of Alice and Henry. Inspired by him she went on to Johns Hopkins in Baltimore, but became, she said, bored and flunked out of medical school. After a time in London voraciously reading in the British Museum, she settled with Leo in Paris where he was trying to be a painter. Together they bought pictures – Cézannes, Matisses and the first of the Picassos which were to become so important to her; on these Leo expounded to their growing number of visitors. Having written two short novels – one, *Q.E.D.*, figuring the tangled triangle of emotions between herself and May Bookstaver, a fellow student who could not or would not abandon her attachment to a third, Mabel Haynes – Gertrude continued to write, despite Leo's lack of encouragement. She translated Flaubert's *Trois Contes* and around the same time, 1905–6, began to write *Three Lives*, related in their subjects of simple lives to Flaubert's but emphatically different in technique.

The three women whose life stories Stein presents stand as representative instances of ordinariness. The good Anna, who scolds, organises and kindheartedly teases a succession of employers; the gentle Lena, who is married to a reluctant husband, and Melanctha, who is attracted to a steady doctor but cannot abandon excitement – one could see in this trio a lightly schematic rendering of the obstacles that women face, the plights they are pushed into, the constrictions which unsettle them. One could make it read more schematically as an investigation of those areas traditionally seen as containing special oppressions for women: domestic work, marriage and maternity, and sexual choice or restriction. The radical effects of this are, though, countered by Stein's racist conformity, as she stereotypically associates sexual waywardness with the Black woman Melanctha. All three women die: Anna from overwork, Lena in childbirth and Melanctha from consumption which symbolises her self-consuming, unfixable desires. The dislocation between the narrative voice and the grim implications of what it announces could be seen as mimetic, since people who have difficult lives are often stoical. But the texts posit a disjunction between their representations and the minutely rendered voices they set loose, which frustrates realism. For instance, one formal characteristic which distinguishes first from third person fiction is that a first person voice cannot describe its own death. Stein's text incorporates an authorial element into stream-of-consciousness which catalyses it, shapes it, rhythmically empowers it yet without destroying its simplicity or closing off its narrative possibilities. Here, for example, is the unfolding and interleaving of time and desire as Melanctha meets the doctor:

> During the year before she met Jefferson Campbell, Melanctha had tried many kinds of men but they had none of them interested Melanctha very deeply. She met them, she was much with them, she left them, she would think perhaps this next time it would be more exciting, and always she found for her it all had no real meaning. She could now do everything she wanted, she knew now everything that everybody wanted, and yet it all had no excitement for her. With these men she knew she could learn nothing. She wanted someone that could teach her very deeply and now at last she was sure that she had found him, yes she really had it, before she thought to look if in this man she would find it.[4]

In *The Making of Americans*, Stein's next project, she expanded and abstracted subjectivity, from three particular lives to one being alive, anyone being alive, everyone being alive. This enormous novel does not completely abandon narrative: ostensibly it chronicles two families, the Dehnings and the Herslands, loosely based on Stein's own. But despite the reappearance of individual existences affected by attraction, stalemate and failure the characters function as representatives of universal psychic identity. Stein envisioned the book as a history of everybody who ever did, would or could live, a compendium of behaviour which would express once and for all the nature of existence in all its nuances. Context becomes irrelevant in this schematic representation of humanity in the same way that water is invisible to fish. With content minimised, Stein concentrated on constructing a prose style which by repetition and fractional shifts of meaning would enumerate particularity while establishing commonality. Here she discusses changes in identity:

> Some are certain that sometime some could be different ones in being in being living, some are certain that sometime everyone will be a different one in being in being living, some are hoping that sometime some one will be a different one, some are certain that they are believing that something can be different in living sometime for some, some are certain that they are believing that something can be different in each one, some are believing this thing about men some are believing this thing about women, some are believing this thing about men and women, some are thinking that they are believing this thing, some are not believing that they are believing this thing, some are always believing this thing, some are not always believing this thing, I am not believing this thing, another one is not believing this thing, another is believing this thing, another one is believing this thing, another one is believing this thing, another one is believing this thing, another one is not believing this thing, another one is not believing this thing, another one is not believing this thing, another one is believing this thing, another one is believing this thing.[5]

The lexical vagueness and insistent syntax make Stein's meanings difficult to paraphrase and diminishing to fix. Throughout her formulaic expositions, her use of verbal nouns makes words absorb extra significations and compels the reader to accept the suspension of specific evocation. 'Telling' in the next quotation could be any kind of discourse, from fiction to gossip, and it cannot be confined to just one:

> Certainly very many are together and very many are telling about this thing about very many being together and very many are willing that very many are telling about this thing about very many being together and very many are not very willing and very many are not at all willing that very many are telling about being very many together.[6]

In order to expel the limiting concerns of where and when to make way for why and how, Stein changed narrative into process. As she put it, 'The business of art is to live in the actual present, that is the complete actual present and to express that complete actual present.' The resulting coincidence of action with representation so that the writing becomes dramatic, itself part of the continuous present in which characters supposedly exist, has an unexpected precedent in the epistolary novel's 'writing to the moment', especially Samuel Richardson's *Clarissa*, a favourite novel of Stein's. But more importantly it relates to the ideas about time and language of Stein's mentor, William James. He blamed nouns as tyrannical particles which tied representation to a material reality at the expense of perceptual possibility – and he suggested the means of escape from their bondage:

> There is not a conjunction or a preposition, and hardly an adverbial phrase, syntactic form or inflection of voice, in human speech, that does not express some shading or other of relation which we at some moment do not actually feel to exist between the larger objects of our thought. . . . So inveterate has our habit become of recognising the existence of the substantive parts [of speech] alone, that language almost refuses to lend itself to other uses.[7]

Stein's language refuses to accept that refusal. In its most revisionist forms it sheds all but one indeterminate noun, that thing, and takes instead flexible, floating verbal nouns which establish a present vibrant in its own right, not as the oscillating narrow gap between past and future. Identity is melted down into non-specific forms – one, anybody, everybody. Though in long paragraphs it can become draining, this mode has its subversive attractions. For one thing, it is anti-hierarchical. As she put it, 'what I am singling out is that one thing has the same value as another'.[8] Insisting on its own incremental rhythms, stressing likeness in preference to difference, the prose refuses phallogocentric signification with its divisions, opposites and hierarchies. Differentiation need not amount to difference. In this insistent style, moreover, which she was to deploy in *A Long Gay Book* and elsewhere, Stein refuses the patriarchal author's privilege as progenitor of meaning. Syntactical neutrality, though it will not valorise the feminine, will not valorise the masculine either: as she put it musingly, 'I like one I am very fond of that one that has many meanings many ways of being used to make different ways of meaning to every one.'[9] The making of Americans is an act shared by the reader, who builds up meaning as gradually as the text appears to do. It is not dissimilar to the gradual revelations of stream-of-consciousness, except that that ultimately valorises subjectivity as a state of perception, and this, the agency of language, in constituting perception. The process is not linear except in so far as the act of reading is linear, and Stein tries to break even that structure by working in blocks, paragraphs rather than sentences. Paragraphs, she thought, were emotional in a helpful way; sentences were not. This she had discovered while listening to her dog drinking: the lap-lap-lap-lap-lap is not emotional but the sequence is, in that the action is begun because the dog has a need and stops when it has had enough. In so far as prose required divisions, paragraphs offered it – frames as borders rather than enclosures.

Stein found analogies for this in two other art forms:

the cinema and cubist painting. Film as one sees it is continuous portrayal. Were one to experience its construction as part of its content one would see it frame by frame, with only minute variations between one frame and the next. Supposedly Stein's only visit to the cinema was to see a Charlie Chaplin film: she thought she could not see better so she never went again. Cubism, however, she did a great deal of looking at. What cubism tried to do, she suggested, was to destroy the hierarchy of the fixed viewpoint and the single perspective. Cubists did so by rearranging composition, arriving at movement by destroying centralisation. They destabilised vision into fragments, repeating uniform pieces of visual information such as shape, line and colour.[10] This parallels Stein's use of repetition in phrasing, though as she said there is no such thing as repetition – every time you repeat something some change, if only that of a different moment, makes it different. So with a cubist painting: your understanding of certain curves or lines is affected by adjacent curves, or lines you have understood the moment before, though they may be identical in shape. And like Stein's prose, a cubist painting does not employ a centre: the corners of a canvas can be as important as its middle. Francis Rose, an English painter whose pictures Stein bought plentifully, put it thus: 'Today, the art of painting is largely concerned with giving life to the medium and texture of paint, rather than to the subject.'[11] So Stein ignored conventional representation in order to give energy to language.

*The Making of Americans* is important as a site of another of Stein's long-term preoccupations. Its title not only insists on art's construction sharing life's process, but also stresses Stein's identification with her fellow nationals. Throughout her life, and however long domiciled in France, she insisted on her Americanness. In this is more than an emigrée's nostalgia for a homeland. Many Americans went to the bohemian oasis of 'gay Paree' in the early twentieth century; some stayed and, as Shari Benstock's book *Women of the Left Bank: Paris, 1900-1940* documents, lesbian women especially found it a hospitable place to be. Stein's motives for staying, though undoubtedly partly social, were not simply so. She expressed her enjoyment and appreciation of France and the French in her late book, *Paris France* (actually more about provincial than Parisian life) but she saw herself as creating an American aesthetic. As she declared in an interview in 1931, 'The natural line of descent is the big four: Poe to Whitman to James to myself. I am the last.'[12] American literature, she asserted, 'is signalized by the consistent tendency toward abstraction without mysticism'. Elsewhere, she explained it roughly as follows. America, because it invented the motor car and mass production, was the first country to begin upon, indeed invent, the twentieth century. Mass production perfectly exemplifies Stein's belief that everything was the same but different. Thousands of motor cars come off the production line and each one is both uniform and unique. Stein owned an early Ford (optimistically called Pauline after a notably reliable aunt) and spent much time over the years doing her writing in garages (so much for the aunt). She was particularly interested in the principle of active sameness embodied by engines. A whirring engine is itself both moving and a source of movement; every repeated action it makes contributes to the motion of the thing it drives. 'We in this period have not lived in remembering, we have living in moving', said Stein, and she defined her work in relation to her time: 'my business my ultimate business as an artist was not with where the car goes as it goes but with the movement inside that is of the essence of its going'.[13]

Movement, moreover, is something which fuses space and time. You cannot move through space without also moving through time. Having worked out a mode of language which recreated time as a succession of moments holding both flux and continuity, Stein tried to explain why an American sense of time incorporated space:

> Think of anything, of cowboys, of movies, of detective stories, of anybody who goes anywhere or stays at home and is an American and you will realize that it is something strictly American to conceive a space that is filled with moving, a space of time that is filled always filled with moving and my first real effort to express this thing which is an American thing began in writing *The Making of Americans*.[14]

It is easier to see what she means if one thinks of why she says time and space not time and place. Space already incorporates an element of time: in outer space we measure space by time – a light year, for example, is distance measured by how long it takes light to travel a certain time. Similarly, in talk of a space race the implication is not only how far can rockets be sent but also how soon can they be sent off.

Stein's dictum that 'it is something strictly American to conceive a space that is filled with moving', whether or not it is true, illustrates the consistent underlying concerns of her work and helps to explain why she saw herself as *the* literary genius of the twentieth century. To be American was to qualify for modernity which was movement. This principle runs through her portraits, operas and plays, landscape writing and memoirs; it also underlies many of her essays and lectures.

The other significant textual site of Stein's radical undertaking of overthrowing patriarchally ordered language is *Tender Buttons*, written in 1911 and published in 1914. It is tempting to link its manifest changes with her personal life. During the lonely writing of much of *The Making of Americans*, Stein met Alice Toklas. Toklas had grown up in San Francisco, toyed with a career as a pianist and had at last exchanged the drudgery of housekeeping for her father and family for the excitement of Europe. Soon after they met, Stein made a passionate declaration of love and what is probably best described as a lesbian proposal of marriage. Toklas cried copiously and accepted. After the depressing frustrations of the May Bookstaver relationship, Stein had at last found someone who not only rejoiced in her but believed in her absolutely as a writer of genius. This helped to precipitate Stein's break with her brother Leo, a break she described and analysed in the portrait *Two* and her autobiographies. Leo concealed a confused personality behind a dogmatic mask; he had taken to lecturing everyone about art and aesthetics, ignoring or disparaging Gertrude's efforts to rebuild language afresh in her writing. She played dumb to his deaf, saying nothing, sitting quietly by until one day she simply stopped listening. This point marked liberation: significantly she describes it in terms of rejecting patriarchal language. She finished off the character in *The Making of Americans* loosely modelled on Leo, ended that attempt to create a universal typology of existence and began another, *A Long Gay Book*, which would this time also celebrate connection. It 'was to describe not only every possible kind of a human being, but every possible kind of pairs of human beings and every possible threes and fours and fives of human beings and every possible kind of crowds of human beings'.[15] Cheered and encouraged by her relationship with Alice she obliquely commemorated it:

> It is naturally gayer describing what any one feels acts and does in relation to any other one than to describe what they just are what they are inside them.
>     And as I naturally found it livelier, I myself was becoming livelier just then. One does you know, when one has come to the conclusion that what is inside every one is not all there is of any one.[16]

Eventually Alice moved in and Leo moved out.

Liveliness then manifested itself in Stein's writing by a flurry of texts and a new genre, that of the portrait, which as in painting celebrates something, usually an individual, through the act of perceiving it. This suited Stein's desire to keep art as process, and though many of the portraits refuse conventional representation they do designate their subjects through their titles, a vestige of recognisable language, in much the same way as Picasso's portraits of this period include a detail or two which identify the subject as subject. But the rejection of representation becomes most startling in *Tender Buttons.*

### COLD CLIMATE

A season in yellow sold extra strings makes lying places.

### WAY LAY VEGETABLE

Leaves in grass and mow potatoes, have skip, hurry you up flutter.

Suppose it is ex a cake suppose it is new mercy and leave charlotte and nervous bed rows. Suppose it is meal. Suppose it is sam.

### CHICKEN

Alas a doubt in case of more go to say what it is cress. What is it. Mean. Potato. Loaves.[17]

Teasingly, Stein uses mostly explanatory titles and there are three groupings into domestic and recognisable categories: Objects, Food and Rooms. But the titles' key is useless to explain the material appended to them. This is all part of Stein's striking new strategy of using the language of signification against itself, rather than trying to reform it. In *The Making of Americans* she got rid of nouns as the most obvious way of releasing language from conventional signification. As she explained in *Poetry and Grammar*:

A noun is a name of anything, why after a thing is named

write about it. A name is adequate or it is not. If it is
adequate then why go on calling it, if it is not then calling it
by its name does no good.[18]

As precedent for this she cited Shakespeare, who evoked
the Forest of Arden without naming things, like trees,
which constitute forests. She had then gone farther,
shedding adjectives and all but minimal punctuation
(the question mark especially she denounced as 'positively revolting') and promoting instead prepositions,
verbs, adverbs, gerunds, articles and pronouns. The
result took on neither conventional representation nor,
thereby, conventional reality. Rather than continuing to
exclude words with descriptive, material connotations,
Stein's new tactic is to include them with a vengeance,
packing them in so energetically that they explode
conventional signification. What 'absence' could not do,
'excess' would. Nouns came back in because, she said,
'poetry is essentially the discovery, the love, the passion
for anything.' [19]

In *Tender Buttons* passionate naming appears random. But there are two possible constructions which
make it intelligible, though not in a conventional sense.
They need not be mutually exclusive. First, Stein has a
private set of referents, a code of personal meanings
which would, if we knew it, enable us to translate back
into standard language. There are points at which this
may be true, but it does not get one far. An alternative
reading does – this would suggest that Stein draws a
creative utopia by writing the humblest constituents of
life (the weather, vegetables, chickens) as polyphonous,
polysemous plenitude. She lays words together like
fireworks, or different kinds of explosive; the reader
detonates them into an aural spectacle. In the 1920s and
1930s, other subversives enacted a more violent form of
Stein's equation of words with explosions: in the
gangster movie *Scarface* (1932), Paul Muni tries out a
machine gun and exclaims delightedly, 'some little

typewriter, eh!' It may be no coincidence that Toklas typed all Stein's manuscripts.

What matters to Stein is not the purpose of words, so much as their effect. The essence of words has been so long monopolised by meaning that their other values as sounds, or graphic relations to each other as shapes, are hard to recover. Some literature has specialised in this – children's rhymes, so-called nonsense verse and so on – but Stein did not want to be marginalised by generic announcements into acceptable specialities, especially those perceived as harmless.

The trouble is that readers are so used to words having purpose that it can be difficult to let go of connotation. Stein seems to allow alternative rather than anti-signification:

> I took individual words and thought about them until I got their weight and volume complete and put them next to another word, and at this same time I found out very soon that there is no such thing as putting them together without sense. It is impossible to put them together without sense. I made innumerable efforts to make words write without sense and found it impossible. Any human being putting down words had to make sense of them.[20]

Codes of meaning may arise in discourse as much from a sense of context, or coexistence between words as from their singular import. This is particularly relevant in texts in which Stein implants disguised sexuality, such as the long and joyous poem 'Lifting Belly' or 'As a Wife has a Cow. A Love Story'. In the latter playfully erotic text, 'cow' can be read as an unusual but comprehensible sexual trope. In conventional signification, it generates associations of warmth, milkiness, velvety gentleness, heavy breathing and so on. But 'cow' is a word Stein uses in a number of texts as a euphemism for orgasm: it is, as Catherine R. Stimpson points out, 'The word that rhymes with wow and now and ow and pow!'[21] This second reading still puts meaning as a textual goal, but one which is not dependent on conventional significa- tion. Her erotic identity, however, does employ in- determinacy, substitution and evasion, not least in her choice of heterosexual terminology, casting herself as husband and Alice as wife, or herself as Baby and Alice as mother. Some may prefer to see this instead as ironic mockery, a parody rather than an adoption of the constrictive roles available.

Stein remarked that portrait writing was difficult 'because you have to refuse so much'. A desire to control a text testifies to the text's instability. As the lighter side of gangsterism would have it, Stein in the speakeasy beating prohibition felt unnervingly disorientated: 'I did begin to think I was rather drunk with what I had done. And I am always one to prefer being sober.' [22] The headiness of being drunk, however, does survive in Stein's gaiety. Though on the surface her *jouissance* appears to resemble Joyce's hermetic disruptions, and to share modernism's delight in enigma, Stein's is of a different order on two counts. First, Joyce's punning games and portmanteau words could be said to reinforce signification by splicing meanings together, and he sites his linguistic rebellion within narrative structures of patriarchal myths and rituals (the odyssey and the wake). He multiplies and condenses sense, whereas Stein revises the relationship between signifier and signified, filtering it through a sensuality common to both, avoiding representation in favour of expansive, evocative in- determinacy. Secondly, Stein's writing is largely informed by cheerfulness. Like HD, she rejects a modernism of despair. Ironically and predictably, male writers did not reflect this aspect of her work when they absorbed her as an influence. [23]

Portraits of objects and people involved Stein in a project of looking. In this she tried to incorporate movement in the form of vibrancy: each word resonates as it detonates. But the First World War interfered with this – one could suggest because war disturbs the ordinary rhythm of sequence and causality which Stein's writing was trying to disturb in its own way. Instead, war imposes a contradictory rhythm of ennui and action, and Stein's writing reflects this. She and Toklas spent most of the war in Mallorca, restless and tense; they then returned to mainland France where they helped in Red Cross work, delivering supplies from the battered Ford. Stein's poems deal obliquely with daily subjects but begin to make more of everyday language, especially courtesies: thank you so much, how do you do. One could see this as a recovery of simple communication made in response to wartime fracture; such phrases recover the kindness and concern which long conventional use, indeed over-use, has leached out of them. The old refurbished can look startlingly new. It also dissolves literary hierarchy by using staples of everyday speech as poetic. This strand in Stein's writing lasts well on into the plays and work of the 1920s, culminating in her *A Novel of Thank You* (1925). Here one suspects it is also or alternatively used as parodic, representing patriarchal speech as banality. Instead of making old signification catch alight from the friction of juxtaposed words she humorously, perhaps also indulgently, uses its now meaningless formulations to expose its exhaustion. Moreover, courtesies have a further function for Stein. They are on the whole used rhythmically in ordinary speech: 'how do you do' is an opening gambit, 'thank you very much' inclines to closure. Stein's uneasiness during and after the war was textually controlled by latent structures of dialogue. 'Lifting Belly', for instance, works conversationally, suggesting, confirming, qualifying, absorbing the views of a second protagonist in order to establish agreement or resolution. Stein could use 'please' and 'thank you' courtesies to mark textual conciliation. 'How do you do' she uses in several ways: displacedly, to mark not openings but beginnings again within texts; paradoxically, for closure; and ironically, for reassuring a reader that the ellipses of her texts are not impenetrably narcissistic. Courtesies express reception of something or recognition of somebody; as linguistic gestures of greeting or gratitude, they supply verbal movement which relieves texts from being static.

Movement was again the characteristic which Stein foregrounded in her operas and plays. She had trouble, she said, with conventional theatre because an audience was always fractionally behind the action and straining to keep up.

> Then I began vaguely to wonder whether I could see and hear at the same time and which helped or interfered with the other and which helped or interfered with the things on stage having been over before it really commenced. Could I see and hear and feel at the same time and did I.[24]

Her solution, as it had been for her fictional prose and portraits, was to replace narrative with spectacle:

> in my portraits I had tried to tell what each one is without telling stories and now in my early plays I tried to tell what happened without telling stories so that the essence of what happened would be like the essence of the portraits, what made what happened be what it was.[25]

Mischievously entitling her first play *What Happened. A Play.*, Stein dismantled existing dramatic conventions, making acts a few lines long and characters not interacting personalities but polyphonous voices. Musical analogies are helpful here – just as in opera narrative is usually exaggerated as a device to render it subservient to the music, so in Stein's operas and plays it was minimised for the same purpose. Similarly, her registration of voice made language as neutral a system of notation as a musical scale – which is not to say that, as in music, notes neutral in themselves cannot produce dramatic effects.

Stein found most help in two non-musical economies: numbers and saints. Numbers designate pure quantity with no emotional connotation at all; at the same time they express irrefutable difference. Five is a different quantity from seven and one of Stein's best known plays, *Four Saints in Three Acts,* turns in its title quantative difference into qualitative relation. That is, the particles are different numbers but both are defined by numbers. Composition and content are thereby formally linked as they had been in the portraits. Saints seem at first a surprising source of neutrality, but in fact they suit Stein's purposes admirably. Even in conventional representation they circulate by virtue of one defining characteristic, and that characteristic can be made and for ideological reasons has to be made simple: St Catherine and her wheel, St Francis and his birds. The iconographically simple can be simplified to the iconically static: in church, saints are often presented as statues. As Stein put it, saints do not *do* anything. Once made a saint, a saint's only function is to be an intercessor, to mediate language. This neatly answers Stein's desire to do away with stories while focusing on language. Furthermore, saints originate from the ordinary: conventional hagiography is as much at pains to stress the worldliness of saints when sinners as their otherworldliness when saints. Thus their apparently static essence is predicated on the transitional. They further embody duality by being simultaneously mortal and divine, body and spirit and, as Stein works it, paired by complementary gender. *Four Saints in Three Acts* stars St Teresa of Avila and St Ignatius Loyola with a chorus of saints and others whose plurality diffuses the numerical determinism of the title. There is not plot but movement through the expressive, echoing speeches hovering round St Teresa as the visionary whose mysticism enfolds all patriarchally constructed differences and resolves them into unity. St Ignatius, founder of the Jesuits, is a figurehead of order, intellect and violence; to him is given the famous theme and variations, 'pigeons on the grass alas'. His system of separation, violated as he sees it by the birds' intrusion, is overcome, absorbed into St Teresa's inclusive celebrations.

In this play, Stein said, saints were landscape. Landscape was another trope for simultaneous relation of coexistent things. When you look at a landscape you see it all at once. As she put it:

> The landscape has its formation and as after all a play has to have formation and be in relation one thing to the other thing and as the story is not the thing as anyone is always telling something then the landscape not moving but being always in relation, the trees to the hills the hills to the fields the trees to each other any piece of it to any sky and then any detail to any other detail, the story is only of importance if you like to tell or like to hear a story but the relation is there anyway.[26]

This relation she expressed for its own sake as a principle of harmonious unity in her 1927 novel *Lucy Church Amiably*. Lucy Church is both a fictional character and a real place – the church of Lucey, a little village near Belley where Stein and Toklas spent their summers between the wars. It has a strange and beautiful onion-shaped spire, whose shape pleasingly unites and defies conventional taxonomies of masculine and feminine. Stein's characters too have integral gender: Simon Therese and John Mary, whose strongly ecclesiastical names relate them to saints. This pastoral novel prefers larger moments of cohesion to coherence; it celebrates nature as something humans experience rather than view as spectacle:

> To bring them back to an experience of natural beauty of nature hills valleys fields and birds. They will say it is beautiful but will they sit in it.[27]

This integration, despite or perhaps because of all the

transformations and disguises it employs, can be seen as Stein's version of 'writing the body' – a textual physicality protected by its disarming title, *Lucy Church Amiably* (my emphasis).

This novel is, it must be said, a difficult text to read, but one which deploys feminism within an *écriture féminine*. Stein's more conventional use of landscape in *Wars I Have Seen* (1944) includes latent feminist content as well. In this book, written part as consoling meditation and part as diary during the Second World War, Stein is at her most accessible and engaging. In war, she suggested, 'there is a mingling there is not children's lives and grown up lives there is just lives'.[28] Since age distinctions disappear, Stein can integrate thoughts on wars she has seen since a child and thoughts on this war, which she is trying to survive by childlike responses. She and Toklas had left Paris and their pictures to spend most of the war near Billignan. As American Jews they were in some danger, but encouraged by the support of the local community they decided to stay put. Living in the landscape, Stein recorded its wartime redefinition as a site of passage, occupation and concealment, its topography charged with tension as troops travelled its valleys and the Resistance hid out in its mountains. Figures in the landscape acquired symbolic potential as threatening, peaceful, patrolling, wandering entities in which gender difference is initially blurred by distance. Viewed closer, it is strangely disempowered: men are largely defined through their relationships to women, as husbands, sons, fathers and brothers. Stein is particularly responsive to the psychic resistance and emotional wounds of women caught up in the war: in the many conversations she has with the mayor's wife, for example, she recounts their anxiety and stoical sturdiness as a matter of course. Stein herself spent much of the war characteristically in motion: most days she walked twelve kilometres to the only baker who still stocked white bread and cakes. In reporting personal conversations on the mountainous road, she valorised the anecdotal as a mode which protected the individual humanity threatened by the war. This atmosphere of integration is ironically counterpointed with the national differences which produced it: men and women share a common cause only when French and German people are on opposing sides.

Throughout this book Stein refers half playfully, half seriously to the prophecies of Sainte Odile and how they correspond to the fortunes of the Allies; the mystical feminine, she implies, can comfort and inspire. Comparable feminist symbolism can be found in her late play *The Mother of Us All*, about Susan B. Anthony, the tireless worker for women's suffrage in nineteenth-century America. Stein is arguably most traditionally feminist when engaged in explicit critiques of patriarchy – to be feminist in content is to have to employ less radical styles. As long as patriarchy controls representation, being intelligible in conventional ways is to participate in a struggle loaded against women. Stein can afford to use ordinary language, albeit singularly adapted, in her autobiographies and lectures, because those genres allow her to inscribe her identity and expound her uniqueness with minimal apology. Stein's sympathetic dramatisation of Susan B. Anthony and the historical opposition she faced includes moments of anger familiarly expressed:

> How can anything be really mixed when men are conservative, dull, monotonous, deceived, stupid, unchanging and bullies, how said Susan B. how when men are men can they be mixed.[29]

Resistance too is upliftingly couched in rhetoric with familarly politicised rhythms of defiance:

> I know that we suffer, and as we suffer we grow strong, I know that we wait and as we wait we are bold, I know that

we are beaten and as we are beaten we win, I know that men
know that this is not so but it is so, I know, yes I know.[30]

In this play Stein made concessions to the oppressors'
language in order to make political points about oppression. In 'Patriarchal Poetry', a long poem of 1927, she
makes almost none, except in a few inspired lines, such
as the witty suggestion that she should ignore the whole
phenomenon completely: 'Never to mention patriarchal
poetry altogether'. But for the most part the text wilfully
enacts everything its subject has excluded, refusing to
adopt any of its positions or procedures, and elusively
switching tactics between sections. She hints at its sinister complacency: 'patriarchal poetry makes no mistake',
and its restrictive dualism: 'Two . . . had such an effect
that only one out of a great many believe in three
relatively.' She spotlights the voices that patriarchal
poetry has stifled by passages of command and demand:

> Let her be let her be let her be to be to be shy let her be to be
> let her be to be let her try.
> Let her try.
> Let her be let her be let her be let her be to be to be let her be
> let her try.
> To be shy.
> Let her be.
> Let her try.[31]

The insistence is imperative rather than pleading, and
extraordinarily effective. Within fractional variations of
simple components, Stein presses for women's autonomy – 'to be', implies that constriction has so destroyed
women's confidence that the first free step will have to be
one of self-consciousness – 'to be shy', and that women's
exclusion from everything makes endeavour applicable
everywhere – 'let her try'. There is also a sound game: 'let
her be' is 'letter b', the one after 'a'. Propositions of
formal logic employ rhetorical formulae such as 'if a,
then b'. Stein's text chants the letter b which patriarchy

casting itself as a has ignored. B necessarily becomes antithesis if a defines itself as thesis, and is forced into unwanted and distorting binary opposition. Extension of the syllogism, if a then b then c, something which leaves behind the categories of a and b, is a cultural transformation almost too far off for Stein to contemplate, though she does permit a moment's cheerful optimism: 'Patriarchal Poetry might be finished tomorrow.'[32]

In the late 1920s and 1930s Stein took on a new role, that of explicating her texts. In 1926 the Sitwells invited her to give a lecture in Cambridge; initially nervous, she enjoyed the experience enough to repeat it in Oxford and in the autumn of 1934 she and Alice embarked on a lecture tour of America. The reversal of her status, from being unread to barely read, then being read by a small but loyal audience and then, with the publication in 1933 of *The Autobiography of Alice B. Toklas*, becoming a best-seller, is still a little puzzling. Her curious status as a celebrity, her name put up in lights on her arrival in New York, was partly the effect of being visited by numerous Americans, many with literary connections, during the 1920s. They came to see her art collection and to meet this weird woman who wrote notoriously weird books. They found her an ample, maternal figure (which reassured all the young men) – hospitable, lively and amusing. Sherwood Anderson, who with Hemingway became one of her literary protégés, experienced a typical revelation. He had expected an exotic creature but when he actually met her, as he wrote in 1921 with silly surprise, he found her

> the very symbol of health and strength. She laughs, she smokes cigarettes. She tells stories with an American shrewdness in getting the tang and the kick into the telling.[33]

These qualities of gusto, animation and entertainment were present in *The Autobiography*, cleverly filtered through the supposed medium of another. That in itself increased her charm: if Stein was this engaging when projected through Alice, her personality unmediated had surely even more charisma. Stein's subversion of conventional frames and her double-edged joke upon identity was thereby deflected as she became celebrated as a lecturer. Those lucky enough to hear her were further enthralled by her wit, her amiability, her patriotism and her ready enjoyment of life. From a critical point of view, Stein's lectures do not always explicate her ideas consistently but they undoubtedly add clarity. Each seemed to demonstrate the principle of her first one, disarmingly entitled *Composition as Explanation*. Adopting the rhythmic accretions of her *Making of Americans* style to build up arguments which ensured her audience or readers followed every step, she also recognised the limits of explanation and appealed with simplicity to their co-operation: 'I hope you like what I say.'[34] But it was not their approval she sought; she wanted them to comprehend her primary writings: 'now I am trying in these lectures to tell what it is by telling about how it happened that I told about what it is'.[35]

These lectures are important not just because they are explanations as compositions in their own right – Stein wrote a series of other compositions published in 1931 as *How to Write* which treat the same ideas in creative, non-representational ways. They are important because they share with the autobiographies, that supposedly by Alice and in 1937 *Everybody's Autobiography* openly by herself, the project of 'telling what it is by telling about how it happened that I told about what it is'. And like the autobiographies, this proselytising project partly backfired. It tangled up promotion of the writing with the personality of the writer and because much of the writing is so baffling, so uncompromisingly different, readers turned with relief to the comfortable personality. There are still awkward relations between biography and critical writing on Stein.

*The Autobiography of Alice B. Toklas* is a textual joke which the reader is let in on at the end. The final paragraph runs thus:

> About six weeks ago Gertrude Stein said, it does not look to me as if you were ever going to write that autobiography. You know what I am going to do. I am going to write it for you. I am going to write it as simply as Defoe did the autobiography of Robinson Crusoe. And she has and this is it.[36]

There is a serious point to this. However much she drew on people she knew for the portraits or places she lived in for the landscapes, Stein insisted that the process of creation was one in which personality was suspended. Perception, she said, required you to step out of identity and time, as Crusoe did when he saw the footprint in the sand. In writing *The Autobiography of Alice B. Toklas*, Stein comically points up unmediated identity as a fiction. Absorbing Alice's persona into her story (just as Alice was absorbed in life to be a willing and devoted wife) arguably makes the text self-engrossed, but also disturbs conventional boundaries to identity. Though Alice in her actual autobiography, *What is Remembered* (1963), set parameters to her history to make it coincide almost exactly with the years spent with Stein, and her voice in this text and her cookbooks matches that which Stein projects for her, yet one might doubt whether the use of Alice as speaker escapes appropriation. The deconstruction can from some angles look like ordinary paradox: as Richard Bridgman remarks, 'This pre-eminently a-historical woman rediscovered her energies in her own history'.[37] It is as if all the stories she had avoided hitherto came together in the autobiographies.

In part this appearance of narrative has to do with Stein's view of literary history. The next generation of male American authors had learnt from her the liberating possibilities of rhythm and simplicity, an appropriation which obscures the politics of gender and sexual orientation in Stein's subversion. In a 1946 interview she remarked that the twentieth century was not successful at the novel because its writers do not create characters you can get het up about. Citing Anderson, Hemingway and Fitzgerald as proof, she observed 'in all these it is the title and the form of the book that you remember rather than the characters in the book'.[38] Arguing from this that the twentieth century finds character in biography more exciting, she autobiographically inscribed herself into that genre very neatly by placing Toklas as a supposed filter in one text and humorously enlarging herself to universal and third person identity in another, *Everybody's Autobiography*. 'By everybody I do of course include myself but always I do of course include myself.'[39] The second autobiography is, though, for all its egotism a textual act of reassurance. Tumultuous recognition had initially affirmed Stein's sense of identity: 'I am I because my little dog knows me.' Now she was not so sure; as she put it, being known by one's dog, alias the outside world, 'only proved the dog was he and not that I was I'. In 1940 she published *Ida*, 'a novel about publicity', throughout which she ponders identity, asking at the end: 'If Ida goes on, does she go on even when she does not go on any more. / No and yes.'[40] Identity could survive the writer's block brought on by fame, and perhaps even the personal erasure of death.

Stein died swiftly and unexpectedly from stomach cancer in 1946. Her last book, *Brewsie and Willie*, was published a few days before her death. Cast as a series of idiomatic, informal discussions between nurses and GIs loitering around in France after the war, waiting to go home, it is a study in national malaise. In keeping with the more political and broadly conservative content of Stein's later works, it suggests that state intervention (in the form of Roosevelt's policies) was at odds with the independent and self-reliant nature of Americans. The younger generation Stein saw as 'spoiled babies', and she

remarked sharply on their sexism ('they don't really
notice a thing not a thing when it is a girl'), their lack of
direction and their complacent insensitivity:

> all American soldiers are just so sure they have to have wine
> women and song. American soldiers think life is a movie
> and they got to dream the parts in their feelings.[41]

Wryly including herself in the text as 'that Stein woman
who says things', she advocates a revival of pioneering.
As one of the nurses puts it, 'you got to break down what
has been built up, that's pioneering'.[42]

In this sense, Stein in her writing had been very much
a pioneer; her revisions of language concentrated on
breaking down the old systems of signification. Pioneering is an activity which consists of motion, in pushing
boundaries forward, and Stein's reworking of language
to incorporate movement, to make writing simultaneously embody and express movement, does open up
new horizons of figuration. *The Autobiography of Alice
B. Toklas* declares that

> Gertrude Stein, in her work, had always been possessed by
> the intellectual passion for exactitude in the description of
> inner and outer reality. She has produced a simplification
> by this concentration, and as a result the destruction of
> associational emotion in poetry and prose.[43]

This meant stripping familiar connotations from words
in order to let new dynamics loose to play. Old predetermined, overdetermined forms of sense were radically reinvented. Stein caught the violence of modernism
and her own merciless version or subversion of it when
in *Wars I Have Seen* she comically described her contribution to culture:

> The nineteenth century was completely lacking in logic, it
> had cosmic terms and hopes, and aspirations, and discover-
> ies, and ideals but it had no logic, and I like logic I really do,

I suppose that it is the reason that I so naturally had my part in killing the nineteenth century and killing it dead, quite like a gangster with a mitraillette, if that is the same as a tommy gun.[44]

The sad fact remains that literary history chose to cite Stein almost entirely as an eccentric personality or an influence on male writers who displaced her inventiveness. As Marianne DeKoven puts it, we still know her as a literary figure rather than a writer. It is time we read her as an innovator whom nobody can imitate, but whose innovations coincide in many places with the feminist project of a new kind of writing.

# Notes

1. *The Autobiography of Alice B. Toklas* (Middlesex, Penguin, 1987), 85.
2. Quoted in Ray Lewis White, *Gertrude Stein and Alice B. Toklas: a reference guide* (Boston, G. K. Hall, 1984), 90.
3. *ibid.*, 7.
4. *Three Lives* (Middlesex, Penguin, 1985), 99.
5. *The Making of Americans being a history of a familys progress* (London, Peter Owen, 1968), 728.
6. *ibid.*, 839.
7. Quoted in John Malcolm Brinnin, *The Third Rose: Gertrude Stein and her World* (London, Weidenfeld and Nicolson, 1960), 64.
8. 'A Transatlantic Interview' (1946), in Robert Bartlett Haas, *A Primer for the Gradual Understanding of Gertrude Stein* (Los Angeles, Black Sparrow Press, 1971), 16.
9. *The Making of Americans*, 306.
10. For a full discussion of this see Randa Dubnick, *The Structure of Obscurity: Gertrude Stein, Language, and Cubism* (Urbana and Chicago, University of Illinois Press, 1984).
11. Sir Francis Rose, *Gertrude Stein and Painting* (London, Book Collecting and Library Monthly, 1968), 31.
12. White, 31.
13. 'Portraits and Repetition', in *Look at Me Now and Here I*

*am: Writings and Lectures 1909-1945*, ed. Patricia Meyerowitz (Middlesex, Penguin, 1984), 109, 117.

14. 'The Gradual Making of *The Making of Americans*': *ibid.*, 98.
15. *ibid.*, 91.
16. *ibid.*, 92.
17. 'Tender Buttons', *ibid.*, 171, 191, 192.
18. 'Poetry and Grammar', *ibid.*, 125.
19. *ibid.*, 140.
20. Haas, 18.
21. 'Gertrude Stein and the Transposition of Gender', in *The Poetics of Gender*, ed. Nancy K. Miller (New York, Columbia University Press, 1986), 1-18.
22. 'Portraits and Repetition', *Look at Me Now*, 118.
23. For example, T. S. Eliot in *The Waste Land*.
24. 'Plays', *Look at Me Now*, 72.
25. *ibid.*, 76-7.
26. *ibid.*, 78.
27. *Lucy Church Amiably* (Paris, Plain Edition, 1930), 47.
28. *Wars I Have Seen* (London, Brilliance Books, 1984), 7.
29. *Last Operas and Plays*, ed. Carl van Vechten (New York, Rinehart, 1949), 61.
30. *ibid.*, 71.
31. 'Patriarchal Poetry', in *Bee Time Vine and Other Pieces, 1913-27* (New Haven, Yale University Press, 1953), 268.
32. *ibid.*, 294.
33. White, xi.
34. 'The Gradual Making of *The Making of Americans*', *Look at Me Now*, 96.
35. 'Portraits and Repetitions', *Look at Me Now*, 123-4.
36. *The Autobiography of Alice B. Toklas* (Middlesex, Penguin, 1987), 272.
37. *Gertrude Stein in Pieces* (New York, Oxford University Press, 1970), 204.
38. Haas, 21.
39. 'Plays', *Look at Me Now*, 75.
40. 'Ida', *Look at Me Now*, 423.
41. *Brewsie and Willie* (New York, Random House, 1946).
42. *ibid.*, 83.
43. *Autobiography*, 228.
44. *Wars I Have Seen*, 91.

# Chronological Table of Works
## Willa Cather

*Born Winchester, Virginia, USA, 1873*
*Died New York City, USA, 1947*

### Poetry
1903  *April Twilights*

### Novels
1912  *Alexander's Bridge*
1913  *O Pioneers!*
1915  *The Song of the Lark* (second edn., 1937)
1918  *My Ántonia*
1922  *One of Ours*
1923  *A Lost Lady*
1925  *The Professor's House*
1926  *My Mortal Enemy*
1927  *Death Comes for the Archbishop*
1931  *Shadows on the Rock*
1935  *Lucy Gayheart*
1940  *Sapphira and the Slave Girl*

### Short Stories
1905  *The Troll Garden*
1920  *Youth and the Bright Medusa*
1932  *Obscure Destinies*
1948  *The Old Beauty and Others*
1965  *Collected Shorter Fiction, 1892–1912*, ed. Virginia Faulkner
1973  *Uncle Valentine and Other Stories: Willa Cather's Uncollected Short Fiction, 1915–1929*, ed. Bernice Slote

### Non-Fiction
1936  *Not Under Forty*
1949  *Willa Cather on Writing*
1966  *The Kingdom of Art: Willa Cather's First Principles and Critical Statements 1893–6*, ed. Bernice Slote
1970  *The World and the Parish: Willa Cather's Articles and Reviews, 1893–1902*, ed. William M. Curtin
1987  *Willa Cather in Person: Interviews, Speeches and Letters*, ed. L. Brent Bohlke

# 2

# Willa Cather

## The Woman as Artist

### *Julia Briggs*

> Has any woman ever really had the art instinct, the art necessity? Is it not with them a substitute, a transferred enthusiasm, an escape valve for what has sought or is seeking another channel? But no, there was Sappho and the two great Georges [Sand and Eliot]; they had it genuinely; they tried other things and none could satisfy them.[1]

In this passage of self-interrogation, the young Willa Cather revealed her anxieties as to whether a woman could become an artist. At twenty-three, already burdened by 'the art instinct, the art necessity', she also recognised that there was no way in which it could be accommodated to the life of wife and mother that society had destined her for and expected of her and which, since puberty, she had energetically repudiated.

Her reflections were occasioned by the renunciation of one particular woman artist, the actress Mary Anderson, who six years before had abandoned the stage to get married and who had just published *Some Memories* (1896). Her reversion to domesticity drew from Cather a response that mingled ostensible admiration with underlying unease: Anderson had left the stage to follow 'a higher calling'; this was her 'greatest creation'. She had retained a clear vision, she had estimated worldly success at its true value and turned her back on it to live her own life, 'for what shall it profit a woman if she gain the whole world and lose – what she wants?' Cather avoided completing the phrase with the words 'her own soul', since to be an artist is supposedly to gain, rather than to lose a soul. Instead she substituted the more enigmatic 'what she wants', traditionally the riddle no one can answer: what Mary Anderson had apparently wanted was marriage. What Willa Cather wanted was to be an artist.

The conflict between 'life' and 'art', what she ought to do and what she did, continued to exercise Cather's imagination for the rest of her life and her fiction constantly returns to the issue, examining it from a variety of different angles. But her first and strongest instinct was always to try to reconcile its damagingly opposed terms, as she does at the end of this review when she observes that while Anderson's book is not literary, 'it is human experience, from which all literature is made'. In an interview with Eleanor Hinman a quarter of a century later, she was to make the same point: 'Art springs out of the very stuff that life is made of'.[2] A statement of this kind might be intended as a deliberate rejection of those contemporary movements in literature such as aestheticism or modernism, which sought to release 'art' from any obligation to reflect 'life', or else insisted upon an antagonism between the two. Yet taken in context, this passage seems primarily concerned to collapse the differences between the woman artist and the woman who has accepted a traditional domestic role: 'The very best cooks I have ever known have been prima donnas', she observes and, a few sentences earlier, 'The farmer's wife . . . contributes more to art than all the culture clubs.'

In such artificial reconciliations Cather attempted to

bury the scars of old wounds incurred during the slow process of her self-construction as an artist, a process in which she learnt to redefine women's creativity in terms other than those of her own earliest experiences of it in the kitchen and the home – in terms of artistic values that necessarily deviated from those of the family and the provincial town in which she had grown up. Yet her writing continued to celebrate the domestic tasks from which she had escaped: she exchanged the warmth and communal life of the kitchen, the creativity of cooking and familiar local narratives for privacy and a room of her own, for writing and narratives of heroic action, but not without many backward glances. Her art grew out of the tension between the values of the society that had nurtured her and those that she had to acquire in order to become a writer at all.

Cather's repression of the conflict between these two roles required that she idealise the creativity of the *materfamilias*; in sustaining her family and ordering their environment, the mother became a figure of the artist, while cooking became a trope for the processes of artistic making and transformation – out of the warmth of the kitchen came food to nourish the body and stories to feed the imagination. Symbolically and imaginatively, she re-appropriated the most creative aspects of that destiny she had resisted when she graduated from college and became a journalist and an independent woman whose passional life was directed towards other women. Behind her uneasy elision of art and life lay doubts about the value of art itself: the fear that art might be merely tangential to life; that it performed no useful function (her first ambition had been to become a doctor); that it held little interest or value for the kind of community in which she had grown up.

Inevitably some of her most potent images of womanhood derived from childhood memories – Cather acknowledged that the first fifteen years of her life had provided her with all the material she needed as a writer.[3] Two scenes, both fictionalised memories, bring together storytelling and domesticity and both have a primal quality: the first, dating from her earliest childhood in Virginia, is evoked in the epilogue to her last novel, *Sapphira and the Slave Girl*. The second dates from her family's move west to the Divide, a plateau on the Nebraska prairies. Here Cather acquired new freedoms, began to make friends among the neighbouring families, and found surrogate mothers to talk to:

> [T]hese old women on the farms were the first people who ever gave me the real feeling of an older world across the sea. Even when they spoke very little English, the old women somehow managed to tell me a great many stories about the old country. They talk more freely to a child than to grown people, and I always felt as if every word they said to me counted for twenty.
>
> I have never found an intellectual excitement any more intense than I used to feel when I spent a morning with one of those old women at her baking or butter making. I used to ride home in the most unreasonable state of excitement; I always felt as if they told me so much more than they said – as if I had actually got inside another person's skin.[4]

In this passage, Cather brings together cooking, the most life-giving of the domestic arts, and storytelling, relating both, in their ethnic distinctiveness, to the speakers' remote European background, seen as an endless source of fascinating fictions. It also introduces several other ideas that coloured Cather's concept of art. The first was that of imaginative sympathy or identification – 'I had actually got inside another person's skin'. Many years later, in writing of her friend and mentor, the New England writer Sarah Orne Jewett, Cather defined the writer's essential quality as that of

> giving himself absolutely to his material. And this gift of sympathy is his great gift; it is the fine thing in him that alone can make his work fine.[5]

While Cather conforms to the stylistic convention of her day in employing a masculine pronoun even though she is referring to her favourite woman writer, her definition of artistry as a matter of identification rather than imposition, of self-surrender rather than self-assertion suggests a repudiation on one hand of the images of domination or mastery commonly associated with (male) creativity, and on the other of that detachment thought to be necessary for artistic distance.

Another key element in this passage is Cather's sense that 'they told me much more than they said', that the speakers' linguistic limitations nevertheless conveyed an experience beyond words, something at once palpable yet elusive, '[w]hatever is felt . . . without being specifically named . . .'.[6] They possessed a force that mere fluency could never have conferred. Listening to them, the young Cather was simultaneously conscious of their power to open new horizons to her and the awkward turns of phrase in which they did so. There was a peculiar poignancy in their clumsy English, which Cather was later to draw on in her fiction: Ántonia Shimerda's grief at her father's death is the more painful because it cannot find adequate release in words:

> 'Oh, Jimmy,' she sobbed, 'what you tink for my lovely papa!' It seemed to me that I could feel her heart breaking as she clung to me.[7]

Cather's relationship with the farmers' wives on the Divide is a reflexive one: she is a woman telling a story about women telling stories. They displayed what was for her a crucial characteristic of the [woman] artist in that they expressed more than they actually said. She displayed another in relating to them through an act of creative sympathy. For these women were more than story-tellers – they themselves were living out their own stories on the Divide, sometimes in a pastoral, sometimes a heroic mode. Their stories of old Europe, like the inset story in *My Ántonia* of the wedding party hounded down by wolves, had a remote, legendary quality, which sets off the domestic drama of the main narrative in which they are related, a narrative about the heroism of the immigrant women forging new lives for themselves. From an early stage in her work, Cather made use of inset stories to illuminate, by contrast, their surrounding context, while also possessing a force and point of their own – for example the story of the Aztec Queen and her captive in 'Coming, Aphrodite!', Tom Outland's Story in *The Professor's House* or 'The Legend of Fray Baltazar' in *Death Comes for the Archbishop*. This device may have had its origin in her memories of the story-tellers of the Divide.[8]

Cather's imagination was deeply engaged by the processes of transformation that she witnessed as part of daily life on the Divide. There were the small-scale kitchen transformations of raw ingredients into food, of flour and cream into bread and butter, of dirt and disorder into comfort and cleanliness wrought by women's labour; but far more significant was the great outdoor transformation, achieved largely by men, by which the rolling red grass of the Nebraska prairies was replaced by heavy ears of corn. Eighteen inches of grass roots had to be removed before the land could be ploughed, and some families survived the long cold winters in homes that were little more than dug-outs, roofed with the cut-away turves. The transformation wrought by that first generation of farmers remained a fundamental source of inspiration to her, and the communal heroism of those who at once told and lived their stories continued to be an active ideal for the solitary writer, engaged in an altogether more metaphysical remaking of the world about her.

The transformation of the prairies by ploughing and road-building was a vivid illustration of the way in which man could impose himself on his surroundings, could write upon the face of the land, as it were. But

Cather was equally moved by the refusal to do so, by the consideration for the land shown, for example, by the Navajo Indians. Father Latour observing Jacinto burying the embers of the camp fire, in *Death Comes for the Archbishop*, is struck by this aspect of Indian culture:

> [T]heir conception of decoration did not extend to the landscape. They seemed to have none of the European's desire to 'master' nature, to arrange and re-create. They spent their ingenuity in the other direction; in accommodating themselves to the scene in which they found themselves.
> (236–7)

The Indian way has analogies with that sympathy that Cather considered to be the artist's great gift. It contrasts with 'the white man's way to assert himself in any landscape' (235–6); it implies observation and respect.

It is tempting to read the white man's imposition of himself on his surroundings as inherently masculine, while the self-effacing Indians, moulding themselves to their setting, might be regarded as feminine. Yet the contrast between the active mastery of circumstances, on one hand, and passivity or endurance on the other, is presented by Cather not in terms of gender but of character difference: the two heroines who make their lives on the Divide display contrasting characteristics, in this respect, though they share a capacity for heroic endurance. Alexandra Bergson, in Cather's second novel, *O Pioneers!*, is herself a farmer who puts out all her power to transform the wilderness into a prosperous farm and garden, shouldering male burdens and responsibilities. *My Ántonia*, heroine of Cather's fourth novel, is victim rather than agent. Like Hardy's Tess, she works as a hired girl and finds herself seduced and abandoned. Though she too ends up farming on the Divide, she is presented rather as a wife and mother of sons than as an independent landowner and the equal of any man, as Alexandra Bergson is.

Willa Cather's second novel *O Pioneers!* (1913) takes its title from Whitman's poem, and like Whitman it celebrates America, the rich potential of the land and the courage of its first settlers: the Bergsons are Swedish immigrants who have left the old world and its ways behind them to start a new life:

> When the road began to climb the first long swells of the Divide, Alexandra hummed an old Swedish hymn, and Emil wondered why his sister looked so happy. Her face was so radiant that he felt shy about asking her. For the first time, perhaps, since that land emerged from the waters of geologic ages, a human face was set toward it with love and yearning. It seemed beautiful to her, rich and strong and glorious. Her eyes drank in the breadth of it, until her tears blinded her. Then the Genius of the Divide, the great, free spirit which breathes across it, must have bent lower than it ever bent to a human will before. The history of every country begins in the heart of a man or a woman.[9]

Sixteen years pass and when the story resumes we learn that 'Any one thereabouts would have told you that this was one of the richest farms on the Divide, and that the farmer was a woman . . .' (83).

Alexandra represents a familiar American ideal, one of self-reliance as outlined by Emerson, and of mystic closeness and sympathy with the land as portrayed by Thoreau. An American hero in every respect but her sex, she lacks that vulnerable element that arouses male desire and protective instincts. Feminine sexuality is associated rather with Marie Shabata whose doll-like prettiness proves fatal to herself as well as to others. The story of Marie's illicit love affair with Alexandra's beloved younger brother Emil, and their tragic love-tryst under the white mulberry tree, presents the strong passions aroused by helpless femininity as potentially destructive. Their story is related with the dignity and simplicity of a traditional ballad, and its identification of sexual love with danger belongs in the same key.

Sexuality continues to be felt as a destructive force in
*My Ántonia* (1918), whose heroine is left with an
illegitimate baby, her life apparently in ruins. In this
novel Cather celebrates in greater detail the hardships,
courage and endurance of the immigrants. It was
inspired by affection for a particular Bohemian girl,
Annie Sadilek, whose father had committed suicide. But
Annie survived to marry a farmer, raise a brood of
children and be immortalised by Cather in a novel whose
transformation of experience into fiction is as masterful
and life-giving as any of the processes she herself
witnessed on the Divide.

Ántonia's parents come to America not knowing what
to expect; they are cheated and defrauded; the cruel
winter and the uncongenial work drive old Anton
Shimerda, amateur musician and professional weaver, to
suicide. Ántonia, tomboyish and strong in the early
sections of the novel, is now left helpless and vulnerable
without her father's protection. She narrowly escapes
rape, only to succumb to passion for a shiftless rogue.
The last section of the story makes good her losses:
twenty years further on, family harmony and faith in the
land have been recovered and restored; Ántonia herself
becomes a figure for the rich mother earth, surrounded
by her devoted Bohemian husband Cuzak and growing
family. The eldest, the illegitimate son, is now a loved
and valued member of this large and united family:

> All the strong things of her heart came out in her body, that
> had been so tireless in serving generous emotions.
> It was no wonder that her sons stood tall and straight. She
> was a rich mine of life, like the founders of early races.
>
> (353)

Ántonia's farm and family, celebrated in terms of a
primitive ideal, serve to recoup what had been damaged,
broken or lost during the earlier stages of the book.

*My Ántonia* has a literary self-consciousness that is

less apparent in *O Pioneers!*. It is a version of pastoral, since its narrator, Jim Burden, deliberately evokes life on the Divide from an urban, even a cosmopolitan perspective. At the University of Lincoln Jim reads Virgil's *Georgics*, recognising in them that love for a particular spot of land which is home: ' "Primus ego in patriam mecum . . . deducam Musas"; "for I shall be the first, if I live, to bring the Muse into my country" ' (264). By alluding to several bucolic classics – Hardy's *Tess* and George Eliot's *Mill on the Floss* – the book's final vision of unity and plenitude takes on an archetypal quality that prevents it from becoming a mere gesture, an overdetermined and sentimental resolution.

Cather drew on the myth of the happy family to provide a reward in the form of a 'genre picture' at the end of this novel of feminine fortitude, but she never for a moment subscribed to it unthinkingly. Indeed she was thoroughly alert to the individual stresses created by close communal life, and even painfully conscious of what sacrifices in the way of personal or artistic fulfilment the land could exact. In an essay on Katherine Mansfield in *Not Under Forty*, Cather brilliantly diagnosed the unresolvable tensions that lie beneath the surface of all family life:

> One realizes that even in harmonious families there is this double life: the group life, which is the one we can observe in our neighbour's household, and, underneath, another – secret and passionate and intense – which is the real life that stamps the faces and gives character to the voices of our friends. Always in his mind each member of these social units is escaping, running away, trying to break the net which circumstances and his own affections have woven about him. One realizes that human relationships are the tragic necessity of human life; that they can never be wholly satisfactory, that every ego is half the time greedily seeking them, and half the time pulling away from them.
>
> (153-4)

Tensions between the family and the young woman

growing up within it, especially if that young woman is already innately an artist, as Katherine Mansfield was, can be intense, even unbearable. Traditionally these provide the main theme of the *bildungsroman* or the *kunstlerroman*, novels in which the artist must reject both family and immediate society in order to find artistic fulfilment. Cather's third novel, *The Song of the Lark* (1915), written between *O Pioneers!* and *My Antonia*, belongs to this type. Its heroine Thea Kronborg, destined to become a great singer, is torn between her background and her ambitions. Such a story inevitably embodies a number of autobiographical features.

*The Song of the Lark* is sometimes regarded as a variant on the traditional plot according to which a hero rejects the temptation to find happiness with a loving woman in order to follow his destiny. If so, Thea combines within herself both the roles of aspiring hero and tempting home-maker. Like Cather, she has to reject her own potential wifehood and motherhood in order to serve her art with full commitment. Thea is thus the character who most fully articulates the conflict at the heart of Cather's work. Her first and fiercest struggle is with her own family who resent her arrogance, her contempt for their narrow values, her rejection of the petty conventions that govern their lives. She rejects her commitments to them in order to free herself to pursue her ambition. When her mother, who alone within the family has given her unquestioning love, lies dying, Thea does not go back to visit her because she has an opportunity of singing Elizabeth in *Tannhäuser* at Dresden.

Like Alexandra Bergson of *O Pioneers!* Thea possesses strength, vision and creative power, but these are directed towards a more obviously selfish goal. The life of the pioneers was an urgent struggle for survival that rendered art and its disciplines irrelevant, unaffordable luxuries. While Moonstone/Red Cloud was merely philistine in its inability to distinguish good art from bad, beyond it lay the prairies and the Divide where only the most practical arts had any place. What had made the sad tale of Sadilek's (or Shimerda's) suicide even more poignant for Cather had been the waste of his musical skills. Ántonia tells Jim Burden, in the novel,

> 'My papa . . . never make music any more. At home he play violin all the time; for weddings and for dance. Here never. When I beg him for play, he shake his head no. Some days he take his violin out of his box and make with his fingers on the strings, like this, but never he make the music.'
>
> (89)

In Cather's earliest version of this story, 'Peter', Sadilek was portrayed as a Prague violinist who had suffered a stroke and was driven to suicide when his wife and son threatened to sell the violin he could not use. Several of the short stories in her first collection, *The Troll Garden* (1905) – notably 'A Wagner Matinée' and 'The Sculptor's Funeral' – dramatise the conflict between artistic needs and a frontier society that has little time for them.

Thea Kronborg rejects her family and Moonstone to follow her calling, though she continues to return to them in her imagination as the safe, lost home. She abandons any hopes of private happiness or the gratification of those nearest to her, saving her energies and gifts for a wider audience. Like her creator, she is in revolt against the small satisfaction women have learnt to seek. The men in her circle admire and even worship her; they do not want to reduce her to ordinariness, to neutralise what is exceptional in her, as in a later novel Harry Gordon wants to neutralise what is exceptional in Lucy Gayheart. Her admirers are fascinated, as we are, by Thea's ruthlessness, that hard element of ambition, determination and rejection of intimate ties which is indistinguishable from artistic commitment. Yet her singing nevertheless involves a kind of selflessness; an act of absorption into the music comparable to that act of sympathy that Willa Cather saw as characterising the true artist.

At the centre of *The Song of the Lark,* its conflicts are momentarily harmonised in an imaginative act of healing and restoration, such as all her novels include somewhere, however briefly. This moment occurs when Thea visits the South West and finds in the abandoned Indian cliff-dwellings on the Mesa a deeply restorative power. The landscape of Panther Canyon, folded and grooved, is subtly suggestive of the female body and helps to promote an atmosphere of female creativity. For Thea the ancient culture effects a reconciliation between her incompatible needs: 'When she felt so keenly alive, lying on that insensible shelf of stone . . ., then she could sing.'[10] Here she finds the remains of pottery designed and made by the Pueblo Indian women. In these ancient artefacts the conflicting imperatives of the frontier – the need for art and the need to live – are re-integrated:

> Nearly every afternoon she went to the chambers which contained the most interesting fragments of pottery, sat and looked at them for a while. Some of them were beautifully decorated. This care, expended upon vessels that could not hold food or water any better for the additional labour put upon them, made her heart go out to those ancient potters. They had not only expressed their desire, but they had expressed it as beautifully as they could.
>
> (379)

The pottery of the Indians annihilates the wounding differences between art and life, humanity and nature. It was made by simple people who possessed a just appreciation of beauty and a need for art. Above all it was made by women, and brings Thea a glimpse of the essentially feminine nature of creativity:

> The stream and the broken pottery: what was any art but an effort to make a sheath, a mould in which to imprison for a moment the shining elusive element which is life itself. . . .

The Indian women had held it in their jars. . . . In singing, one made a vessel of one's throat and nostrils and held it on one's breath, caught the stream in a scale of natural intervals.

(378)

Here and in subsequent accounts of the finding of these ancient Indian jars, Cather seeks to establish a myth of a feminine point of origin for the arts. Yet each time she imagines the process of their making an unease creeps in which undermines the fullness of her vision. In making the jars, the Indian women are prompted by a longing which life itself has failed to satisfy; in trying to define what that longing might mean, Cather's hard-won equation of life and art begins to disintegrate: if life is essentially functional then art must be the outcome of unsatisfied desire, a desire for something beyond life, something required to amend or complete it or confer meaning on it. Writing twenty years later on the theme of art as an escape, she observed of the Indians:

These people lived under the perpetual threat of drought and famine; they often shaped their graceful cooking pots when they had nothing to cook in them. . . . [T]he potters experimented with form and colour to gratify something that had no concern with food and shelter. The major arts (poetry, painting, architecture, sculpture, music) have a pedigree all their own. They did not come into being as a means of increasing the game supply or promoting tribal security. They sprang from an unaccountable predilection of the one unaccountable thing in man.[11]

The desire that drives the ancient potters on is for Cather 'the seed of sorrow and of so much delight' (379); if it compensates for something felt to be missing from life, it may also disclose its absence. Implicit in Cather's myth is the historic distance of the unifying culture that produced the jars; it is alien, absent, desired but unattainable. What survives of it are merely shards and relics; like the jars themselves, the culture is lost, fragmented. Thea, as Tom Outland was later to do in *The Professor's House*, explores the wonderful rock-hung villages and curls up on their warm stone shelves, but the villages and their pottery are empty and hollow as a sea-shell. The vision they briefly suggest of life at one with itself, possessing 'unity of being', is located elsewhere.

The ambiguous status of art in Cather, at once the product of life and yet something felt as a lack seems to echo the sexual symbolism of the jars as empty vessels that can nevertheless be filled with water, even by 'the shining elusive element which is life itself'. Women's bodies have the potential to give life, yet may be experienced as empty, or incomplete. The jars are associated with maternal power. Sheath-like, they hold life within them and are unknowably ancient. They also carry something of the danger associated with maternal power which can be felt as mysteriously threatening, thus provoking violent revenge. Tom Outland in *The Professor's House* describes his discovery of the Blue Mesa (in fact the *Mesa Verde*), with its 'beautifully shaped water jars', small bone instruments and houses carefully built into the rock. Finally he comes upon 'one of the original inhabitants', apparently a young woman whom they refer to as 'Mother Eve'. Her body has mummified in the dry air of the canyon:

> We thought she had been murdered; there was a great wound in her side, the ribs stuck out through the dried flesh. Her mouth was open as if she were screaming, and her face, through all those years, had kept a look of terrible agony.
>
> (206)

In *Death Comes for the Archbishop* Father Latour is led through a snow storm to take shelter in a secret Indian cave whose topography, like that of Panther Canyon, suggests the intimate places of a woman's body – the cave lies between two stone lips, with an underground river flowing far within. It induces in the celibate priest a deep and inexplicable horror (128–35).[12]

The imagery of the jars is associated not only with feminine sexuality (as 'sheath') but also with the use of the voice ('in singing, one had made a vessel of one's own throat and nostrils . . .'). An opera singer is essentially an executive artist rather than a primary creator, an instrument that turns air or a musical score into living song. Cather, with extensive experience of theatrical reviewing, was drawn to actresses and opera singers, their energy and single-minded devotion to their careers offered her one kind of role-model. But if they were self-assertive in some respects, they were self-effacing in others: 'Novelists, opera singers, even doctors have in common the unique and marvellous experience of entering the very skin of another human being.'[13] It was that experience, of getting 'inside another person's skin', that she had first felt in the kitchens on the Divide. But opera-singers and writers have something more specific in common: a voice. Thea discovers that she is an artist when her teacher discovers her voice, for she had begun her musical career by playing the piano. Finding out that she can sing is for her as crucial a discovery as her talent for writing must have been to Willa Cather.

In discussing literature, the metaphor of 'voice' is commonly used to describe the individuality of a particular author or work: a story, Cather claims, 'must leave in the mind of the sensitive reader . . . a cadence, a quality of voice that is exclusively the writer's own, individual, unique'.[14] The individuality of the writer consists in 'the thing that is his very own, his timbre, this cannot be defined or explained any more than the quality of a beautiful speaking voice can be'.[15] It is this essential yet fugitive quality that for Cather distinguishes the true artist: 'It is just the thing in him which escapes analysis that makes him first-rate'.[16] This element of greatness defies definition; it does not correspond to particular words or what is printed on the page, any more than the magic of their stories correspond to the broken English of the immigrant women. As with their speech or the Indian jars something broken or elusive stimulates the imagination to supply a felt absence, to fill an emptiness; once again, Cather's concept of art points towards something outside itself, something unattainable. She admires Katherine Mansfield for her ability to evoke this absent presence – 'She communicates vastly more than she actually writes'.[17] Cather's best-known critical essay, 'The Novel Démeublé', attempts to pin this element down:

> Whatever is felt upon the page without being specifically named there – that, one might say, is created. It is the inexplicable presence of the thing not named, of the overtone divined by the ear but not heard by it, the verbal mood, the emotional aura of the fact or the thing or the deed, that gives high quality to the novel or the drama, as well as to poetry itself.[18]

The language of this, with its anxieties about naming and its emphasis on the metaphysical, gestures towards a feminist poetics that cannot itself be conceived or 'named'. Furthermore it implicitly passes on to the reader the responsibility of deciding whether this particular level of communication has been achieved.

Sometimes Cather seems to have thought that this mysterious intensity might be achieved by quite humdrum methods, for example by a deliberate process of stringent simplification and concentration, 'so that all that one has suppressed and cut away is there to the reader's consciousness as much as if it were in type on the page'.[19] Such an editing process is akin to Kipling's concept of 'draining', that is, beginning with an expansive draft which is gradually reduced to its essentials, yet cut in such a way that the pressure of the deleted material can somehow still be felt.[20] Cather drastically reduced the text of her final novel, *Sapphira and the Slave Girl*, perhaps with her own strictures in mind.[21] Yet this concept of deliberate concision is substantially different as well as evidently more prosaic than her sense of an art mysteriously prompting the reader to supply something more than itself.

It was only a matter of time before Cather adapted her technique of unfurnishing the house of fiction to the presentation of her heroines. In using Jim Burden as narrator, *My Ántonia* had made use of a limited viewpoint, requiring the reader to make allowances for his particular angle of vision, to recognise what was partial in Jim's act of appropriation and reconstruction of 'his' Ántonia. But it was not until *A Lost Lady* (1923) that Cather placed at the centre of a book a character seen only through other people's eyes, a woman who is 'lost' not merely in the Victorian sense of fallen, but is genuinely missing, a felt absence, rather than a presence: 'in order to portray Mrs. Forrester it was necessary to show her as she was reflected in the minds of a number of men'.[22] Chief of these is the backwoods boy Niel Herbert who acts as 'a peephole into that world . . . a point of view'.[23] He begins by worshipping her but comes to hate her for destroying his illusions. To his eyes she appears as a series of female stereotypes: the angel in the house; the fallen woman; the cast-off mistress; the victim of a scoundrel; the alcoholic slut. The last illustration in the sequence, her successful second marriage, interrupts this feminine rake's progress and reveals it as illusory, the imposition of a punitive moral judgement. Marian Forrester herself is patently a construct and thus can share with Cather's ideal of art that quality of conveying more than can merely be stated: 'Beautiful women whose beauty meant more than it said . . . was their brilliancy always fed by something coarse and concealed? Was that their secret?'.[24] What is coarse and concealed and yet also nourishing is, of course, sex. Like Cather's own earlier fiction, Niel displays a fear and distrust of sexuality, but his creator has herself moved on, to the recognition that Marian Forrester's vital energies and *joie de vivre*, her ability to confer happiness on the men around her, are inseparable from her sexuality and lie at the core of her being.

Marian Forrester shares with Cather's earlier heroines qualities of courage and endurance; she maintains the little arts of civilisation even in the wilderness. Cather's next heroine, Myra Henshawe of *My Mortal Enemy* (1926), is, if anything, even more disturbing. She too is the victim of a romantic passion, but it is a passion that she has come bitterly to regret. Though she is presented more fully in her own words than Marian Forrester, she remains as mysterious a figure, poised between the relentless materialism that ruined her love-match and a deep and touching spirituality shown in her commitment to her faith and her final romantic determination to die watching the sun rise over the sea, a symbol of hope or even resurrection.

Myra Henshawe's hunger for an expansive and expensive life style has some parallels with that of the wife and daughters of Godfrey St Peter, hero of *The Professor's House* (1925). Here Cather is preoccupied with the struggle to retain integrity, order and meaning in life in the context of an increasingly materialistic society, for so America had come to seem to her in the years following the Great War: 'the world broke in two in 1922 or thereabouts'.[25] In *Death Comes for the Archbishop* (1927) and *Shadows on the Rock* (1931), the struggle to preserve the values of civilisation is enacted with greater decency and dignity at the old frontiers – by two missionary priests among the Spaniards and Indians on the Southern border, and by the first French settlers on the Rock of Quebec. In these harsh settings, the old life-giving routines that she had observed on the Divide, the preparation of food, the washing, cleansing and ordering of the home still act as a bulwark against chaos and share with art the power to confer meaning:

These coppers, big and little, these brooms and clouts and brushes, were tools; and with them one made, not shoes or cabinet-work, but life itself. One made a climate within a climate: one made the days, – the complexion, the special flavour, the special happiness of each day as it passed; one made life.[26]

Cather's late fiction, focused upon lost frontiers and lonely men, seems coloured by a disillusion with post-war America and its women, with Ántonia's grand-daughters, as it were. No longer required to perform heroic tasks, their care for others, their maintenance of the fugitive values of civilisation, even their femininity are fast disappearing. The aggressive girls who cause an accident in 'The Old Beauty' smoke and drive: 'They were Americans; bobbed and hatless, clad in dirty white knickers and sweaters. They addressed each other as "Marge" and "Jim".'[27]

Yet Cather had not abandoned her old concern to define the nature of feminine creativity and to chart its fulfilment or frustration in domestic tasks. Two late fictions return to confront that paradigmatic representative of it – the mother, a figure that her earlier fiction had usually avoided, except to provide the idyll at the end of *My Ántonia*; motherhood offered a closeness abandoned in *The Song of the Lark*, and lost in *Shadows on the Rock*. The death of her own mother in 1931, after a long illness, finally released her to depict that relationship, and to do so she drew from her own experience, writing both her mother and her grandmother into her last fictions. 'Old Mrs. Harris' (in *Obscure Destinies*, 1932) describes three generations of women: Grandma Harris whose selfless love rejoices in whatever she can give or do for her handsome, thoughtless daughter Victoria Templeton, and her grand-daughter Vickie who stands for Cather at the outset of her life, a young woman, preoccupied with going to college. Vickie, eager to begin packing, arrives home to find both her mother and grandmother lying down:

Nobody but Mr. Rosen seemed to take the least interest, 'when my whole life hangs by a thread,' she told herself fiercely. What were families for, anyway?[28]

In fact it is her grandmother's life that hangs by a thread, even at the same moment as her mother reluctantly recognises that she is pregnant again and has brought a new life into being. The isolation of individuals within the family unit which Cather had observed in her essay on Katherine Mansfield is painfully conveyed. The three generations stand for contrasting aspects of feminine creativity: Grandma Harris cooks, cleans and attends to the children's needs; Victoria, still breast-feeding the youngest, is resentfully preoccupied with maternity; Vickie is studying and longing for the world beyond.

In Cather's last novel, *Sapphira and the Slave Girl* (1940), written after a gap of several years, she returns to her own family and to Virginia, where she had spent her earliest childhood. Those qualities of feminine authority and feminine stoicism that had empowered Alexandra Bergson and Ántonia Shimerda are once more at the centre of the action, but now they are flawed or darkened and pitted against one another in a bitter conflict that splits the family, and would soon split the American nation, for this is the ante-Bellum South. The authority belongs to Sapphira Dodderidge Colbert, a Southern matriarch who, though crippled with dropsy, nevertheless keeps herself and her household in apple-pie order. The stoicism is that of the slave girl Nancy whose gentle loving nature is misconstrued and abused. Hers is the stoicism of black women, suffering under the double burden of race and gender. Cather's presentation of her black characters has dated and at times is uncomfortably patronising, yet the book as whole is animated by a strong sense of their oppression.

As in 'Old Mrs. Harris', Cather dramatises maternal power through the interaction of three generations:

Sapphira, her daughter Rachel and her young grand-daughters are set against the four generations of their servants: Jezebel, ninety-five years old, is dying. She can recall having been brought over in a slave ship from Guinea where she had seen her family slaughtered before her eyes. Her grand-daughter Till has internalised white values and accepts all that Miss Sapphy does without question, including an arranged marriage to an impotent husband, so that she will not be distracted from her duties by child-bearing. Till's beautiful illegitimate daughter Nancy is the book's central victim, for Sapphira unjustly suspects her husband's affection for Nancy and is determined that she be resold or else debauched by her libertine nephew. While the book invites our admiration for Nancy's courage and dignity in the face of persecution, it also shows how relentlessly cruel women in authority can be to other women: the great matriarchs of the South possessed a power open to terrible misuse. As Sapphira becomes steadily more helpless and physically dependent, losing her freedom and mobility, so she becomes steadily more vicious, spiteful and vengeful.

Like so much of Cather's fiction, *Sapphira and the Slave Girl* is a book about women and the way they accept or repudiate the roles allotted them by society. The male characters, Henry, Sapphira's well-meaning husband, and the aspiring rapist, Martin, remain marginal to the action. Outside the unequal conflict between Sapphira and Nancy and vainly attempting to mediate between them is Rachel Blake, Sapphira's widowed daughter, who is disgusted by the slave system. She eventually intervenes to save Nancy from Martin by smuggling her up the line, and over the border to freedom. By a subtle transformation, Rachel Blake is revealed, in the last pages of the book, as Rachel Boak, Willa Cather's own maternal grandmother, and thus the original of 'Old Mrs. Harris', though she is there por-trayed very differently.

In the epilogue to *Sapphira* Willa Cather herself, aged five, is carried to the window to watch the legendary figure of Nancy return, after twenty-five years in which she has made a new life for herself in Montreal. *Sapphira* is a book about matriarchal power and in this epilogue, which is also the author's own farewell to her readers, her version of Prospero's final speech, she recreates some of her own earliest memories, recalling the warmth and comfort of mother and grandmother, but most of all the storytelling of women as they sit round the kitchen table, sewing or knitting or watching the rising dough, pursuing the further destinies of the various men and women who had worked in and around Colbert's mill. While the small narrator sews her patchwork Till, Nancy and Rachel follow up other threads and as they do so, an unending and endlessly absorbing sequence of stories unfolds in which national and family history are woven into a seamless, mythical web. Today this epilogue is distanced from us by its self-conscious presentation of black conversation, yet in its blending of maternal love with women's tales, women's society, women's gifts to and love for one another, it might well be Willa Cather's final comment on her own narrative art.

# Notes

1. *Nebraska State Journal*, 3 May 1896, 13, reprinted in *The Kingdom of Art: Willa Cather's First Principles and Critical Statements 1893–1896*, ed. Bernice Slote (Lincoln, University of Nebraska Press, 1966), 158. This essay is particularly indebted to discussions of Cather by Sharon O'Brien, *Willa Cather – The Emerging Voice* (New York and Oxford, Oxford University Press); Sandra M. Gilbert and Susan Gubar, *No Man's Land – The Place of the Woman Writer in the Twentieth Century*, vol. 2, *Sexchanges* (New Haven and London, Yale University Press, 1989); and Ellen Moers, *Literary Women* (London, Allen, 1977).

2. *Lincoln Sunday Star,* 6 November 1921, reprinted in *Willa Cather in Person,* ed. L. Brent Bohlke (Lincoln, University of Nebraska Press, 1986), 47.

3. 'All my stories have been written with material that was gathered . . . before I was fifteen years old. Other authors tell me it is the same way with them. Sarah Orne Jewett insisted to me that she had used nothing in all her short stories which she did not remember before she was eight years old.' From the interview with Hinman, cited above and reprinted in *Willa Cather in Person,* 43; see also 31, 37.

4. Interview in the *Philadelphia Record,* 10 August 1913, reprinted in *Willa Cather in Person,* 10. See also 20: 'Their stories used to go round and round in my head at night. This was, with me, the initial impulse.'

5. 'Miss Jewett', in *Not Under Forty* (London, Cassell, 1936), 89.

6. 'The Novel Démeublé', *Not Under Forty,* 54.

7. *My Ántonia* (Boston and New York, Houghton Mifflin, 1918), 115.

8. *My Ántonia,* 56–60; 'Coming, Aphrodite!', in *Youth and the Bright Medusa* (New York, 1920, London, Heinemann, 1921), 55–9; *The Professor's House* (New York, London, Heinemann, 1925), 171–245; *Death Comes for the Archbishop* (New York, Alfred A. Knopf, 1926), 105–17.

9. *O Pioneers!* (Boston and New York, Houghton Mifflin, 1913), 65.

10. *The Song of the Lark* (Boston and New York, Houghton Mifflin, 1915; second edition London, Cassell, 1938), 381.

11. 'Escapism', a letter, 17 April 1936, in *On Writing: Critical Studies on Writing as an Art* (New York, Alfred A. Knopf, 1949), 19.

12. The significance of these images in Cather's work has been extensively examined. Ellen Moers (*Literary Women*) describes Panther Canyon as 'the most thoroughly elaborated female landscape in literature', 258–9; Sandra M. Gilbert and Susan Gubar in *No Man's Land – The Place of the Woman Writer in the Twentieth Century, vol. 1, The War of the Words* (New Haven and London, Yale University Press, 1988) discuss the Canyon and the 'stone lips', 120–1; and further in vol. 2, *Sexchanges,* 180–1, 208–9; see also Sharon O'Brien, 202–3, 408–11, 415–6.

13. Elizabeth Sergeant, *Willa Cather - A Memoir* (Lincoln, University of Nebraska Press, 1963), 111, cited by Sharon O'Brien, 92, who also discusses 'voice' in relation to Cather's conception of the artist; see esp. 171-4.
14. 'Miss Jewett', *Not Under Forty*, 87-8.
15. 'Katherine Mansfield', *Not Under Forty*, 152.
16. *ibid.*, 152.
17. *ibid.*, 155.
18. 'The Novel Démeublé', *Not Under Forty*, 54.
19. 'On the Art of Fiction' (from *The Borzoi*, 1920); *On Writing*, 102; see also 'Katherine Mansfield', *Not Under Forty*, 155.
20. See Rudyard Kipling, *Something of Myself* (London, Macmillan 1937; reprinted Harmondsworth, Penguin, 1977), 135-60.
21. Interview in the *New York Herald Tribune* (*Books*), 15 December 1940, reprinted in *Willa Cather in Person*, 135-6.
22. *New York Herald Tribune*, 22 February 1924, reprinted in *Willa Cather in Person*, 64.
23. *New York World*, 19 April 1925, reprinted in *Willa Cather in Person*, 77.
24. *A Lost Lady* (New York, Alfred A. Knopf, 1923), 84.
25. Prefatory Note to *Not Under Forty*, v.
26. *Shadows on the Rock* (New York and London, Hamish Hamilton, 1931), 198.
27. 'The Old Beauty', in *The Old Beauty and Others* (New York, Alfred A. Knopf, 1948; London, Cassell, 1956), 67.
28. 'Old Mrs. Harris', in *Obscure Destinies* (New York and London, Alfred A. Knopf, 1932), 181-2.

# Chronological Table of Works
# HD (Hilda Doolittle)
### *1886–1961*

### Poetry

| | |
|---|---|
| 1916 | *Sea Garden* |
| 1921 | *Hymen* |
| 1924 | *Heliodora and Other Poems* |
| 1925 | *Collected Poems* |
| 1931 | *Red Roses for Bronze* |
| 1944 (1942) | *The Walls Do Not Fall* (Part I, *Trilogy*) |
| 1945 (1944) | *Tribute to the Angels* (Part II, *Trilogy*) |
| 1946 (1944) | *Flowering of the Rod* (Part III, *Trilogy*) |
| 1961 (1952–1956) | *Helen in Egypt* |
| 1972 (1957) | 'Sagesse' (in *Hermetic Definition*) |
| 1972 (1959) | 'Winter Love' (in *Hermetic Definition*) |
| 1972 (1960–1961) | 'Hermetic Definition' (in *Hermetic Definition*) |

### Prose

| | |
|---|---|
| 1926 | *Palimpsest* |
| 1928 | *Hedylus* |
| 1935 | *Nights* |
| 1936 | *The Hedgehog* |
| 1956 (1944) | *Writing on the Wall* (major part of *Tribute to Freud*) |
| 1960 (1939, 1949) | *Bid Me to Live* |
| 1974 (1933, 1948) | *Advent* (revised journal now part of *Tribute to Freud*) |
| 1979 (1958) | *End to Torment* |
| 1981 (1927) | *Her* |
| 1982 (1919) | *Notes on Thought and Vision* |

### Translations

| | |
|---|---|
| 1916 | *Choruses from Iphigenia at Aulis* |
| 1919 | *Choruses from the Iphigenia in Aulis and the Hippolytus of Euripides* |
| 1937 | *Euripides Ion* |

### Critical

| | |
|---|---|
| 1927 | 'The Cinema and the Classics' |
| 1949 (1945–1946) | *By Avon River* |

*Note:* Brackets enclose the date of writing when they vary with the date of publication.

# 3

# HD's *Autre*Biography

## *Dianne Chisholm*

More than a decade has passed since Susan Stanford Friedman launched a feminist revaluation of HD with her breakthrough query, 'Who Buried HD? The Poet, Her Critics, and "The Literary Tradition".'[1] During this time, feminist scholarship has successfully retrieved the poet and her poetry from masculist judges and canon-builders who failed to appreciate the poetics because they failed to recognise the woman and her writing (of) difference. 'The Emergence of HD' in the canon of twentieth-century women writers testifies to the collaborative effort of feminist scholars, culminating in the production of three book-length critical biographies (Friedman; Robinson; DuPlessis).[2] These biographies perform the difficult task of introducing the poet and her work simultaneously and they imply certain causal (historical, psychological, genealogical, national) connections between the self who writes and her written text. Each of these studies proceeds on the assumption that writing is an 'effect' of an autobiographical intention or the 'product' of a writer's life, that it functions as an autograph, identifying a 'transcendental signified' – the self-signifying signatory. These works interpret writ-

ing, in general, as an 'epiphenomenon' of mind or spirit,
a dynamic recording of poeticised feelings, aspirations,
identifications, conflicts and transgressions of a more or
less self-conscious subject. They attribute the 'developments' they chart in HD's *oeuvre* to either a dialectic of
self-knowledge and its automatic articulation, to the
'auto' of the autographer, or to the contingencies of
'life', to the mediation between the 'auto' and the 'graph'
by the 'bio' of auto-bio-graphy.

Such critical assumptions have recently been
challenged or at least supplemented by a structuralist
and/or post-structuralist shift of emphasis from 'self' and
'life' to 'writing'. Advances in psychoanalytic criticism
and deconstruction have sought a radical de-mystifica-
tion of the idealist (variously referred to as 'trans-
cendentalist', 'romantic', 'liberal humanist') notions of
the autonomous, automatic, writing subject and have
replaced the concept of autography with auto-hetero-
graphy, the inscription of 'the other'. The term 'the other'
does not necessarily signify an identifiable entity or a
codifiable process; in (post-)structuralist readings of
literary texts it is used to refer to various possible ways of
rethinking the complex act of poetic articulation, taking
into account (a) the heterogeneous system(s) of writing
which constitute(s) the authorial subject in an inscription of grammatical and generic laws, of graphic technique, of idiomatic style, of rules of metaphor, of esoteric
or hermetic signs, of poetic characters (ideograms,
hieroglyphs, cryptograms); (b) the 'language(s)' of writing, which include(s) the poet's mother tongue, the traces
of bilingual- or polylingual-ism and the play of translation, non-speaking or non-communicating, 'pre-
symbolic language' (what Julia Kristeva calls 'the
semiotic'), 'symptomatic language' (what semanalysts
refer to as 'dream language' or as 'hysterical discourse');
(c) rhetorical and linguistic conventions which are
systematically but not fixedly bound to political and
prejudicial ideologies (what Luce Irigaray refers to as

'Master Discourse', what Jacques Derrida and Hélène Cixous refer to as 'phallogocentrism' and what HD refers to as 'the palimpsest of misadventure'); (d) the uncanny subject 'who' is not inscribed, not spoken for, not identified, not adequately or sufficiently signified, a semiotic or grammatological 'excess' which is neither wholly expressed nor repressed by any communal language, literary tradition or finite speech act (Irigaray's 'other (woman)', Kristeva's 'feminine or maternal semiotic', Derrida's 'difference').

Does this (post-)structuralist critique of the 'unified subject' or of the autonomous self offer HD criticism a radical point of departure? If, as HD's readers, we take this criticism to heart and no longer trust the autobiographer to be herself or the poet to be giving vital and direct vent to her (un)conscious will, lived experience, desire for self-formulation and self-criticism, then 'who' are we dealing with? 'Who' is HD if not 'Herself Defined', when by self we mean self-originating, self-authorising, self-reliant; 'who' is HD if not the woman who, with a writing of her own (self-)making, transcends the severe limitations imposed on her autobiography by a patriarchal, linguistic/literary community?

This essay makes an attempt to reconsider HD, or more precisely her prose and poetry (not the least of which is, in the conventional sense, autobiographical) in the light of (post)structuralist thought. I regard this venture as supplemental to, and not a substitution for, the kind of critical work which Friedman and others have undertaken and I remain indebted to their pioneering efforts, which in some ways are more adventuresome and less derivative than the theoretically self-conscious criticism of the present.

# HD, Who is He?

It is still timely to wonder at the question, 'HD, who is he?', the question asked by readers of the canon who have yet to appreciate the arrival of 'HD, Woman and Poet'; we might guess that it is prompted by a conventional, hermeneutic desire to trace the meaning of the poem to the identify of the poet. We might also guess that the gender-bias of this question is prompted by the expectations of a patriarchal community which authorises all symbolic transactions in the name of the father. In the face of these expectations and assumptions which overrule the enigmatic anonymity of HD's cryptic signature it is still highly politic to consider the power of the proper name, the gender of *author*ity, the en*gender*ing of authorship, the possible inscription of feminine difference in the text of one of the few women poets of this century to try her hand at writing Cantos-length auto-mythology.

The discovery that the signatory 'is not a man' poses further questions to the feminist reader: does HD choose to sign without 'the mark of gender'? Does 'HD' strategically draw attention to the text without at the same time drawing upon the usual prejudices which attend the idea of a 'woman writer'?[3] Does 'HD' provide a c(l)ue to the hermeneutic feminist that there is this 'other' woman who writes elusively behind the veil of these curious initials but who cannot be positively named or identified? Does HD sign her name with two hieroglyphic letters like the mystic AE (George Russell), in preference to using a masculine pseudonym like the sceptical feminist, George Eliot, in order to signify her feminine difference as an otherworldliness? 'Who' is this cryptographer, this anagrammatist, who inscribes her signature into the titles of her books (H*edylus*, H*ermetic Definition*) and who is as much 'inscribed' by them as they are by her? How do we trace the identity of a writer who graphs her name into at least one feminine pseudonym (*H*elga *D*orn), into the name of her autobio/biblio/ graphical protaganist, *H*enry *D*ohna, who already undertakes the task of tracing the poet's (Dohna's, HD's) genealogy and who arrives at the same mystical, Moravian script which inspired the great poet Goethe.[4] 'Who' is this 'HD' who signals to biographers in search of HD that there is nowhere to look beyond the reinscription of archives and the engraving of palimpsests? Can we disentangle the poet from the lives of her characters when they, too, are searching for their author whom they know can be found in repetitious rewriting of her life story? What do we make of the testimony of HD's 'Helen', that exemplary grammatologist who underlines for the collaborating reader of *Helen in Egypt* that 'she herself is the writing'?

Until the advent of feminist literary criticism, modernist studies had been content to represent HD as one of Ezra Pound's creations. In particular, malestream canon-builders are fond of recapturing that magic moment in 1912 in the teashop of the British Museum where Pound enthusiastically received a poem, freshly scored by the novice Hilda Doolittle, proclaiming prophetically 'but dryad, this is poetry!' and scratching 'HD, Imagiste' at the bottom of the page.[5] HD's recollection of this moment reconsiders the authority of the master craftsman to which masculist critics attribute the creation of the first Imagist poem, 'Hermes of the Ways', and the forthcoming success of HD's Imagism. As she sees it, this was the crucial moment of the birth of 'HD – Hermes – Hermeticism and all the rest of it.'[6] 'Hermeticism and all the rest of it' was not on Pound's agenda and has remained outside the curriculum of modern English studies. It is time that HD criticism should attempt to introduce this heterodoxical modernist and her *autre*biography.

# From Imagism to Hermeticism, Tracing the Signature of the Other (Woman)

HD's 'Oread' appeared in *Some Imagist Poets* (1915) and was used by Pound in his definition of Vorticism as the ultimate Imagist creation. Taking his cue from Pound, anthologist Peter Jones turns to 'Oread' to supply a self-illustrating description of Imagist poetry. 'There are no similes in the poem', he observes,

> no symbols, presentation rather than representation; no moralizing tone; no reflection on human experience (a danger here in lack of human concern); no striving for the spiritual; no fixed metre or rhyme – but a rhythm organic to the image itself; no narrative – it needs none; no vagueness of abstractions – it would destroy the image . . . and no form but the poem itself. It is not forced to take upon itself a fixed shape, except that of the image in isolation ecstatically held. It is not merely description but evocation; and to use Pound's words: 'The gulf between evocation and description . . . is the unbridgeable difference between genius and talent'.[7]

In short, this exemplary imagist poem presents the Image in its 'transparency', no mediating symbolism, or narrative, or morality, no thinking on human issues, no striving for the spiritual, no representation, though we must concede at least an implicit reference to that Imagist doctrine, whose authorial 'genius' engendered this seminal form of *vers libre*. But to whose genius do the critics pay explicit tribute? Several feminist critics point to the subsequent erasure of the significance of HD's contribution to the making of an Imagist aesthetic, the first chapter in the history of English modernism. And one critic in particular points to HD's unrecognised *tour de force* which propelled Pound's otherwise static formulation of poetic form towards a vorticist aesthetic. In her reading of 'Hermes of the

Ways', Cyrena N. Pondrom contends that it was HD's poetry which inspired Pound's Vorticism, and not vice versa, that:

> the poem anticipates more than the prescriptions of Imagism. Its method is more fully described by the discussion of poetic form in Pound's essay on 'Vorticism' than by the early Imagist documents, which focus chiefly on metric, economy, the use of ordinary language, the preference for metaphor over simile, and the avoidance of imprecision and abstraction. The way form . . . itself becomes an image is not explicitly considered in the first explanations of Imagism in March, 1913. Thus [HD's] poems do more than offer models for the description of Imagism. They actually provide early poetic models for the important transformation of the static form of Imagist doctrine into Vorticism.[8]

But even if and when we establish HD as a *tour de force* of early modernism, how do we explain her disappearance from 'the rostrum of the literary establishment' in the history of twentieth-century poetics which follows the dissolution of the Imagist movement? Like her male colleagues, Pound, Richard Aldington and D. H. Lawrence, HD left the confines of Imagism to experiment with other poetic forms, altering the genre of her artistic practice and writing industriously until the end of her life in 1961. Yet her contribution to post-Imagist modernism remains unsung outside feminist literary circles. Why? Since with Pound she shares a pagan mythopoeia; with Eliot a 'striving for spirituality'; with Aldington a notion of literary autobiography; with Lawrence a revision of psychoanalysis; with Mallarmé a mystical symbolism; and with Joyce a Flaubertian or 'decadent' aestheticising of common language and specialised discourses. But while HD's writing encompasses all the distinctive features of modernism, it does so with a critical difference. In search of stranger gods than Pound, HD's mythopoeia 'invokes' not Priapus, Pound's favourite phallic deity, but Thetis, metaphoric, metamorphic sea-goddess, creatrix-of-all-things and muse of her first collection of poems, *Sea Garden* (1916). Against Eliot's Anglicanism, rooted in the English heritage of his forefathers, HD draws from a hermeticism rooted in her maternal, Moravian genealogy. Against Aldington's presentation of auto-biography as a scandalous tale of the (anti-) hero HD's autobiography tells the tale of '*personne*', of the poet-nobody, of the writing woman, known to no one, not even to herself and especially not to the writing men who would mythologise her. Against Lawrence's Oedipal narratives of mother–son relations HD's narratives elaborate Freud's highly suggestive notion of 'pre-Oedipal' mother–daughter relations. Against Mal-larmé's *poésie pur* and its absolute disregard for refer-entiality (beyond poetic self-reference) HD employs a mystic symbolism to 'invoke' other worlds, particularly the other world of 'the mothers' which she found in the 'alchemical' texts of Goethe and Freud. Against word-wizard Joyce and his polyphonic, polyglottal choruses HD abandons the realm of the word and calls upon the 'hieroglyph of the unconscious', the 'language of dreams', the primitive, unspoken language of a repressed and forgotten personal or racial pre-history. While Joyce subverts the notion of a pure, national language with a polylingual mother tongue HD subverts the very notions of 'language' and of 'speech' by attempting to articulate the imaginary, primary world of child and woman outside the discourse of nations, of the exchange of signs between citizen–men, the talk of patriots and/or patriarchs. Her invocation of a primal poetics recalls Nietzsche's defence of a 'primitivist' art:

one must overlook it in the artist himself if he does not stand in the foremost ranks of the Enlightenment and the progres-sive *masculinization* of man: he has remained a child or a youth all his life, stuck at the point he was first assailed by his drive to artistic production; [invoking] feelings belonging to the first stages of life which are, however, admitted to be closer to those of earlier times than to those of the present century.[9]

HD's modernist art looks back to antiquity; but it risks looking even further back than that of her male colleagues, beyond Joyce's 'Ulysses', Eliot's 'Ecclesiastes', Pound's 'Confucius', Lawrence's and Nietzsche's 'Dionysos', and even beyond Freud's 'Moses', who 'arose' in the reign of the Egyptian Sun King, Akhenaton. HD's 'Helen' descends from Isis, who is not to be confused with the phallic, sun/son-worshipping 'Isis' of Lawrence's later years and who signifies a 'dark age' not yet illuminated by a humanist Enlightenment or repressed and surpassed by 'the progressive masculinization of man'.

Various reflexive devices in HD's text alert the reader to the poet's transition from Imagism to Hermeticism, to the fabrication of a mythic (w)rite of passage, to the 'becoming' of a woman *autre*biographer. Consider the difference between 'Oread' and the excerpt from the long poem, *Hermetic Definition*, transcribed below:

| | |
|---|---|
| whirl up sea, | why must I write? |
|   whirl your pointed pines, |   you would not care for this |
| splash your great pines |   but She draws the veil |
| on our rocks, | aside, |
| hurl your green over us, |   unbinds my eyes, |
| cover us with your pools of |   commands, |
| fur. |   write, write or die. |
| 'Oread', 1914 | *Hermetic Definition*, 1961 |

In 'Oread' there is no poetic persona; the subject is invisible, transparent, given in an artificial immediacy, 'free' of historical, ideological, political, economic,

racial and sexual definition. The reader is implied but
only in a covert and disinterested gesture – 'O read' –
pointing towards the poem's stylistics. We note the
syntactical 'dance' between two metaphorical objects,
'sea' and 'pines', along the rocky rhetorical border where
we find an unlocatable 'us'. The choreography entwines
the figures of 'sea' and 'pines' and 'fur' so inextricably
that no distinct entity or unified subject emerges. In
contrast to the unfocused, I-/eye-less 'Oread', the 'visionary' *Hermetic Definition* demands that the poet be seen
behind the impersonal veil of her writing, that she be
recognised and authorised by her Muse, the empowering
and en-gendering 'She'. This later text clearly has focus,
a feminist goal whose stakes are no less than life and
death; gone is indeterminacy, the disinterestedness and
the deconstructive anonymity of the imagist lyric.

Critical reception of HD's 'model' Imagist poem may
be read as a fetishisation of a woman's potential to write
as women are conditioned to write – without the proper
name, its power to signify what is 'proper' to it (the
paternal genealogy of poetic generations, traditions
styles and differences). 'Oread' itself may be read as a
fetish object, marking the gap at the 'centre' of dancing
images where a 'woman' (some sign of en-gendered
writing) could have appeared and whose abyss is concealed by the choreographed veils of illusory in-differ-
ence. Phallocentric critics would especially approve of a
poem whose 'superimposition' of images (to use a term
of Pound's) could solicit the reader's mastering gaze
without looking him in the eye from an identifiable
subject position. No eye, no I, no identity: hence 'HD,
Imagiste', no further signature needed. Is 'Oread' the
exemplary Imagist poem sponsored by the self-styled,
exemplary poet warranting the death of the (woman)
author? In marked contrast the passage from *Hermetic
Definition* unveils its subject and indicates the desire of
the woman poet or of her self-authorising muse to the
annoyance of the reader, the 'you [who] would not care

for this' (the doctrinal, Imagist reader? Pound?). The rhetoric of immediacy in the former poem is overruled by the rhetoric of deferral in the latter one, which we know, from reading the entire text of 'HD', emerges only after a lifetime of self-definition in writing.

Cyrena Pondrom attributes HD's Imagist 'genius' to her lack of 'positionality': 'An expatriate for [. . .] a year's length, HD', she writes,

> surely stood on the boundaries between two cultures. She [also] stood on the boundary between two definitions of her sexual identity, and was shaping with pain an identity which relinquished neither role. She stood poised between a traditional childhood as the daughter of a distinguished professor and the unstable life of the expatriate abroad.[10]

She concludes that it was HD's shaping of a myth that allowed her to dance along the borders of identity without falling into line or losing control. 'The myth of Hermes', she claims, 'embodies those skills to which [HD] turned for the strength to remain at the boundaries of her life.'

Pondrom's reading of HD's Imagism revalues a woman's contribution to literary history without considering the historical and ideological conditions of women's writing, and without considering women's need to designate a position from which to authorise entry into history as a speaking, knowing, self-signifying and significantly different, feminine subject. That the Imagist poem permits, as Peter Jones glibly outlines, no symbols, no representation, no reflection of human experience, no striving for the spiritual, no narrative, is surely advantageous to the male poet–entrepreneur who would exploit, consciously or unconsciously, women's lack of symbolic identity within established public institutions, including all specialised disciplines and discourses, in order to attract a following among those women who turn to poetry as the most accommodating medium of self-expression. It is not surprising that

Pound lost his two most influential Imagist practitioners, HD and Amy Lowell, when he began to expound upon his theory of the seminal force of poetic creation, the explicitly phallic nature of the Vortex. The greatest 'danger' of Imagism is not its 'lack of human concern', as Jones suggests, but its seductive capacity to distract women from their pursuit of symbolic self-representation, its lack of concern for the woman writer and for her struggle to write against the suppressive historical, material and ideological conditions which govern her artistic production. Unlike Pondrom, I read 'Oread' as a symptom of women's lack of authoritative position, of self-signification – *as women* – in the public, symbolic order and I read the transition from imagism to hermeticism as a lifelong struggle to materialise the vital, imperious desire to forge a definition and find a sign – however esoteric – with which to signify herself, to stamp her mark upon the world and to re-mark upon her erasure from the world text.

If life could be lived in the rarefied environ of the Imagist poem, the woman poet could revel in the dissolution of positionality, endlessly recirculate a dithyrambic ecstasy at the expense of self-determination and definition. But beyond the confining boundaries of this poetic form in a larger, social and political context, the undesignated subject flounders in a phenomenological mud of symbolically unmediated experience. The Imagist lyric affords the woman writer no focal point, no point from which to launch into history or to narrate her life story. HD's autobiographical novel, *Her*, translates 'Oread's' whirling round an I-less core into hysterical narrative whose 'concentric' motions belie the narrator's deliriously desperate desire to locate the ground of identity, some sign, some mark of difference, some point of view, some position, to mark her off from the enveloping, nebulous world:

Her Gart went round in circles. . . . she cried in her

dementia, 'I am Her, Her, Her.' . . . She said, 'I am
Hermione Gart,' but Her Gart was not that. She was
nebulous, gazing into the branches of liriodendron. . . . Her
eyes peered up into the branches . . . Her Gart peered far, to
follow [a] bird, she lost the bird, tried to focus on one leaf to
hold her on to all leaves . . . She was nothing . . . She tried
to drag in personal infantile reflection . . . Sylvania. I was
born here. Pennsylvania. I am part of Sylvania. Trees.
Trees. Trees. . . . Liriodendron. . . . Pennsylvania whirled
round in cones of concentric colour. . . . [a] concentric
gelatinous substance that was her perception of trees, grown
closer, grown near like celluloid. The circles of the trees
were tree green; she wanted the inner lining of an Atlantic
breaker. . . . She wanted the Point. She wanted to get to
Point Pleasant.[11]

'Oread's' whirling up of 'pointed pines' now appears
disastrously pointless when seen outside the vortex from
the yet unarticulated point of view of a woman writer in
search of narrative or authorial identity. As a writing
subject, Oread/Her 'is nothing', a non-being, a non-
entity in the text of the world and its inscription of
history, ideology, nationality. She is without means of
representing her place in the world or of speaking for
herself as one of its citizens. She helplessly embodies the
object of the Imagist movement, its determination to
dissolve political and personal identity, to shift ground
into no man's land and to shift focus onto the site/sight
of the subject's undoing, the undoing of any and all
points of view. She is Pound's exemplary *poem,* his
'Oread', his *her,* recalling a quotation Pound derisively
flung at HD, 'you are a poem though your poem's
naught'. Without a style, a 'stylus', a signature of her
own, she cannot designate landmarks in her imaginary
or phenomenal landscape, losing herself instead in
perceptual immediacy, suffocating in the greenness of
trees, the translucent viscosity of sensory data, of 'Sylvania' without the 'Penn' to demarcate boundaries of
symbolic identity, as if she were unborn, existing but no

one, no where, not yet having crossed the symbolic barrier. With a feminist rereading, 'Oread's' whirling dervish becomes *Her*'s female hysteric.

What Her lacks, however, is not necessarily the stylus/phallus of Pound's phallocentric Vortex but the medium to accommodate her specific need of self-signification. She considers painting, but fears the provincial reaction of the Pennsylvanian artistic community which is still new and hostile to expressionism. She considers music but hesitates before its pure notation, its lack of gender and figure with which to symbolise her experience of the world, thus implying a withdrawal from the 'decadent' creed that 'all art aspires to the condition of music' and from the purist Imagist intention of attaining the pure ecstasy of 'melos', to paint in words the de*lirio*us Bolero-like dance of the dryad, the lyric of '*lirio*dendron'.

The shift of genres from short lyric poem to fictional autobiography is not an easy one; *Her* might be read as a study and demonstration of just how difficult this transition necessarily is for the woman who writes without access to conventional autobiographical forms. The novel opens with confession of narratorial anxiety over the inadequacy of the *Bildungsroman* and *Kunstler-roman*, which seem designed to record and measure the progress of (self-)enlightenment along normative lines to which she has not and could never conform. 'Her development', the story begins,

> forced along slippery lines of exact definition, marked supernorm, marked subnorm, on some sort of chart. . . . She could not distinguish the supernorm, dragging herself up from the subnorm, letting her down. She could not see the way out of the marsh and bog. She said, 'I am Hermione Gart precisely' . . . but Her Gart was not that, she was nebulous. . . . Her Gart said, 'I am certifiable or soon will be.'[12]

Later, in her 'memoir', *Tribute to Freud*, HD records Freud's diagnosis of her 'writer's block' as a dangerous megalomania, bordering on a psychotically 'suppressed desire for forbidden signs'. But the implicit diagnosis in *Her* points towards (a) woman's exclusion from the universal, symbolic order:

> Her Gart had no a, b, c Esperanto of world expression. She was not of the world, she was not in the world, unhappily she was not out of the world. She wanted to be out, get out, but even as her mind filmed over with grey gelatinous substance of some sort of nonthinking, nonbeing or of nonentity, she felt . . . herself clutch at something that had no name yet.[13]

This testimony of symbolic deprivation resembles Luce Irigaray's reinterpretation of the symptoms of the female hysteric/psychotic as diagnosed by psychoanalysis. According to Lacan/Freud, observes Irigaray, woman 'functions as a hole . . . in the elaboration of imaginary and symbolic processes'; woman's lack or deficiency constitutes sexual difference and supplies the blank text on which man can trace his positive, phallic identity. But what the psychoanalysts fail to acknowledge, she goes on to say, is that:

> this fault, this deficiency, inevitably affords woman too few figurations, images, or representations by which to represent herself. It is not that she lacks some 'master signifier' or that none is imposed upon her, but rather that access to a signifying economy, to a coining of signifiers, is difficult, even impossible for her because she remains an outsider, herself (a) subject to [men's] norms. She borrows signifiers but cannot make her mark, or re-mark upon them. Which all surely keeps her deficient, empty, lacking in a way that could be labeled 'psychotic': a *latent* but not actual psychosis, for want of a practical signifying system.[14]

While it might be said of Her Gart who 'had no a, b, c Esperanto of world expression', it might also be said that it 'is not that she lacks a master signifier or that none is imposed on her'; Her is assigned her position in the linguistic community according to the law of the father and the power of his name to command public recognition. As a woman, she must bear his patronym without inheriting his power to signify autonomy, authority or property. Deprived of a sign or of a discourse with which to represent herself, to mark her difference, to distinguish her aspirations from Gart's, and from patriarchal, self-signifying schemes in general, she wallows in debilitating anonymity. She is barred from self-definition by the imposition of a 'master signifier', emblematised by the dominant appearance of the letter 'G', the first letter of the proper names attached to the men in her life – her father, Dr Carl Gart, her brother, Bertrand Gart, who together work on 'the Gart formula' and whose name commands respect in the scientific community and her poet-fiancé, George.

'Gart' alienates and oppresses Her. Father, brother and formula constitute a closed and imperious, symbolic organisation. She feels forced to translate and legitimate her sense of the world according to Gart's abstract and reductive 'mathematical – biological definition', and she lacks the signifying means with which to articulate a phenomenological substitute. As she sees it, she has been systematically denied access to even her own perceptions:

> Seeing in a head that had been pushed too far toward a mathematical–biological definition of the universe . . . and science, as she saw it eluded her perception. Science as Carl Gart, as Bertrand Gart defined it, had eluded her perception. Her Gart went on, 'I must hurry with the letters'.[15]

Her's sole occupation is to carry her father's 'letters', correspondence between men, an enactment of woman's socially sanctioned, symbolic function of bearing the letters of her father's name, not only exchanging signs between fathers and sons, but also being the sign of exchange between fathers and fiancés. Her's surname

signifies the legal right of the father to contract align-
ments with other men, including the one who will
collaborate in serving his patrilineal and patrimonial
prerogatives which he brandishes like an old testament
prophet in the all-powerful name of God.

Her realises that she must 'do something' besides
'marry' to make her (re)mark upon the world. In order to
articulate her own, '*Her*metic definition', she looks to
literature as an alternative, self-signifying medium. But
the chauvinistic Shavian, George, also her lover and
literary mentor, already occupies the centre of her poetic
world and appropriates for himself the position of poetic
subject, assigning to his personae and to writing in
general an exclusively masculine, profoundly virile
('seminal') character. He manages to seduce her into
playing the part of Galatea in their love affair which he
directs as his version of *Pygmalion* thereby overruling
and displacing her needs to articulate poetic aspirations
and amorous feelings, mastering her as his object of
desire, his art (ifact), his 'Her'. 'George' alludes not only
to George Bernard Shaw and to the overwhelming
popularity of *Pygmalion* in her Pennsylvanian locality
in 1910 but also to Ezra Pound who, in his memoir to the
French sculptor Henri Gaudier-Brzeska in 1916, writes
in the name of the universal *masculine* artistic subject
that:

> We all of us like the caressable, but we most of us prefer the
> woman to the statue. That is the romance of Galatea. We
> prefer – if it is contest in caressabilities – we prefer the figure
> in silk on the stairs to the 'Victory' aloft on her pedestal-
> prow. We know that the 'Victory' will be there whenever we
> want her, and that the young lady in silk will pass on to the
> Salon Carré, and thence on toward the unknown and
> undefinable. That is the trouble with the caressable in art.
> The carressable is always a substitute.[16]

All of these 'G's', 'G' for *G*art, for *G*eorge, for *G*od, for

Gaudier, for *Galatea*, point to that 'master signifier' which administers men's symbolic self-reproductions while militating against Her self-signification in art:

*Her* / ¯G / *art*

Given her wholly alienated, mediated position, what does Her/HD propose to do? What textual strategies are available to her? While *Her* traces the poet's attempted transition from Imagism to narrative, it formulates a serious problem of self-representation confronted by women writers who wish to inscribe a specifically feminine, autobiographical and/or authorial subject. This is no easy transition for which there was no literary model. By the time HD began writing *Her* in 1927 Virginia Woolf had published *Voyage Out* (1915) and more recently, *Orlando* (1928); Radclyffe Hall was about to publish her 'scandalous' *Well of Loneliness* (1929); Bryher had completed her 'case histories', *Development* (1920) and *Two Selves* (1923); Dorothy Richardson, nine volumes of *Pilgrimage*. Charlotte Perkins Gilman's *Yellow Wallpaper* had been out since 1892, though the diary of Alice James (1934) was still at the printers. All these books inscribe a woman's symptomatic narrative, problematising the construction of a feminine writing subject without proposing a way out of a confinement within patriarchal discourse beyond the 'silence' of stream of consciousness, the inscription of madness or death, the renunciation of femininity or transgressive, but not transformative, gender-bending. In writing *Her*, HD considers these narrative subversions and more; she ventures to tell the unrecorded story of 'the other woman', the woman behind the veils of masculine discourse, the woman trapped in fetish artifacts, whether in writing or in silks. Her *autre*biography revises, relives the story of self-becoming from the point of view of the 'overwritten' and overruled 'other' – of Pound's Galatea, of Shakespeare's Hermione, of Shaw's Eliza *Doolittle*, and moreover, the other 'Anna O.' and the 'Dora' whom Breuer and Freud could not wholly objectify.

The ending of *Her*, like the ending of *Voyage Out*, features a passage of delirious speech to represent a young woman's otherwise unsignifiable protest of marriage; but unlike Woolf's en-fevered Rachel Vinrace, HD's hysteric survives to begin another journey. Her's delirium is presented as 'a latent but not actual psychosis, for want of a practical signifying system'. Her *ludic*rous speech re-enacts Anna O.'s 'talking cure', and records the translation of 'the posthysteric subject' from symptomatic silence to engaged public speaking.

Why does HD turn to Freud when his *Studies on Hysteria* do not draw an account of the recovery of the most famous of his hysterics? Partly, I suggest, because his case histories provide the closest thing to a literary model for a woman writer who wants to articulate woman's struggle for self-representation. Moreover, these histories engage scientific observation with such (self-conscious) poetic licence that Freud himself offered to confess that they read like 'short stories [which] lack the serious stamp of science'.[17] Though psychoanalysis narrates the story of a woman's hysteria up to the point of the termination of her treatment and does not chart the course of her (further) recovery, not even the remarkable recovery of Anna O., who we now know went on to become a powerful speaker on the stage of international feminism, the characters in Freud's hysterical plots at least give an idea of where to look. As the feminist critic Peggy Kamuf observes, Breuer's and Freud's case histories are virtually a cue to the creative woman writer:

What if one of [their female hysterics] had left a written account of her passage out of a closed hysterical silence? As a record of this passage, the account would have to substitute for the conventions of case history the conventions of autobiography, so that to imagine such a text is to imagine the interlocutor as the silent pole through which passes the invention of the writing subject. The analytic scene would, in a sense, return to its point of departure with Anna's discovery of 'the talking cure' but displace Breuer's intervening narrative point of view.[18]

HD's *autre*biography returns to the scene of hysteria in the life of its protagonist, taking as its point of departure her discovery of a talking cure. But HD's hysteric exceeds the limit of talk which the Freudian physician normally en-treats. 'Don't you think you've talked yourself out, Miss Gart?' asks Her's psychiatric nurse and to which she responds with a flagrant, 'I have only just begun.' Moreover, what she 'talks out' is:

. . . psychoanalysis, German books . . .

In an ironic reversal of Breuer's translation of Anna O.'s hysterical 'English', HD's 'hysteric' translates the German of psychoanalytic discourse:

Now German came clear and ritterspuren and hummingbird blue . . . German that ran on and on and the translations that read odd, didn't mean the same thing. German had caught one in a mesh, it was inferiority complex if you translated it . . .; it was mother and father and Oedipus complex and it made pattern on a brain that rose from a black mesh. A white spider rose from a black mesh; there were people who loved . . . differently.[19]

Her 'translation' scrambles the letters on the page so that black print is no longer foregrounded on white paper but just the opposite, with a white background emerging, spider-like, from a 'black mesh'. The psychoanalytic text is turned inside out by the resisting woman reader who is on her way to becoming a woman writer, the symptomatic 'white spider' signalling her emergence from the normative historiography of psychoanalysis, from the narrative traps of Oedipus and the patriarchal, familial order to tell the untold story of a daughter's disease. Her 'feminine protest' marks the first step in reformulating Freud's theory of sexuality towards an unorthodox definition of desire and re-transcription of the story of those so-called hysterics 'who loved . . . differently'.

## HD's Freudian Poetics

*Her* marks the beginning of a lifelong writing on quest(ion)s of woman's symbolic power, including the power to authorise, to narrate her writer's life. While at this still early stage of her career HD outlines an esoteric, 'star-signed', writing project, it is the 'medium' of psychoanalysis, not hermeticism, that designates her point of departure into *autre*biography. 'Hermes, Hermeticism and all the rest of it', includes psycho-analysis which is also not on Pound's agenda. 'I can't blow everybodies' noses for 'em', writes Pound in a letter to HD; 'Have felt yr / vile Freud all bunk . . . / You got into the wrong pig stye, *ma chère*. But not too late to climb out.' [20]

The psychoanalytic turn HD's writing takes indicates not so much a conversion to the new psychology as a defection from the conventions of established scientific discourse and also from the poetic discourses of Pound and Lawrence, which (they believed) dominated English modernism. 'Lawrence was', HD writes, 'instinctively against Sigmund Freud, Frieda was intelligently for him.' [21] Her *Notes on Thought and Vision*, written in 1919, forges a post-Imagist 'psychological' aesthetics which precedes Lawrence's publication of *Psycho-analysis of the Unconscious* in 1921 and *Fantasia of the Unconscious* in 1922. Here, HD sketches a typography of the artist's psyche which bears resemblance to Freud's schematic description of the unconscious in 1915. Her phenomenological and genealogical description of artistic consciousness as the 'womb-brain' of artistic inspiration distinguishes her poet, however, not only from Pound's 'seminal' Vorticist,[22] and from Lawrence's masculist, 'eternal protaganist',[23] but also from Freud's 'creative writer', who subjects his 'infantile' fantasies to the prescriptions and prohibitions of the paternal ego.[24]

At the start of her *autre*biographical project, HD's writing makes overt, if not ironic, use of psychoanalytic lexicons. *Her*'s complex, third person narrator uses a pseudo-psychoanalytic vocabulary to refer to the hysterical condition of her narrative subject-in-the-making, her self-less writing self. Both the language and the theories of psychoanalysis are being tested here and technical terms are frequently put in quotations. The novel opens with this passage:

> Her Gart had no word for her dementia. . . . But Her Gart was then no prophet. She could not predict later uncommon syllogisms: 'failure complex,' 'compensation reflex,' and that conniving phrase 'arrested development' had opened no door for her. . . . In those days, those astounding Freudian and post-Freudian volumes had not found their way into the common library.[25]

*Her*, however, *is* prophetic: while, here, the use of quotation marks and technical jargon draw attention to the ambiguous representation of psychoanalysis in HD's text, HD's later writing drops the quotation marks and clichés and assimilates certain of Freud's tropes and themes, notably his optic, graphic and archeological concept-metaphors which I shall discuss later.

*Her* is prophetic in another sense: in foreseeing how psychoanalytic names and wordplay signal a route to finding those star signs which *would* open doors in her journey towards *Her*metic *D*efinition. Thirty years later she charts her movement through the labyrinth of Paris's Notre Dame cathedral, guided by her sibyl, 'Our Lady', St Anne, through the three doors of '*Astrologie, Alchimie, Magie*' that open onto mystical self-revelation.[26] In her (w)rite of passage, HD's poet displays an overt indifference to the orthodox reaction she provokes among her imagined followers and mentors, including her deceased astronomer father who, in the auspicious year of her birth, had published the popular guidebook *Practical Astronomy As Applied Geodesy and Navigation.* HD felt encouraged to pursue her heterodox semiotics because, I suggest, she found authoritative, if marginal, support outside the literary establishment. She found in Sigmund Freud, during her analytic sessions with him in 1933–4, an empowering 'colleague' who gave audience to her self-signifying doubts and desires and who 'collaborated' with her in translating the hieroglyphics of her dream-visions. Moreover, it was Freud who gave her the cue to articulate 'what it is to be a woman'.[27]

How essential is psychoanalysis to this passage from hysteria to hermeticism? Freud's texts offer HD, if nothing else, a guidebook to writing 'the uncanny feminine'. In his seminal work *The Interpretation of Dreams* (1900), Freud notes having suggested to a female patient that she read Rider Haggard's *She*; ' "A strange book", he tells her, "but full of hidden meaning, the eternal feminine, the immortality of our emotions".' It is a book which, for Freud, features a strange woman who undertakes a 'perilous journey . . . leading to undiscovered regions' and who, having left the confines of the printed page, comes back to haunt him in his dreams.[28] 'She', in fact, haunts Freud's entire *oeuvre*; from *Studies on Hysteria* in 1895 to his essay entitled 'Femininity' in 1933. She makes her variable appearances as the medieval witch cum modern hysteric in Freud's case histories; as the terrible triple goddess – birth/love/death – in 'The Theme of the Three Caskets' (1913); as that eternally 'incomprehensible and mysterious, strange and therefore apparently hostile' femininity, which strikes a 'generalized dread of woman' in men who cannot account for her sexual 'difference', her deviation from the anthropological norm in 'The Taboo of Virginity' (1918); as the most uncanny of uncanny phenomena, that 'home' become 'unhomely', nutritive womb and hospitable vagina 'transmortified' into mother earth's cold tomb, as he sees it, in his essay 'The Uncanny' (1919); as the mysterious 'harbourer of an undiscovered region', the pre-Oedipal phase in women and girls, which Freud likens to the Minoan–Mycenean layer of civilisation in his essay, 'Female Sexuality' (1931); and finally as the Sphinx-like 'riddle of femininity', the 'enigma of woman', the scientifically unpresentable 'other' which psychoanalysis, in the last analysis, hands over to the poets in mock defeat.[29]

Freud prompts the poets to collaborate with psychoanalysis in its attempts to draw (out) the 'other woman' who survives civilised [female] sexuality and its nervous illnesses[30] in the repressed memory traces of individual and racial prehistory. HD 'responds' not merely by drawing a matriarchal image of her own depth psychology; she revises 'the case study', studies 'the language of dreams', adapts 'the transference narrative' and of self-analysis, restages the 'Oedipal drama', stylises a rhetoric of 'the uncanny' and retraces the configuration of the 'enigmatic woman' of Freudian literature.

I would venture the claim that HD's writing transcribes a 'Freudian poetics', that it displays such 'techniques' as dream-analysis, 'reconstruction' (of memory and fantasy), transference and counter-transference, narrative speculation. The result is the production of a woman's lifestory which does not conform to the design of those Enlightenment genres, the *Bildungsroman* and *Kunstlerroman*.

HD's *autre*biography, I suggest, takes as its model not Freud's *Autobiographical Study,* a first person narrative which chronicles the making of a great man and his legacy, but *The Interpretation of Dreams,* Freud's own '*autre*biography' whereby he discloses the other 'self' of which he is unconscious, the self 'who' dreams in a

hieroglyphic language and subliminally subverts the
censor of conscious dialogue. Her narratology elaborates
Freud's writing on such parapsychological subjects as
occultism, telepathy, animism, totemism, magic and
primal languages; it also covertly exploits the facts of
Freud's undiscussed, maternal – Moravian – heritage and
the seldom-mentioned Semitic culture of his forefathers,[31] for their genealogical suggestiveness, their
indication of a powerful, alternative 'source' of writing
in Moravian mystic texts and kabbalistic script.

I propose that we read HD's narratives as a rewriting
and re-vision of psychoanalysis and not simply as a
psychoanalysis disguised as poetry. If we consider those
of HD's narratives which self-consciously conform to the
genres of the *romans à clef*, the 'memoir' or the diary, we
can easily identify a Freudian rhetoric, an Oedipal plot
and/or a therapeutic analysis of traumatic memories,
fantasies, dreams. Norman Holland suggests that we
read *Tribute to Freud* as 'psychobiography', an innovation in the line of Freudian case histories. Undertaken
at Freud's bidding, HD's *Bid Me to Live* demonstrates or
enacts a 'working through' of dangerously repressed and
oppressively remembered experiences of the traumatic
years of the First World War, when HD was passionately
(dis)engaged with Aldington and Lawrence. It is
followed by *End to Torment, A Memoir of Ezra Pound*,
another 'writing out' from within the asylum of walled-
up, indiscriminate feelings about the first and the most
formidable of her literary lovers and (tor)mentors. But
what concerns me is not HD's possible application of
psychoanalytic therapy but rather the possible, dramatic
adaptation or poetic translation of Freud's psychoanalytic text, its split narrative subject which we might
interpret as the opening onto a new genre of autobiography in women's writing.

I detect a progressive change in HD's narrative treatment of psychoanalysis, and I also observe a critical
difference between the intertextual styles of those

narratives (what HD calls 'straight narratives') which self-consciously apply Freud's therapeutic strategies and those which present themselves as exceptional, ground-breaking 'case studies' to Freud's expanding science, or as additional, seminal chapters in the formulation of psychoanalytic theory. Before her analysis with Freud in 1933, HD's writing displays an ironic use of Freud's text as narrative model; after her analysis in 1934 it displays a critical engagement with psychoanalytic rhetoric and speculation;[32] and, after Freud's death in 1939, it displays a particular interest in the poetics of 'the uncanny'.

HD's novel, *Nights* (1935) (an experimental text, not one of the 'straight narratives') marks the middle transition. Much less sceptical than *Her*, it shows a subtle, sympathetic appreciation of such technicalities as ' "inhibition" ' and ' "repression" ' and a new sensitivity to ' "the language of the unconscious" ' in a half-ironic bid to champion the ' "much abused medium of psychoanalysis" '.

In this novel, the first narrative production to appear in the wake of HD's sessions with Freud, Her makes her comeback as a bewitching 'she', the self-dramatising subject of (her own) erotic fantasies and poetic aspirations. Like Her, 'Natalia' occupies the centre-stage of a theatre as psychological spectacle. But unlike Her, whose 'hysteria' displays the frustration of a woman dispossessed of any language or media to express her desire, 'Nat' entertains night after night of erotic carnival, fired by her own, all-consuming passion. Moreover, the wild performances she directs in her bedroom-boudoir she also conducts in writing in a double act of expressive authority.

The text is divided into two sections, the second of which is the 'primary text', Natalia's diary of twelve 'Nights' of love-making while the first, entitled 'Prologue', is the 'secondary text', a critique or (p)review of this diary as supplied by John Helforth, amateur analyst with a literary 'bent'. Following Natalia's bizarre death

the diary is brought to Helforth, whose job it is to judge
the writing for its psychological and/or literary value.
His reception of the manuscript suggests a form of
'thought-transference' and he regards himself and
deceased to be 'of like mind':

> I knew enough about Natalie, to know that her problems
> would have been my problems, but for my somewhat
> tantalising scientific habits, I had lost much and gained
> little, perhaps, in my explanations into the new doctrines of
> the unconscious . . .[33]

Helforth is also of two minds, 'a half and half sort of
person', an aspiring, creative writer with 'enlightened'
reservations ('my psychological investigations were
marred by my own imagination, and when I wanted to
write a purely popular . . . tale or novel, my scientific
training spoiled it'). Yet Helforth is willing to lay aside
his 'catholic' fears in his reading of Natalia's wholly
unreserved, if innovative, exhibitionism, whose medium
he describes as otherworldly, demonic: 'Every line
seemed to bleed fire. . . . She was presenting truth . . . in
some other medium.'

While death (fortuitous? suicidal?) delivers the woman
writer from face to face confrontation with criticism and
possible rejection, her 'resurrection' into the public
sphere ultimately depends upon his judgement.
Helforth must choose between commending 'Nights' for
publication as a significant contribution to (psychoanalytic) literature and shelving it as the 'blazing illumi-
nism of lucid madness'. His occasional ambivalence
reflects the writer's own (un)willingness to accept
psychoanalytic speculations on the subject of feminine
desire as well as her (dis)belief in the power of her
writing to explore and subvert.

*Nights* might best be read as a self-mocking attempt to
construct an ideal reader, literally a 'reader-in-the-text',
as a woman's strategy of self-authorisation. Helforth is

not only vulnerable to the diabolical posthumous charm
of her erotic inscriptions, to the 'power' of her writing
no less than to the power of her sex, but he is also
conscious of his need to read *as a woman*, to become her
feminine 'medium', a reader–seer of the mysteries and
ecstasies of that other, sexual/textual body. He invokes
the collaboration of his master/muse, a certain Viennese
clairvoyant whose name, 'Dr. Frank', barely conceals a
joke played on the founder of psychoanalysis, a con-
densation of the names 'Freud' and (Otto) 'Rank',
suggesting an unorthodox hybrid of a strictly scientific
psychoanalysis and a mystifying, mythopoeic one.
Freud's first reference to Rank appears in his inaugural
study of the uncanny, 'The Theme of the Three Caskets'.
In her *Tribute to Freud*, HD mentions Freud's instruction to her that she read Rank's study of the myth of the
hero, an instruction which neither clearly ascertains nor
doubts the demystifying, wholly 'scientific' potential of
psychoanalysis.

*The Gift* (1943) is the first of HD's *autre*biographies to
represent the poet 'herself' as a self-referring, speaking
subject. An older 'Hilda', trapped in her London flat
during the blitz, finds herself compelled to record suddenly released, shell-shocked memories of childhood.
Each of the seven chapters, 'Dark Room', 'The Fortune
Teller', 'The Dream', 'Because One Is Happy', 'The
Secret', 'What It Was', 'Morning Star', illustrate Freud's
analysis of uncanny theme(s) while dramatising the
rhetorical/mystical evocation of uncanny feelings.

The novel opens on the poet's childhood at home in
her father's house and in her grandfather's seminary. But
the scene darkens with the appearance of the mothers
who haunt unknown recesses of otherwise familiar
settings and who make unhomely the homely, like
blacked-out chapters of personal memory or like un-
developed negatives in the family photograph album. It
is women and girls who occupy Hilda's uncanny imaginary: chief among the ghosts of her childhood past are

her 'morbidly, self-effacing' mother and her mysterious other-worldly grandmother, who has been secreted away in the crevices of the family house. There is also that shade of herself, the pre-pubertal adolescent, whose intellectual and creative imagination had been 'buried alive' with her sexual awakening by the repressive administration of feminity. It is the *paterfamilias* which figures as the agency of repression – or 'oppression' – a 'home rule' of Puritan and scientific (fore)fathers in whose domain the Moravian mother and grandmother have no voice of their own, have lost their inherited musical and mystical gifts of self-expression.

*The Gift* performs an experimental recovery/articulation of these lost expressive powers. An uncanny art of writing, it exploits psychoanalytic technique 'on the spot', recalling and reconstructing buried memories or fantasies, analysing the 'hieroglyphs' of Hilda's continuous daydream of childhood, of (grand)motherhood, enacting a play of transference between an imaginary past self and an imaginary analyst–reader who (it is imagined) takes on the personae of mother and grandmother so that their ghosts may acquire a 'living', dialogical, self-disclosing presence, recovering and releasing the expressive powers of an encrypted, cryptic 'mother tongue'.

*Trilogy* (1944) and *Helen in Egypt* (1954) are long narrative poems which chronicle the process of dreaming, remembering and reconstructing the life stories of two, mythographic female figures – 'Mary' of the Scriptures and 'Helen' of the classical Greek text. Wordplay and the recall of trans-personal memory traces extend *autre*biography beyond the limit of individual recollection, opening doors onto racial and biological memory and looking back as far as the common dream of 'matriarchal prehistory'. The tracing of the gram or the glyph is the 'key' to HD's hermetic recall: her later *autre*biography combines the Imagist 'ideogrammic method' with Freud's analysis of the dream–hieroglyph to produce c(l)ues to the (re)production and (re)presentation of the trans-historical female unconscious. Grafting of signifier to signifier, heedless of proprieties of the word, the Logos, splitting and recombining lexical, figural and structural items, exploiting the double capacity of writing to evoke and deconstruct the iconography of meaning and memory. That HD believed in the occult power of her style of deconstruction was essential to her art of self-recovery, of tracing her lost genealogy to its first, cryptic inscriptions. In a meditative passage of *The Gift*, she muses:

> A bit of me can really 'live' something of word or phrase, cut on a wall at Karnak. . . . Then, I am for a moment . . . Egyptian, a little cell of my brain responds to a cell of someone's brain, who died a thousand years ago. A word opens a door . . .[34]

*Trilogy* deploys a writing metaphor/metaphorical writing – the 'palimpsest' – which might be likened to Freud's figure of the 'mystic writing pad'. Freud's magic pad diagrams the topography and dynamics of repression, a complex function which involves the engraving of permanent (but not fixed) memory traces on unconscious, archival layers in the same instance that these traces undergo censorious erasure from a conscious, surface text. The poem opens with a 'dream' of a stylus dipped in 'corrosive sublimate' which her dreampoet, a hallucinated, hieroglyphic scribe would 'scratch out/ indelible ink of the palimpsest of misadventure' – the censored, canonical text of Western literature. The poem re-presents the cryptic, 'manifest text' of the poet's unconscious wish to restore to mankind's Enlightened consciousness the powerful, primitive magic of hermetic script.

At one point, this wish appears in the uncanny, occult figure of a poet–alchemist, an enigmatic 'She' who carries in her arms a book, 'the blank pages/ of the

unwritten volume of the new'.[35] The dream hovers
momentarily over this trace of a forbidden wish before it
is 'erased'; yet it lingers long enough to leave with the
feminist reader an impression of an ideal 'archetrace', a
woman's 'originary' writing which blanks out 'the
indelible ink' of patriarchal poetry at the same time that
it restores or re-transcribes the 'corrupt text' of an
ancient, other world.

The last book of *Trilogy*, entitled 'Flowering of the
Rod', recontextualises this dream in a narrative reconstruction of the fabled, apocryphal 'Gospel of Mary'.
The 'narrative' has no identifiable narrator and the
'subject' of the story is a subversive, intertextual inter-
weaving of the 'Revelations' of John with gnostic,
hermetic, alchemical and cult sources: a semiotic wizar-
dry whose occult product is an ideogrammic tracing of
'Mary': of the Virgin Mary, of Mary Magdalene and of all
those (other) Marys who appear, not always as distinct
and discrete entities, in the Bible and its 'margins'. The
spellbinding, iconoclastic charm of this writing
represents the release (of woman's symbolic power) that
comes with the liberating re-transcription of female
iconography/pornography. A legitimising, if marginalised, reader appears in the figure of Semitic Kaspar, a
kabbalist–psychoanalyst in whose 'dream-vision' and
hermetic dream-analysis 'Mary' makes a hieroglyphic
appearance, bringing with her repressed memory traces
of a censored and forgotten matriarchal prehistory.

While HD's late poetry acquires a less personal, more
universal character, the poet still writes with the convic-
tion that 'one must, of necessity, begin with one's own
private inheritance'. *Helen in Egypt* is an intertextual
weaving of 'autobiographical fantasy' and classical
mythology. Taking the relay from male mythographers,
Homer, Steisichorus, Euripides, Goethe and Pound, the
poem traces yet another legendary inscription of Helen
of Troy. But HD's *Helen* traces the legend beyond its
pre-Hel(l)enic sources, back to 'Egypt', to the pre-

historical archives of Western literary culture. Posing as Helen's 'medium', the poet 'HD' mediates imaginary dialogues between Helen and her equally legendary lovers (Theseus, Achilles, Paris); the 'writing' of *Helen* conducts scenes of analysis, transcribes the narratives of transference/counter-transference, interprets the reconstruction of dreams, solicits and translates the 'indecipherable' hieroglyphs of the censored, primary text of maternal (matriarchal) prehistory from Helen's 'female' unconscious.

*Helen in Egypt* presents an ideal reader, this time in the figure of a woman – 'Helen', who is also 'the writing' – with the implication that woman's 'true' autobiography entails a radical critique or deconstruction of the autobiographical subject which is always already inscribed in patriarchal culture, in its fetishes and fixations. 'We' are asked to collaborate with Helen and with 'HD' in the *autre*biography of the legendary woman, to 'travel' with Helen to the 'ruins of Egypt' where we encounter her first 'written character'. With Helen we trace the origins of the representation of 'femininity' to an earlier source than that of ancient Greece, back to *The Book of the Dead*; in the process of re-reading and remembering the textual body of Helen, we re-enact the writing of the task of the Egyptian mythographer, Thoth, whose scripture formulates the occult remembering and rebirth of Osiris.

It is useful to read *Helen in Egypt* as a critical rejoinder to Freud's *Moses and Monotheism*. According to Freud, 'Moses' marks the first establishment (patriarchal) civilisation and the proper end of an epoch of (matriarchal) chaos and decadence following the fall from the first father's absolute rule. The event which accordingly brought about the fall was a patricidal battle between father and sons for the (ultimately incenstuous) possession of women. It is an Egyptian 'Moses' who sets about restoring order, re-establishing patriarchal rule in real, cultural terms (in place of the corrupted 'ideal') –

the strict administration of the incest taboo and the severe control, suppression of female sexuality.

Against this mythic historiography, *Helen and Egypt* traces the sources of Western civilisation's progressive discontent to a progressive masculinisation of mankind and, more specifically, to patriarchal imperialism beginning with the domination and suppression of the Egyptians by the Greeks. Helen's earliest memories of 'racial and biological prehistory' (as recalled by the hieroglyphic writing on physical, trans-historical walls) refers to an age of Egyptian culture which pre-dates that of Moses and the Monotheistic Sun King. She learns that she descends from the age of Isis, where sexual difference was not formulated in terms of sexual opposition or hierarchy, but where the sexual initiation into woman's mysteries, into the rites of passage inscribed in the *Book of the Dead*, engaged both sexes in ecstatic renunciation of self and rebirth in communal, conjugal 'ego'. Again and again, Helen concludes her interminable analysis with the determination to resurrect the Egyptian mysteries as antidote to a modern, misogynist civilisation and its deadly discontents.

With the completion of *Hermetic Definition* in the year of her death (1961), HD sees the end of a writing (of) life. As the anagram hidden in the cryptogrammic title of the poem suggests, 'Hermetic Definition' traces the poet's 'coming into her own' as a self-authorising, defining or 'divining' medium. The title easily reads as a sign of hermeneutic closure but the autobiographial (w)rite of passage which began with *Her* defies summation and continues to subvert established codes and conventions which inhibit women's poetic imagination.

The poem circumscribes a wholly unconventional love story which begins with an 'enigmatic encounter' between an ageing, seventy-year-old HD and an 'ordinary stranger', a certain Lionel Durand, a forty-year-old newspaper reporter. To her shock and delight, HD records feeling the resurgence of desire. But her poem is more than a testimony of her outrageous love: it is also a deconstruction of patriarchal culture's sexual/reproductive norms, the same norms which sanction the exploitation, alienation and fetishisation of woman's desire. Her narrative represents love as the inviolable, if illegitimate, attraction of 'eternal affinities', as consummation outside the marriage contract and the reproductive economy, as incestuous desire for a man young enough to be her grandson, as female initiative and maternal prerogative to articulate and nurture (her own) sexual feeling.

*Hermetic Definition* might be read against the definition of society which Freud presents in *Civilization and Its Discontents* whose 'enlightened' enterprise depends on the imposition of severe constraints on Eros, on the 'life instinct', and, in particular, on the sex drive as embodied in women. It might also be read as a late response to the seventy-year-old Freud who once, in analysis, prompted the forty-year-old HD with the retort: ' "The trouble is, I am an old man – *you do not think it worth your while to love me*" '. While defying his prescriptive definition of Eros, she affirms his re-evaluation of love's 'worth', its therapeutic and 'spiritual' value outside of the lover's discourse and reproductive economy of patriarchal capitalism.

*Hermetic Definition* does not merely chronicle an alternative love story; it performs the act of love-making as love-writing, and it displays the power of writing to spur desire. The desiring, narrating subject, the 'HD' of *Hermetic Definition*, is the subject of writing born of desire born of writing. The poem is the product of writing her self-love and of loving her writing self. 'HD' signifies a tautological writing defining her own erotic poetics; it authorises an auto-erotic definition of feminine desire and maternal love. The poem contemplates its own conception and fabrication over a nine-month period which the poet spent mostly in bed, recovering from a broken hip. The act of writing transfigures her convalescence into gestation. The poem is proof of parthenogenesis, the offspring of a mother–muse (Isis, Aphrodite, Cybele, 'She') and of a writing style (stylus, technique, technology) whose birthing would not have been possible without intertextual midwifery, Freud's contribution as *sage femme.*

HD's *autre*biography might finally be understood as a form of therapy which 'delivers' woman's writing from the debilitating structures of patriarchy (phallogocentrism) and which recovers a trace of or a style of tracing a specifically feminine imaginary. What this therapy does not perform is the recovery of an 'other' self, already there, intact but buried, preserved, waiting for exhumation, a raising from the dead. *Autre* may be elsewhere, unsignified, unrecognised by the male-stream canon; but 'she' is not an alternative 'presence', only a prior inscription. No more or less than a pre-text to autobiography, *Autre* 'is herself the writing'.

# Notes

1. Susan Stanford Friedman, 'Who Buried HD? The Poet, Her Critics, and "The Literary Tradition"', *College English*, **36** (March, 1975), 801–14.
2. Susan Stanford Friedman, *Psyche Reborn, The Emergence of HD* (Bloomington, Indiana University Press, 1981); Janice S. Robinson, *HD: The Life and Work of an American Poet* (Boston, Houghton Mifflin, 1982); Rachel Blau DuPlessis, *HD: The Career of That Struggle* (Hemel Hempstead, Harvester Wheatsheaf, 1986).
3. For a discussion of these prejudices see Diana Collecott, 'Remembering Oneself: the reputation and later poetry of HD', *Critical Quarterly*, **27** (1) (Spring 1985), 7–22, 9.
4. Helga Dorn is the pseudonym HD used to sign her unpublished 'autobiographical' novel, 'Paint it Today' (1920–21). Henry Dohna is the chief protaganist of the half-published novel, *The Mystery* (London, Enitharmion Press, 1976).

5. For example, Peter Makin, *Pound's Cantos* (London, George Allen and Unwin, 1985), 29–30. See also Barbara Guest, *Herself Defined, The Poet and Her World* (London, Collins, 1985).Guest describes HD's first entry into the poetry scene as a scene from *Pygmalion*: 'For years Pound has been preparing for this debut. He had a new name for her, tossing away "Doolittle". She was the first charter member of his new *ism* with which Ezra was preparing to startle London. Unlike Professor Higgins, he had not found his Miss Doolittle selling flowers outside Covent Garden, but he planned to transform her from a dedicated scribbler into the poet, HD. . . . He succeeded' (40–1).
6. *End to Torment; A Memoir of Ezra Pound* (Manchester Carcanet Press, 1980), 40.
7. Peter Jones, 'Introduction', *Imagist Poetry*, ed. Peter Jones (Harmondsworth, Penguin, 1972), 31.
8. Cyrena N. Pondrom, 'HD and the Origins of Imagism', *Sagetrieb* 4 (1) (Spring 1985), 73–100, 89.
9. Friedrich Nietzsche, *Human, All Too Human*, trans. P. J. Hollingdale (Cambridge, Cambridge University Press, 1986), 81.
10. Pondrom, 89.
11. *Her* (London, Virago, 1984), 3–6.
12. *ibid.*, 3–6.
13. *ibid.*, 8.
14. Luce Irigaray, *Speculum of the Other Woman*, trans. Gillian G. Gill (Ithaca, Cornell University Press, 1985), 71.
15. *Her*, 6.
16. Ezra Pound, *Gaudier-Brzeska, A Memoir*, 1916 (reprinted London, Marvell, 1960), 97.
17. See Sigmund Freud, 'Studies on Hysteria', *Standard Edition*, 2 (London, Hogarth Press and the Institute of Psycho-Analysis, 1955). 'I have not always been a psycho-therapist', writes Freud; 'it still strikes me myself as strange that the case histories I write should read like short stories and that as one might say, they lack the serious stamp of science' (160–1).
18. Peggy Kamuf, *Fictions of Feminine Desire, Disclosures of Heloise* (London, University of Nebraska Press, 1982), 56.

19. *Her*, 203.
20. Ezra Pound, quoted in Norman Holmes Pearson's 'Foreword' to HD's *Tribute to Freud* (New York, New Directions, 1974), xii.
21. *Tribute to Freud*, xi.
22. See Ezra Pound, *Gaudier-Brzeska; A Memoir*, 23–4.
23. D. H. Lawrence, *Fantasia of the Unconscious*, 1922 (reprinted Harmondsworth, Penguin, 1977), 98.
24. Sigmund Freud, 'Creative Writers and Day-Dreaming', trans. I. F. Grant Duff, *Standard Edition*, 9 (London, Hogarth Press and the Institute of Psycho-Analysis, 1959), 141–53.
25. *Her*, 3, 18.
26. *Hermetic Definition* (New York, New Directions, 1972), 51.
27. Quoted from HD's poem 'The Master' (*c.* 1934–5), in *HD, Collected Poems, 1912–1944*, ed. Louis Martz (Manchester, Carcanet Press, 1984), 451–61, 460.
28. Sigmund Freud, *The Interpretation of Dreams*, trans. James Strachey, *Standard Edition*, 4 and 5 (London, Hogarth Press and the Institute of Psycho-Analysis, 1953), 453.
29. Sigmund Freud, 'Femininity', trans. James Strachey, *Standard Edition* 22 (London, Hogarth Press and the Institute of Psycho-Analysis, 1964), 112–35. Freud ends his essay/lecture rhetorically by saying to his audience of male professionals, '[i]f you want to know more about femininity, inquire from your own experiences of life, or turn to the poets, or wait until science can give you some deeper and more coherent information' (135).
30. See Sigmund Freud, ' "Civilised" Sexuality and Modern Nervous Illness', trans. E. B. Herford and E. C. Mayne, *Standard Edition* 9 (London, Hogarth Press and The Institute of Psycho-Analysis, 1959), 177–204.
31. Critics are just now pointing to the historical importance of this 'other' genealogy in shaping the character of psychoanalysis. See Michel de Certeau, *Herterologies*, trans. Brian Massumi (Manchester, University of Manchester Press, 1986), 3–34, and Estelle Roith, *The Riddle of Freud, Jewish Influence On His Theory of Female Sexuality* (London, Tavistock, 1987).

32. For inquiries into HD's 'duplicitous' critical yet defer-
ential translation of Freud, see the following: Susan
Stanford Friedman, *Psyche Reborn: The Emergence of
HD*; Marilyn B. Arthur, 'Psychomythology: The Case of
HD', *Bucknell Review* (1983), 65–79; Peggy A. Knapp,
'Women's Freud(e): HD's *Tribute to Freud and* Gladys
Schmitt's *Sonnets for an Analyst*', *Massachussetts Review*
(1983), 338–52; Janice S. Robinson, 'What's in a Box?', in
*HD, Woman and Poet*, ed. Michael King (Orono,
University of Maine, 1987), 237–57.
33. *Nights* (New York, New Directions, 1986), 6–7.
34. 'Dark Room', a section of *The Gift*, published separately
in *Montemora*, 8 (August 1981), 57–78, 70.
35. *Trilogy* (Manchester, Carcanet Press, 1973), 103. See
Andrew Howdle, 'Feminine Hermeticism in HD's
*Trilogy*', *Studies in Mystical Literature* (1985), 26–44.

# Chronological Table of Works
# Margaret Atwood

*Born Toronto, Canada, 1939*

### Poetry
1966  *The Circle Game*
1968  *The Animals in That Country*
1970  *The Journals of Susanna Moodie*
1970  *Procedures for Underground*
1971  *Power Politics*
1974  *You Are Happy*
1978  *Selected Poems*
1978  *Two Headed Poems*
1981  *True Stories*
1984  *Murder in the Dark*

### Novels
1969  *The Edible Woman*
1972  *Surfacing*
1976  *Lady Oracle*
1979  *Life Before Man*
1982  *Bodily Harm*
1985  *The Handmaid's Tale*
1989  *Cat's Eye*

### Short Stories
1977  *Dancing Girls*
1983  *Bluebeard's Egg*

### Non-Fiction
1972  *Survival: A Thematic Guide to Canadian Literature*
1983  *Second Words*

# 4

# Margaret Atwood

## Taking the Capital W off Woman

### Harriet Devine Jump

Margaret Atwood has expressed profound reservations about classifying herself as a feminist writer.[1] Nevertheless the chief preoccupation of her writing has always been women and the ways in which they relate to the society in which they live. Her views on this subject have, however, clearly developed and modified over the course of the twenty years of her publishing career.

Interestingly, it is Atwood's earliest novels – *The Edible Woman* (1969), *Surfacing* (1972) and *Lady Oracle* (1976) – which have generated the most interest among feminist critics, possibly because this period of her work can be seen as one of exploration of the female psyche, and of the difficulties experienced by women in defining roles for themselves. *Surfacing*, in particular, continues to offer a fruitful field of exploration for critics working in such diverse areas as gynocriticism and Marxist-feminist criticism.[2] Far from being polemical, however, these novels offer no easy solutions and their conclusions are invariably open-ended and ambiguous.

Her next novels, *Life Before Man* (1979) and *Bodily Harm* (1981), show a marked increase in pessimism, both personal (as in *Life Before Man*) and political (as in

*Bodily Harm*). It was at this period that Atwood became interested in Amnesty International and her increased political awareness produced a darkened view of the dangers and hostility of the world and of man's inhumanity. The human relationships portrayed at this stage seem more than usually unsatisfactory, the male protagonists largely manipulative (either through violence or through weakness), the heroines acquiescing in their own victimisation: secondary female characters (Elizabeth in *Life Before Man* and Lora in *Bodily Harm*) are marginally more 'heroic' only because they adopt brutal strategies of self-preservation.

The *Handmaid's Tale* (1986), however, despite some indications to the contrary, shows signs of a return to qualified optimism and her most recent novel, *Cat's Eye* (1989), shows a noticeable alteration of emphasis. Whether this change represents a departure from feminist principles, or whether it in fact points the way in which women's thinking about themselves and the world could usefully go, will no doubt be decided by individual readers according to their own particular viewpoint. This essay will argue for the second view.

This is not to suggest that the elements of Atwood's refusal to simplify gender issues have not been present in her writing for some time. In a 1978 essay, 'The Curse of Eve - Or, What I Learned in School', she registered her disagreement with what she took to be the view of feminist critics that women in novels should be ideal role models:

> perhaps it is time to take the capital W off Woman. I myself have never known an angel, a harpy, a witch, or an earth mother. I've known a number of real women, not all of whom have been nicer or more noble or more long-suffering or less self-righteous or pompous than men. Increasingly it becomes possible to write about them.
>
> (*Second Words*, 227-8)

Although *Cat's Eye* stands alone among her works for

the fact that female cruelty and inhumanity form the main subject of the novel while the men have faded into insignificance, every previous novel contains one or more secondary female characters who behave at least as badly as the male ones. Admittedly, her heroines are frequently put at a disadvantage in some way by the expectations, the demands, the pressures and sometimes the violence of the male-oriented society in which they find themselves. But simply to complain about the conditions of victimisation is, as Atwood put it in 1972, only the second of three possible 'victim positions' which a woman can take in a sexist society, which are:

> 1. Ignore her victimization, and sings songs like 'I Enjoy Being A Girl'.
> 2. Think it's the fault of Biology, or something, or you can't do anything about it; write literature on How Awful It Is, which may be a very useful activity up to a point.
> 3. Recognize the source of oppression; express anger; suggest ways for change.
>
> (*Second Words*, 145)

In this essay she also postulated a fourth possibility: to be a creative non-victim. It is this possibility which, as a novelist, she seems to be attempting to fulfil in her most recent works.

The applicability of this argument to *The Handmaid's Tale* may not be immediately apparent. The novel is a dystopian satire set in the not-too-distant future, in which the religious, moral and political fanaticism of the governing Fundamentalist regime has suppressed pleasurable sexuality, forbidden women any occupations apart from breeding or domestic servitude, and which encourages ritual public dismemberments and murders. The real name of the main protagonist is never revealed: she is one of the 'Handmaids' kept for breeding purposes and known only by the possessive preposition added to the name of her 'Commander': so, in this case, Offred. Offred has unquestionably been victimised by the system. But Atwood's message here, as elsewhere, seems to be that victims too must take responsibility for their victimisation. Offred herself recognises not only that apathy and non-involvement on the part of society have contributed to the present situation: 'There were marches, of course, a lot of women and some men. But they were smaller than you might have thought . . .' but also that she herself has been guilty of moral cowardice:

> I didn't go on any of the marches . . . I had to think of them, my family, him and her. I did think about my family. I started doing more housework, more baking.[3]

The other women in the novel, too, are clearly implicated to an even greater extent. This may be by passive complicity, as in the case of the barren Commanders' Wives, who have accepted the privileges of their position but who nevertheless suffer an immeasurable loss of dignity as a result. Offred's own Commander's Wife weeps silently at the beginning of each monthly 'Ceremony', the grotesque threesome in which her husband attempts to impregnate his Handmaid, and Ofwarren's Commander's Wife is profoundly discomforted and embarrassed when she has to take her place on the 'birthing stool' while her Handmaid gives birth to her husband's baby. Even more culpable, however, are the Aunts, middle-aged women armed with cattle-prods, who run the re-education centres where the Handmaids are brainwashed into submission and tortured if they rebel. One critic has suggested that the Wives and the Aunts represent two aspects of the anti-feminist movement among women, which began in response to Women's Liberation in the 1960s and is still in evidence today.[4] But even the Aunts admit that the 'Unwomen', as they call the radical feminists of whom

Offred's own mother had been a member, had some ideas which were 'sound enough' (128) – including, presumably, the book-burnings of pornographic material such as the one Offred witnessed as child, which demonstrate the dangers of fanaticism even in a supposedly worthwhile cause.

Grotesque as they are, the Wives and the Aunts have their prototypes in Atwood's earlier writings: Anna, in *Surfacing*, for example, unable to face her husband without the make-up she carefully applies in private each day, a part-willing participant in her husband's degrading and violent movie and unhappily conniving at his sexual infidelities, already has some of the attributes of a Wife, while Joan Foster's violent and arbitrary mother in *Lady Oracle* and Elizabeth's domineering and spiteful Auntie Muriel in *Life Before Man* clearly anticipate the cruelty of the Aunts. Although these are extreme cases, the Aunts seem to be a logical development of a recurring theme throughout Atwood's fiction: the suggestion that the older generation, those responsible for our rearing and our education, have added to our burdens by acquiescing in the oppression of the system, or simply by withholding the knowledge of warmth, of loving, of human contact, like Rennie Wilford's mother in *Bodily Harm*, whose first lesson had been 'how to look at things without touching them'.[5] This theme is extended still further in *Cat's Eye*: all the cruelty and violence which is perpetrated by the female characters can be seen as in some way a result of the example set by their mothers.

There is a sense, however, in which the sufferings of Atwood's heroines may be seen to be partly self-generated; as an indication, in other words, of their own alienation and lack of maturity. This seems to be the message of *Surfacing*, in which part of the protagonist's quest for self-hood, self-recognition and completion is a metaphoric search for her mother, whose 'legacy', if she can attain it, will be 'simple . . . final'.[6] Alienation, isolation, the desire for non-involvement which is admitted by the protagonist of *The Handmaid's Tale*, have been shared by the protagonists of all Atwood's earlier novels. Offred is the first of her heroines to have recognised her own culpability before the start of the novel; one indication of the fact that this book has moved on from Atwood's earlier work. In *Cat's Eye*, which has a double time-structure, the child Elaine escapes her victimisation and becomes a survivor about halfway through the novel, although the narrator (the adult Elaine) comes fully to understand the whole process only at the end. In each of the previous novels, the recognition of responsibility is perhaps the primary lesson which the main character has to learn. As Atwood puts it in *Two-Headed Poems*:

> As for the women, who did not
> want to be involved, they are involved.

> It's that blood on the snow
> which turns out to be not
> some bludgeoned or machine-gunned
> animal's, but your own
> that does it . . .

> Each has a mirror
> which when asked replies Not you.[7]

The image of the mirror in this poem is one which recurs frequently in Atwood's writing. Sometimes it can be a vehicle for self-deception, like the mirror on Anna's gold compact in *Surfacing* which she uses to create her own fictionalised persona, or the triple mirror on Joan Foster's mother's dressing-table where the fascinated child watches her mother colouring herself in. Mirrors, in Atwood's writing, may also reveal the truth, or what the protagonist feels to be the truth: in Joan's dream the three-headed mother reflected in the triple mirror 'seemed merely a confirmation of something I'd always known . . . my mother was a monster'.[8] Joan, however, one of the most self-deceived of all Atwood's leading characters, comes in the end to a half-realisation that what the mirror revealed may only have been half of the truth. The absence of conventional mirrors can sometimes force a realisation of a more accurately reflected reality: in the prison cell in which Rennie finds herself at the end of *Bodily Harm*, the lack of a mirror forces her to see herself reflected through the eyes of her cellmate, Lora, and it is this act that brings her to a state of recognition of their shared humanity, in which she is finally able to transcend the freezing limitations of her restrictive childhood and reach out to touch the other woman.

*Cat's Eye* also contains several sinister and deceptive mirrors. The sadistic Cordelia uses a real one to torment the heroine:

> 'Look at yourself! Just look!' Her voice is disgusted, fed up, as if my face, all by itself, has been up to something, gone too far. I look into the mirror but I don't see anything out of the ordinary . . .[9]

A literary/pictoral mirror – reflecting a monstrous face back at the 'normal' girl who looks into it – also figures in the romantic horror comic read by Cordelia and Elaine (211), and Elaine's self-portrait (entitled 'Cat's Eye' like the novel) contains a mirror which reflects 'a section of the back of my head . . . but the hair is different, younger' (408). Above all, in this novel, the dénouement proves to depend on the realisation that mirroring can be a vehicle for self-recognition: Elaine comes to understand at the end that the pain which Cordelia induced was simply a reflection of the pain which Cordelia herself was suffering. In *Cat's Eye*, possibly the most self-consciously self-reflexive of Atwood's novels, the process of recognition experienced by Elaine is clearly an analogue of what its author sees as the purpose of art. As she wrote in *Survival*:

A piece of art, as well as being a creation to be enjoyed, can also be . . . a mirror. The reader looks at the mirror and sees not the writer but himself; and behind his own image in the foreground, a reflection of the world he lives in.[10]

The recognition of responsibility, in the novels before *The Handmaid's Tale*, comes slowly to the protagonists, if at all. Marion MacAlpin, in *The Edible Woman*, perhaps never really achieves it, although this rather depends on how one interprets what Atwood has called the 'self-indulgent grotesqueries' (*Second Words*, 369) of the final scene where Marion bakes and then consumes a cake made in her own image. Atwood herself admits that in this book the heroine's choices 'remain much the same at the end of the book as they are at the beginning' (370).

In contrast she sees the heroine of *Surfacing* as taking as active step forward,[11] presumably because in this work the ending, although far from conclusive, contains the protagonist's important self-recognition that she must, 'above all':

refuse to be a victim. Unless I can do that I can do nothing. I have to recant, give up the old belief that I am powerless and because of it nothing I can do will ever hurt anyone. A lie which was always more disastrous than the truth would have been.

(191)

The self-deception which the protagonist of *Surfacing* is at last facing up to – in her case, she has lied to herself and others about her past, deliberately falsifying the true facts of her abortion and her failed non-marriage – is a common escape strategy for all Atwood's major characters, up to, but not including, Offred. Joan Foster, who has constructed a whole series of fictive identities for herself both as a writer and as a human being, calls herself 'an escape artist' (334). This description could apply equally to Marion MacAlpin, whose bizarre

fantasy life becomes almost pathological when she
attempts to evade the responsibilities of her femininity
by means of a form of anorexia; to Rennie Wilford, who
runs away from two failed relationships, an unsatisfactory journalistic career and the implications of an
operation for cancer to take refuge on a Caribbean
island; or Lesje, in *Life Before Man,* the scientist who is
unable to participate fully in life and who takes refuge in
fantasies about a lush tropical prehistoric world in
which the 'gargantuan passions'[12] of the dinosaurs
appear to have more substance than her own rather
unsatisfactory personal life.

In all these earlier novels fantasy is seen as an escape,
an evasion of a reality which must in the end be faced if
the protagonist is to realise her potential health and
sanity. The success with which this test is passed varies
considerably from novel to novel; Rennie Wilford and
the protagonist of *Surfacing* seem to pass it more
successfully than do Marian McAlpin, Joan Foster or
Lesje. In *The Handmaid's Tale,* however, the few
fantasies in which Offred is able to indulge serve the
purpose of keeping her sane. As she says herself, 'Sanity
is a valuable possession; I hoard it the way people
hoarded money. I save it, so I will have enough, when
the time comes' (119); and her imagination is a primary
means to that end. She is fortunately possessed of an
ironic humour which comes into play in many of the
bizarre situations in which she finds herself: for example, when the Commander ends his fertilisation attempt,
performed with Offred lying between the legs of his
passive Wife:

> He rests a moment, withdraws, recedes, rezippers. He nods,
> then turns and leaves the room, closing the door with
> exaggerated care behind him, as if both of us are his ailing
> mother. There's something hilarious about this, but I don't
> dare laugh.
>
> (106)

Elsewhere, she consciously makes use of humorous fantasies; when she attends the Prayvaganza which culminates in the group marriage of twenty virgins, for instance, she prevents herself from being impressed by the Commander in charge, in his sober black uniform with the rows of insignia and decorations by making 'an effort':

> I try to imagine him in bed with his Wife and his Handmaid, fertilizing away like mad, like a rutting salmon, pretending to take no pleasure in it.
>
> (230)

Towards the end of the Prayvaganza she recalls the first time she realised the fact that:

> there is something powerful in the whispering of obscenities, about those in power. There's something naughty, secretive, forbidden, thrilling. It's like a spell of sorts. It deflates them, reduces them to the common denominator where they can be dealt with.
>
> (234)

This knowledge has not come to her spontaneously. It has been passed on to her by her friend Moira, who is an example of a woman who chooses not to be a victim. That this is seen as a heroic choice is in no way diminished by the fact that it brings little or nothing but suffering. Moira's first two attempts to escape from the Red Rehabilitation Centre are punished by torture, and when Offred sees her for the last time she has been assigned as a hostess/prostitute to Jezebel's, the Club where the Commanders indulge their male demand for 'variety', which Offred's Commander tells her is 'Nature's plan' (249). Whether this is a victory or a defeat is not clear to Offred, who thinks that she may detect signs of indifference or resignation in Moira, and never discovers what happens to her afterwards:

I'd like to tell a story about how Moira escaped, for good this time. Or if I couldn't tell that, I'd like to say she blew up Jezebel's, with fifty Commanders inside it. I'd like her to end with something daring and spectacular, some outrage, something that would befit her. But as far as I know that didn't happen. I don't know how she ended, or even if she did . . .

(262)

This theme echoes one which is especially noticeable in the novels of Atwood's 'middle period': heroism, the counterpart to victimisation, tends to be punished by suffering. Elizabeth, in *Life Before Man*, despite her domineering toughness, achieves a sort of heroic strength at the end of the novel, if only in the recognition that 'she's still alive' (301), that she will go on and face the realities of her bleak and lonely future; and Lora, in *Bodily Harm*, pays for Rennie's and her own survival in prison by prostituting herself to the guards, only to be beaten in the end, perhaps to death. In *The Handmaid's Tale*, however, the existence of the work is predicated on the fact that Offred herself has progressed to a state of heroism, having made her escape and managed somehow to record her story for later generations. Finally, in *Cat's Eye*, Elaine matures from a frightened, victimised child through a stage of inability even to recall the circumstances of her victimisation (escape fantasy again) to a final point where she can confront and fully deal with the painful facts of her own past. Her success in doing so is almost certainly associated with her successful career as an artist: just as in *The Handmaid's Tale* Offred preserved her sanity through imagination and fantasy, so Elaine paints out her traumas, transmuting them into grotesque and often hilarious but essentially manageable artefacts.

Again, this seems to indicate that Atwood has moved on in her thinking from the stage in which she seemed preoccupied with the fact that what she saw as the purpose of art – to pass on knowledge – may end in punishment or death.[13] This preoccupation initiated the recurring references in her work to the film *Red Shoes*, in which Moira Shearer (whose name perhaps suggested Moira's in *The Handmaid's Tale*) plays a dancer with red shoes who chooses art over ordinary life and ends by dancing herself to death. In the poem about her small daughter, 'A Red Shirt', Atwood expressed her fears about the child's future through this image:

> she should
> keep silent and avoid
> red shoes, red stockings, dancing.
> Dancing in red shoes will kill you.
> (*Two-Headed Poems*, 101)

And Offred, watching the body of a Handmaid who has rebelled suspended from a wall, her red shoes dangling in a grotesque parody of a ballet, thinks to herself: 'I don't want to be a dancer' (298). Nevertheless, Offred comes to realise that it is her duty to pass on her experiences in the hope that some future good may result, and the whole novel is presented as the result of that realisation:

> it hurts me to tell it over, over again. Once was enough: wasn't once enough for me at the time? But I keep on going with this sad and hungry and sordid, this limping and mutilated story, because after all I want you to hear it. . . . Because I'm telling you this story I will your existence. I tell, therefore you are.
> (279)

By telling her story, Offred has transformed herself from a victim into a heroine. In *Cat's Eye* the process goes a stage further, as Elaine has ceased to blame society or other people for her sufferings, choosing instead to identify the final cause with her own immature and confused psyche.

Another way in which Atwood's writing seems to have developed and matured in her most recent fiction is in her presentation of male characters. This is an aspect of her work which has attracted a good deal of negative criticism, most, though not all, of it from male critics. Frank Davey, for example, in his *Margaret Atwood: A Feminist Poetic*, speaks of finding in her work a 'profound mistrust of men',[14] while other male critics have discerned 'a rankling sense of alienation' expressed in 'the neurotic edginess of her prose'; and, in her poetry, 'barely controlled hysteria' which takes 'specifically feminine forms'.[15] It is not difficult to see why some men may feel disturbed and threatened by Atwood's presentation of them, both in her poetry and in her novels: there are clear indications of a decidedly ambivalent attitude towards men expressed in her early and middle work. Perhaps the first suggestion of this is to be found in the powerful and disturbing poem sequence, *Power Politics* (1971), which gives an account of the last painful throes of a relationship characterised by an inability to communicate, and by violence both mental and physical. The most notorious poem of the collection - and also the shortest - is the first:

> You fit into me
> like a hook into an eye
>
> a fish hook
> an open eye.[16]

This could certainly be seen as lending weight to the view that Atwood sees male sexuality as equivalent to violence. But in fairness to this particular collection there is a strong suggestion that women are equally implicated in this: this seems, at least, to be the point of the lines in which the speaker says: 'Next time we commit/love, we ought to/ choose in advance what to kill' (35).

It seems likely, however, that one of the initial results of Atwood's developing political awareness was an increased mistrust of men on the grounds that they are largely responsible for oppression, tyranny and violence. This seems particularly marked in *Bodily Harm* in which Rennie's lover has indulged in rape fantasies, she has been threatened by an actual rapist who has left a coiled-up rope on her bed, she has been shown violent pornography at the police station and witnessed real brutality in prison, so that she comes to realise: 'She's afraid of men and it's simple, it's rational, she's afraid of men because men are frightening' (290). A similar attitude is expressed in the prose poem, 'Liking Men', published in *Murder in the Dark* (1983). Here, the speaker begins by cautiously fantasising about men's feet, 'pinkly toed and innocuous'; moves on to *'Footgear* . . . Golfshoes . . . Workboots . . . Rubber boots'; only to find herself trapped by the thought of 'Jackboots' in a terrifying rape-fantasy:

> Now you see rows of them, marching, marching; yours is the street level view, because you are lying down. Power is the power to smash, two hold your legs, two your arms, the fifth shoves a pointed instrument into you; a bayonet, the neck of a broken bottle, and its not even wartime. . . .[17]

In 'Writing the Male Character', a 1982 essay, Atwood argued that:

> One must conclude that the less than commendable behaviour of male characters in certain novels by women is not necessarily due to a warped view of the opposite sex on behalf of the authors. Could it be . . . that not every man always behaves well?
>
> *(Second Words,* 417-18)

and made the point that women are likely to know more
about men than men themselves, since they have not
only their own experiences but those of their friends to
draw on: men rarely discuss their behaviour towards
women with their male friends (424–5).

In *The Handmaid's Tale*, however, Atwood can be seen
to be moving towards a more positive presentation of the
male character. This may not seem immediately obvious.
After all, men have certainly been largely responsible for
setting up the totalitarian regime of Republic of Gilead:
although Offred herself is unable to discover any information about the highest levels of government the
appendix makes it clear that it was the product of a secret
organisation called the Sons of Jacob. Furthermore,
although Offred's Commander behaves towards her with
perfect courtesy of what she finds to be a rather laughably
old-fashioned kind – she thinks he looks like 'a vodka ad',
'some old come-on from a glossy men's mag' (97, 147),
finds his requests for illicit games of Scrabble and
goodnight kisses 'as if you meant it' (150) sad and bizarre
rather than threatening, and notes that 'I sense in him
none of the animosity I used to sense in men. . . . He's not
saying *bitch* inside his head. In fact he is positively
daddyish' (193) – and although it is revealed at the end of
the novel that he soon afterwards 'met his end . . . in one
of the earliest purges' as a result of his 'liberal tendencies'
(321), these facts are intended, it seems clear, to make him
more, rather than less, sinister. This is undoubtedly the
point of Offred's childhood memory of a documentary
she had once watched with her mother which included an
interview with a woman who had been the mistress of a
Nazi camp commandant:

> He was not a monster, she said. People say he was a
> monster, but he was not one.
> . . . he was not a monster, to her. Probably he had some
> endearing trait; he whistled, off key, in the shower, he had a
> yen for truffles, he called his dog Liebchen and made it sit

up for little pieces of raw steak. How easy it is to invent a
humanity, for anyone at all. What an available temptation.
A big child, she would have said to herself. Her heart would
have melted, she'd have smoothed the hair back from his
forehead, kissed him on the ear, and not just to get something out of him either. . . .
   Several days after this interview with her was filmed, she
killed herself. It said that, right on television.
   Nobody asked her whether or not she had loved him.

(155-6)

Although Offred mistrusts him profoundly, the Commander does present her with the opportunity to
meditate on what his experience of life – a man's
experience of life, and of sex – must be like:

To be a man, watched by women. It must be entirely
strange. To have them watching him all the time. To have
them wondering, What's he going to do next? To have them
flinch when he moves, even when it's a harmless enough
move, to reach for an ashtray perhaps. To have them sizing
him up. To have them thinking, he can't do it, he won't do,
he'll have to do, this last as if he were a garment, out of style
or shoddy, which must be nevertheless put on because
there's nothing else available.
To have them putting him on, trying him on, trying him
out, while he himself puts them on, like a sock over a foot,
onto the stub of himself, his extra, sensitive thumb, his
delicate stalked slug's eye, which extrudes, expands, winces,
and shrivels back into himself when touched wrongly,
grows big again, bulging a little at the tip, travelling
forwards as if along a leaf, into them, avid for vision. To
achieve vision in this way, this journey into a darkness that
is composed of women, a woman, who can see in darkness
while he himself strains blindly forward.

(98-9)

The other male characters in the novel are Offred's
husband Luke, for whom she has only positive feelings
but who exists for her only in her memory, since she has

no idea what has happened to him, whether indeed he is alive or dead; and Nick, the Commander's chauffeur, who becomes her lover, initially as a result of a suggestion by the Commander's Wife (who wants a baby at all costs and fears her husband may be sterile) but later by illicit choice. Neither of these two shows any sign of being either a wimp or a brute, unlike almost any of Atwood's earlier male characters, most of whom seem to possess at least one if not both these characteristics. There are one or two exceptions to this rule: the almost totally silent Joe in *Surfacing*, the lover of the protagonist and later chosen to be the father of her child, seems neutral enough but he is curiously unformed, like one of the 'disagreeable mutant' ceramic pots which he makes, and which because they are unsaleable and unusable simply litter the basement (57); and the mysterious but apparently saintly Dr Minnow in *Bodily Harm*, who is murdered for his political involvement. In her essay 'Writing the Male Character', Atwood discussed the extreme difficulty of writing about a truly good man:

> What, these days, is a believable notion of a good man? . . . Let's suppose that I want him to have some actual good qualities, good in the active, positive sense. What is he to do? And how can I make him . . . interesting in a novel?
> (*Second Words*, 427)

She concluded that 'male characters are more of a challenge', and that she looked forward to trying more of them, if only because 'they force you to imagine what it's like to be somebody else' (430). The passage in which Offred tries to imagine what a man's experience must be like is obviously one example of a response to that challenge. Possibly Nick in *The Handmaid's Tale* is an attempt to create a male character with 'actual good qualities'. Like Dr Minnow, he appears at first to be extremely enigmatic, though this is not surprising given the lack of trust which exists between all members of the society and the impossibility of communication between himself and Offred. Unlike Dr Minnow, however, he is young and obviously sexual. Offred is drawn to him but is profoundly uncertain whether or not she can trust him. She suspects he may be a spy, and also feels he must disapprove of her illicit relations with the Commander. Even when she has begun her visits to his room at night, during which she talks 'too much', and tells him 'things I shouldn't', he still remains mysteriously closed to her:

> He . . . talks little: no more hedging or jokes. He barely asks questions. He seems indifferent to what I have to say, alive only to the possibilities of my body, though he watches me while I'm speaking. He watches my face.
> Impossible to think that anyone for whom I feel such gratitude could betray me.
>
> (282)

Nevertheless, the possibility of betrayal is there, for the reader at least and no doubt for Offred herself, right up to the conclusion of her story. In the end, however, it is Nick who is responsible for rescuing her, although this act is one which involves immense personal risk and may lead to his own capture and death. In other words, in this novel the one truly *useful* heroic act is performed by a man.

This is obviously another way in which the novel seems to represent an advance in optimism over Atwood's previous work. Indeed, the very brutality and inhumanity of the regime of Gilead only serves to highlight the fact that there is still in individual cases a survival of love, of forgiveness, of the need to help others at whatever the cost to oneself. This is demonstrated not only by Nick but by Offred's 'shopping partner' Ofglen, a member of the underground organisation known as Mayday, who not only gives Offred essential nourishment in the way of hope and moral support but also in the end sacrifices herself by her act of humanely finishing off the victim of the ritual dismemberment, whom she has recognised as 'one of ours'. Also notable, though subsidiary, are the nameless members of the Underground organizations who help Moira on her escape attempts and who shelter Offred when she is finally smuggled out of the Commander's house by Nick's efforts.

A recent critic, Barbara Hill Rigney, sees the appendix, in which the book is set as a subject for discussion at an academic conference in the twenty-second century, as indicating 'a further and presumably better future' (Rigney, 119). However, although women are indeed again participating as human beings – the conference is chaired by a female academic – Rigney seems to have missed Atwood's irony here: the male 'Keynote Speaker' indulges in sexist jokes at her expense and at the expense of the document he is discussing, which clearly indicate that men's attitude towards women has changed very little since the 1980s. Nevertheless, I think Rigney is right when she sees the theme of the novel as being 'the persistence of love even in a loveless world' (*ibid.*).

Although this element of forgiveness and human warmth is more marked in *The Handmaid's Tale* than in the writing which immediately preceded it, it has been present to some extent in all her earlier work. It is developed most fully, however, in her latest novel, *Cat's Eye*.

> I began . . . to think of time as having a shape, something you could see, like a series of liquid transparencies, one laid on top of another. You don't look back along time but down through it, like water. Sometimes this comes to the surface, sometimes that, sometimes nothing. Nothing goes away.
>
> (*Cat's Eye*, 3)

This statement seems to me descriptive not only of Atwood's narrative practice in *Cat's Eye* but also of the ways in which the novel relates to her own development as a writer. The novel, that is, is retrospective both because its narrator, Elaine Risley, contemplates her own past in an attempt to make sense of her present and because its author comments on and rewrites the themes and preoccupations of her earlier writings.

Discussing the arrangement of the paintings in her retrospective exhibition Elaine, who favours a chronological approach, becomes nervous when the gallery owner says she 'wants things to go together tonally and resonate and make statements that amplify one another' (87). Atwood's arrangement of her narrative material manages to adopt both approaches. The sections of the book (= gallery catalogue), numbered in Roman numerals and titled after Elaine's paintings, proceed along a double chronological track in which the events of her childhood rise to the surface to resonate with and amplify the account of her return to Toronto in middle age to supervise the opening of her exhibition.

As in Joyce's *Portrait of the Artist,* the childhood portions of *Cat's Eye* are frequently concerned with ways in which the child Elaine acquires knowledge of herself and her relation to society. Unlike Joyce, however, Atwood is most interested in showing the child attempting to make sense of gender differences, an attempt which is forced on her when she first goes to school, aged eight, and encounters girls whose upbringing has been more conventional than her own.

All the members of Elaine's family are natural (or in touch with nature) in ways that none of the other characters is: even her brother, the astrophysicist, at least studies the fundamental laws of creation though he may appear to have little grasp of what is usually thought of as reality. Her mother, who wears slacks rather than the regulation aprons or twin-sets, goes skating, and takes solitary walks, is 'not like the other mothers. . . . She does not inhabit the house, the way the other mothers do; she's airy and hard to pin down' (156). Finally, her father's occupation as an etymologist dictates both the geographical environment in which she spends her earliest years – the far north of Canada, where refinements like permanent houses, possessions, flush toilets, are unknown – and apparently also his broader grasp of essentials: when he becomes a university professor, he laughs and shakes his head over the inability of his students' anatomical drawings to make 'provision for a heart' or to 'tell a male from a female' (34). The child Elaine at this stage judges the drawings 'better or worse depending on the colours'. The novel will show her learning to become as discriminating as her father.

The central action of the novel – woman's inhumanity to woman, demonstrated by the sadism practised by the child Cordelia and her followers on the child Elaine – takes up once again the theme of female cruelty found in the Aunts of the *Handmaid's Tale* and their predecessors. Atwood's treatment of it here constitutes an advance over her earlier fiction, however, since instead of presenting it simply as an ugly fact of life she shows Elaine slowly and painfully coming to an understanding of its sources and causes.

The eight-year-old Elaine's first experience of playing with girls is 'different . . . as if I'm only doing an imitation of a girl' (52). With Carol and Grace she spends hours cutting out figures from old mail-order catalogues and then encumbering them with the trappings of domesticity: ' "My lady's going to have the refrigerator" ' (53). Both girls are clearly carbon copies of their mothers: Carol is already delicate and feminine, like the twin-setted and house-proud Mrs Campbell (a Wife?) while Grace, bossy and domineering, is modelled after the terrifying, hideous (Aunt?) Mrs Smeath (later to figure in so many of Elaine's paintings) who has a 'bad heart' and whose bibbed aprons make her look as if she has only one large central breast. It is Cordelia, however, whose appearance on the scene marshals the other two into the programme of ill-treatment to which Elaine is submitted. Like her namesake, Cordelia has two elder sisters; like her, too, she suffers from the fact that they seem to have been given all the gifts – beauty, charm, talents – while she is 'the third sister . . . the rejected one, the one who was not heard' (263). Lear's passionate, ultimately prophetic appeal to his daughter, 'Nothing will come of nothing' (*King Lear*, I,i,89) finds its full fruition in the Cordelia of Atwood's novel. Unable to admit even to herself her sense that she has, or is, nothing, she attempts to impose that feeling onto the weakest member of her entourage, Elaine. At first meeting with success, her act crumbles to dust in the face of Elaine's eventual realisation that 'I don't have to do what she says, and, worse and better, I've never had to do what she says. I can do what I like' (193).

This is the earliest realisation for any of Atwood's protagonists that it is not necessary to be a victim. Although it leaves her with an instinctive knowledge of how to be a survivor, its initial effect on Elaine is a suppression of even the memory of her victimisation. During this period of amnesia, which lasts almost to the end of the novel, she suffers from time to time from periods of black, unattributable despair, during which she has to 'lie down, expecting nothing, and it arrives, washing over me in a wave of black vacancy' (380). Over the years, however, she comes to understand with increasing clarity the enormous problems which Cordelia has faced in dealing with the demands of her life and the expectations of her family. Their last meeting is in a mental institution to which Cordelia has been committed following a suicide attempt: 'She has let go of her idea of herself. She is lost' (358).

In the final pages of the novel Elaine, having at last recalled the past, finds herself longing to see Cordelia again: her non-appearance at the exhibition leads her to the conclusion that '*You're dead*' (414) – literally as well as figuratively is implied, though unconfirmed. But *Cat's Eye*, like *The Handmaid's Tale*, is a novel about forgiveness despite the fact that 'Forgiving men is so much easier than forgiving women' (267). Forgiveness, in fact, turns out to be synonymous with understanding, as in Elaine's final realisation:

> I know she's looking at me, the lopsided mouth smiling a little, the face closed and defiant. There is the same shame, the sick feeling in my body, the same knowledge of my own wrongness, awkwardness, weakness; the same wish to be loved; the same loneliness; the same fear. But these are not my own emotions any more. They are Cordelia's; as they always were.
>
> (419)

In this novel, Atwood seems to have found ways of moving in the direction of representing something which has interested her since the beginning of her writing life, and which she described to Graeme Gibson in an interview in the early 1970s:

> If the only two kinds of people are killers and victims, then although it may be morally preferable to be a victim, it is obviously preferable from the point of view of survival to be a killer. However, either alternative seems pretty hopeless . . . I think there has to be a third thing again; the ideal would be somebody who would neither be a killer [n]or a victim, who could achieve some kind of harmony with the world, which is a productive or creative harmony, rather than a destructive relationship towards the world.
>
> (Gibson, 27)

The greater tolerance and understanding of the problems faced by both sexes which Atwood seems to have developed in her most recent writing has been called 'post-feminist'. This rather depends what feminism is taken to be. If anger, polemicism and separatism are viewed as its necessary components then the description is apt. If, however, it can be defined as an attempt to live in a state of 'productive or creative harmony' with other human beings without sacrificing one's integrity either as a woman or as an artist then perhaps she is a feminist after all.

# Notes

1. 'On Being a Woman Writer: Paradoxes and Dilemmas', *Second Words* (Toronto, Anansi, 1982), 190–204.
2. See Sara Mills, Lynne Pearce, Sue Spaull, Elaine Millard, *Feminist Readings/Feminists Reading* (Hemel Hempstead, Harvester Wheatsheaf, 1989), 109–16, 195–208.
3. *The Handmaid's Tale*, 1985 (London, Virago, 1987), 189.
4. Barbara Hill Rigney, *Margaret Atwood* (London, Macmillan Education, 1987). Although she does not deal specifically with some of the issues discussed here, I would like to acknowledge a general indebtedness to Rigney's sensitive reading of Atwood's work.
5. *Bodily Harm* (London, Virago, 1983), 54.
6. *Surfacing* (London, Virago, 1979), 149.
7. *Two-Headed Poems* (New York, Simon & Schuster, 1978), 82.
8. *Lady Oracle* (London, Virago, 1982), 67.
9. *Cat's Eye* 1988 (London, Bloomsbury, 1989), 158.
10. *Survival: A Thematic Guide to Canadian Literature* (Toronto, Anansi, 1972), 15.
11. Graeme Gibson, 'Margaret Atwood', in *Eleven Canadian Novelists* (Toronto, Anansi, 1973), 24.
12. *Life Before Man* (London, Virago, 1979), 144.
13. Clearly this preoccupation was to an extent a result of her involvement with Amnesty International.
14. Frank Davey, *Margaret Atwood: A Feminist Poetic* (Vancouver, Talonbooks 1984), 163.
15. Philip Stratford, 'The Uses of Ambiguity: Margaret Atwood and Hubert Aquin', in *Margaret Atwood: Language, Text, and System*, eds. Sherrill E. Grace and Lorraine Weir (Vancouver, University of British Columbia Press, 1983), 113; John Wilson Foster, 'The Poetry of Margaret Atwood', *Canadian Literature*, **74** (1977), 5.
16. *Power Politics* (Toronto, Anansi, 1981), 1.
17. *Murder in the Dark* 1983 (London, Jonathan Cape, 1984), 53–4.

# Chronological Table of Works
## Maya Angelou
*Born St Louis, Missouri, USA, 1928*

1970    *I Know Why the Caged Bird Sings* (UK, 1984)
1971    *Just Give Me a Cool Drink of Water 'Fore I Die* (UK, 1988)
1974    *Gather Together in My Name* (UK, 1985)
1976    *Singin' and Swingin' and Gettin' Merry Like Christmas* (UK, 1985)
1978    *And Still I Rise* (UK, 1986)
1981    *The Heart of a Woman* (UK, 1986)
1986    *All God's Children Need Travelling Shoes* (UK, 1987)
1989    *Conversations with Maya Angelou* (UK, 1989)

## June Jordan
*Born Harlem, USA, 1936*

1977    *Things That I Do in the Dark*
1980    *Passion: New Poems 1977–1980*
1981    *Civil Wars*
1987    *Riding the Moon in Texas*
1989    *Lyrical Campaigns*
1989    *Moving Towards Home*


*Essays*
1985    *On Call: Political Essays* (UK, 1986)

## Ntozake Shange
*Born Trenton, New Jersey, USA, 1948*

1978    *for colored girls who have considered suicide / when the rainbow is enuf*
1979    *Nappy Edges* (UK, 1986)
1981    *Three Pieces* (UK, 1982)
1982    *Sassafrass, Cypres and Indigo* (UK, 1983)
1984    *A Daughter's Geography* (UK, 1984)
1985    *Betsey Brown*

# Alice Walker

*Born Eatonton, Georgia, USA, 1944*

| | |
|---|---|
| 1970 | *The Third Life of Grange Copeland* (UK, 1985) |
| 1973 | *In Love and Trouble* (UK, 1984) |
| 1973 | *Revolutionary Petunias* (UK, 1988) |
| 1976 | *Meridian* (UK, 1982) |
| 1978 | *Once* (UK, 1986) |
| 1979 | *Good Night Willie Lee, I'll See You in the Morning* (UK, 1987) |
| 1981 | *You Can't Keep a Good Woman Down* (UK, 1982) |
| 1982 | *The Color Purple* (UK, 1983) |
| 1984 | *Horses Make a Landscape Look More Beautiful* (UK, 1985) |
| 1987 | *Living by the Word* (UK, 1988) |
| 1989 | *The Temple of My Familiar* (UK, 1989) |

*Essays*

| | |
|---|---|
| 1983 | *In Search of Our Mothers' Gardens: Womanist Prose* (UK, 1984) |

# Audre Lorde

*Born Harlem, USA, 1934*

| | |
|---|---|
| 1968 | *The First Cities* |
| 1970 | *Cables to Rage* |
| 1973 | *From a Land Where Other People Live* |
| 1975 | *New York Head Shop and Museum* |
| 1976 | *Coal* |
| 1976 | *Between Ourselves* |
| 1978 | *The Black Unicorn* |
| 1980 | *The Cancer Journals* (UK, 1986) |
| 1982 | *Chosen Poems* |
| 1982 | *Zami: A New Spelling of My Name* (UK, 1985) |
| 1986 | *Our Dead Behind Us* (UK, 1987) |
| 1989 | *A Burst of Light* |

*Essays*

| | |
|---|---|
| 1984 | *Sister Outsider: Essays and Speeches by Audre Lorde* |

# 5

# And Still I Rise

## Five Contemporary Black Women Poets from North America

### *Helen Kidd*

To begin with a litany:
Ruby McCullem, Beverley Smith, Harriet Tubman, Rashida Woods, Joan Little, Georgia Douglass Johnson, Shirley Chisholm, Phyllis Wheatley, Nella Larson, Assata Shakar, Mary McLeod Bethune, Linda Brent, Rebecca Jackson, Angelina Weld Grimke, Camille Yarborough, Sojourner Truth, Fannie Lou Hamer, Frances Harper, Joan Pidion, Anne Petry, Bernice Regon, Janet Tolliver, Sarah Fabio, Maya Angelou, Adrienne Kennedy, Louise Meriweather, Jane Cortez, Sarah Wright, Eloise Greenfield, Micki Grant, J. E. Franklin, Nikki Giovanni, Gloria Olden, Kristin Hunter, June Jordan, Gayl Jones, Julia Fields, Audre Lorde, Rosa Guy, Paule Marshall, Gloria Naylor, Toni Morrison, Zora Neale Hurston, Carolyn Rodgers, Vare Mae, Ntozake Shange, Katherine Dunham, Charlayne Hunter Gault, Alice Walker, Sherley Anee Williams, Barbara Smith, Paulette Childress White, Lorraine Hansberry, Margaret Donner.

Some of these names will be familiar, some unknown, and you will recognise that this list is only a fragment of the numbers of Black women writers to be found in

*124*

North America. I shall be focusing on five writers in this essay: June Jordan, Maya Angelou, Alice Walker, Ntozake Shange and Audre Lorde. I have chosen five, rather than the statutory one or two that might be found in an essay on European writers, for two reasons; first because all these writers live and work in a context entirely different from our own European experience and, indeed, from that of white American writers and, most importantly, this context is dependent on a sense of community and cultural differences which does not depend on dominant white notions of 'high' culture but on its own artistic roots, folk traditions, music and literature, as well as sense of mutual support and community. This is something that the European reader may be too little aware of. Secondly, and arising from the first, it seems important to establish the sense of a group or collective consciousness which runs through Black writing, and particularly through Black writing women who remain very much in contact with one another and provide mutual support and assistance, both in addressing writing issues and the larger issues of living as women in a man's world, and Blacks in a white world. What emerges from examining these writers together is the sense of political commitment to change and resistance in the face of an oppressive present and a grim past but, despite this, a wide range of techniques and differing approaches. It is important to bear this in mind. Clearly, being Black is not a blanket experience any more than being a woman, gay, Chinese or working class are blanket experiences. We are all aware that to be African or Caribbean is different to the American Black experience, but what tends to be overlooked is that to be a Black woman in California is different, culturally, socially and politically, to being a Black woman in New York or the deep South, just as a Scot from the Gaeltacht[1] is different to an Aberdonian or a Lowlander like Burns. If this cultural diversity is remembered then the dangers of stereotyping can be avoided.

To continue, some biographical sketches:

# June Jordan

Born in Harlem, raised in Brooklyn. Political essayist, journalist, activist, poet and now a Professor of English at SUNY, Stoneybrook, she began writing when she was seven. She is divorced and is a mother. In her poetry she is a drummer of witty and complex rhythms which hold together what she terms her 'New World Vision':

> Let me define my terms in brief: New World does not mean New England. New World means non-European; it means new; it means big; it means heterogeneous; it means unknown; it means free; it means an end to feudalism, caste, privilege, and the violence of power. It means *wild* in the sense that the tree growing away from the earth enacts a wild event. It means *democratic* in the sense that Whitman wrote:

> > 'I believe a leaf of grass no less than the journey-work of the stars . . .
> > And a mouse is miracle enough to stagger sextillions of infidels.'
> > > (Song of Myself)[2]

# Audre Lorde

Born Harlem 1934, of West Indian parents. Describes herself as a Black Lesbian Feminist Warrior poet. She is Professor of English at Hunter College and also a mother of two. She has transformed her experience of breast cancer and a radical mastectomy into *The Cancer Journals*.[3] She is both traveller in and sculptor of poems, crossing edges and barriers, honing the edges of experience:

. . . I have a duty to speak the truth as I see it and to share not just my triumphs, not just the things that felt good, but the pain, the intense, often unmitigating pain . . .[4]

# Ntozake Shange

Born in Trenton, New Jersey, 1948, began writing as a child. She is a poet, novelist, playwright, performer. Her original name, Paulette Williams, she changed as a protest against the West, and her new Zulu name means 'She who comes with her own things' (Ntozake) and 'She who walks as a lion' (Shange). She is the mother of a daughter. She is the dancer with language and describes herself as a 'Jazz poet'; someone whose poetry lives on the page as a visual distortion of formal conventions, grammatical structures, poetic expectations. It becomes the visual equivalent of Black American accents:

. . . a poem shd fill you up with something/cd make you swoon, stop in yr tracks, change yr mind, or make it up. a poem shd happen to you like cold water or a kiss.[5]

# Maya Angelou

Born in St Louis, Missouri 1928, raised in Stamps, Arkansas and California. She is a poet, playwright, actress, dancer, singer and Reynolds Professor at Wake Forest University. She is also a mother, and in poetry she is a singer:

I write for the Black voice and any ear that can hear it. As a composer writes for musical instruments and a choreographer creates for the body, I search for sound, tempos, and rhythms to ride through the vocal cord over the tongue and out the lips of Black people. I love the shades and slashes of light. Its rumbling and passages of magical lyricism. I accept the glory of stridencies and purrings, trumpetings and sombre sonorities.[6]


## Alice Walker

Born in Eatonton, Georgia 1944, and like Maya Angelou she is a Black daughter of the South and also a mother. This poet, novelist, short story writer, essayist and biographer is the artist, the painter in words.[7]

These writers cannot be reduced to a single and comprehensive artistic characteristic; each transforms her world of experience into a particular vision. As Shange puts it in her introduction to *Nappy Edges*:

> my basic premise is that poets address themselves to the same issues as the musicians / but that we give musicians more space to run with / more personal legitimacy than we give our writers.[8]

I believe it to be true that the 'space' allowed to Black writers to 'run with' is considerably more generous across the Atlantic than it is here in Britain and even, indeed, on the Continent, for the 'English Tradition' (that is to say, that which the magazines and publishing houses deem acceptable and, importantly, saleable) still adheres to a lyricism particularly handed on from the Romantics, and has to a large extent shrugged off Modernism or relegated it to one, and one only, historical example, namely Mr Eliot. The Continent, on the other hand, though happy to embrace experimentation, innovation, foregrounding of materials such as language textures, syntax and punctuation, concrete and phonic poetry, has to a large extent tended to forget that there is a world outside the poem from which it comes, to which (however narrow) it speaks and towards which (however randomly assembled) it must gesture. Women poets in Britain, apart from a rare few, have not dared to move into the 'experimental' or 'post-Modernist' modes of writing, for fear of losing poetic content. Unfortunately this places the poetry in a retrospective and rather narrow spectrum. Could women writers only look to poets such as Shange as an example, other possibilities might emerge, such as ways of treating the textures, distortions and rhythms of language which may accompany and convey content without losing it. She also interestingly stresses the importance of identity and experience to Black cultural identity:

we have poets who speak to you of elephants and avenues / we have others who address themselves to worlds having no existence beyond the word. That's fine. we live all those places. but, if we don't know the voice of a writer / the way we know 'oh . . . that's trane' / something is very wrong. we are unfortunately / selling ourselves down the river again. and we aweady know abt that. if we go down the river again / jus cuz we don't know or care to recognize our particularities / wont nobody come / cuz don nobody care / if you dont know yr poets as well as yr tenor horns.[9]

Ntozake's comment brings out the one uniting characteristic of all the Black writers I have encountered so far, and that is the importance of Black musical traditions, the pervasive background of Blues, slave hollers, Rock'n'Roll, Motown, Reggae, Salsa, bar room stomps, Ragtime, Ska, Calypso, Spirituals and latterly, Rapping.
    To continue with another litany:

Bessie Smith, Billie Holiday, Big Mama Thornton, Miss Sassy Vaughan, Josephine Baker, Memphis Minnie, Tina Turner, Ella Fitzgerald, Nina Simone, Odetta, Diahann Carroll, Eartha Kitt, Diana Ross, Mammie Smith, Aretha Franklin, Roberta Flack, Mahalia Jackson. Add your own

favourites to this roll of honour, augment it. Play them to
your friends, pass them on.

In *The Heart of a Woman*, Maya Angelou says: 'I could
moan some salty songs. I had been living with empty
arms and rocks in my bed.'[10] This is an apt description
for June Jordan's 'Alla That's All Right, but',[11] which is
a deceptively simple lament for the lack of love in life.
Maybe it is more than just personal, for it can certainly
be read as a salty moan for rocks in the bed of all Black
women; the need for understanding, for love but also,
and crucially, for a different kind of power:

### Alla That's All Right, but

Somebody come and carry me into a seven-day kiss
I can' use no historic no national no family bliss
I need an absolutely one to one a seven-day kiss
I can read the daily papers
I can even make a speech
But the news is stuff that tapers
down to salt poured in the breach

I been scheming about my people I been scheming about my
sex
I been dreaming about Africa and nightmaring Oedipus the
Rex
But what I need is quite specific
terrifying rough stuff and terrific

I need an absolutely one to one a seven-day kiss
I can' use no more historical no national no bona fide
family bliss
Somebody come and carry me into a seven-day kiss
Somebody come on
Somebody come on and carry me
over there.

This is not then so much a song of the Sleeping Beauty
waiting for the magic kiss as an invitation to engage

with reality on a one-to-one level, to engage with personal and sensual politics rather than the politics of 'over there'. And such direct and relational politics are seen as rough and raw, terrifying in fact, because they are the direct stuff of needs and desires rather than social conventions, which are grouped together by Jordan to suggest ideological formulations – 'national', 'historical', 'family'. Thus love and physical desire are expressed as revolutionary in this bluesy song, with its drawn out lingering hungry lines in the central section. We have in 'over there' both the outsideness of abstract formulations and the over thereness of the implied Promised Land, over the (appropriately named) Jordan. To emphasise this we also have the repetition and embellishments of repeated phrases used by the Southern Baptist preacher, as well as the echo of the Spiritual from which, of course, the Blues has grown.

Songs tend to have two purposes, but because of their nature as performance these functions tend to overlap. First there is the public utterance, then there is the personal and the intimate. There is the lyric and there is the community song. The latter becomes a statement of community of purpose. Therefore it has an easily recognisable pattern; passages and choruses or refrains that can be repeated and shared. Even if it allows for improvisation and elaboration it retains a recognisable framework and rhythmic and musical cues in its choral sections. The pattern of Black Baptist preaching is similar and progresses through various modulations and moods into a culmination of shared hope and affirmation. The above poem demonstrates a song quality which, while containing a rhetorical similarity to preaching, as well as Biblical and hymnic allusions, yet its subject is another kind of intensity, that of the importance of sexual commitment and passion which is a frequent subject of the Blues. Thus we are reminded of Bessie Smith, for example, in the way the lines repeat and repeat and yet improvise on line lengths, until we

get a raunchy drawn-oi moaning effect redolent of the
Blues. But we have also been taken into a political arena,
we have been specifically told, so the preacherly element
and the Blues element combine in what amounts to a
Feminist affirmation of the overwhelming importance
of the personal as political, the erotic and sexual as
revolutionary.

A third element contributing to the poem's effect
which is implied in the preacherly cadences, coupled
with the political undertones, is the oratorical style of
the Civil Rights speakers and leaders. This effect can be
seen working superbly in the following poem:

### Poem about My Rights

Even tonight and I need to take a walk and clear
my head about this poem about why I can't
go out without changing my clothes my shoes
my body posture my gender identity my age
my status as a woman alone in the evening /
alone on the streets / alone not being the point /
the point being that I can't do what I want
to do with my own body because I am the wrong
sex the wrong age the wrong skin and
suppose it was not here in the city but down on the beach /
or far into the woods and I wanted to go
there by myself thinking about God / or thinking
about children or thinking about the world / all of it
disclosed by the stars and the silence:
I could not go and I could not think and I could not
stay there
alone
as I need to be
alone because I can't do what I want with my own
body and
who in the hell set things up
like this
and in France they say if the guy penetrates
but does not ejaculate then he did not rape me
and if after stabbing him if after screams if
after begging the bastard and if even after smashing

a hammer to his head if even after that if he
and his buddies fuck me after that
then I consented and there was
no rape because finally you understand finally
they fucked me over because I was wrong I was
wrong again to be me being me where I was / wrong
to be who I am
which is exactly like South Africa
penetrating into Namibia penetrating into
Angola and does that mean I mean how do you know if
Pretoria ejaculates what will the evidence look like the
proof of the monster jackboot ejaculation on Blackland
and if
after Namibia and if after Angola and if after Zimbabwe
and if after all my kinsmen and women resist even to
self-immolation of the villages and if after that
we lose nevertheless what will the big boys say will they
claim my consent:
Do You Follow Me: We are the wrong people of
the wrong skin on the wrong continent and what
in the hell is everybody being reasonable about
and according to the *Times* this week
back in 1966 the C.I.A. decided that they had this problem
and the problem was a man named Nkrumah so they
killed him and before that it was Patrice Lumumba
and before that it was my father on the campus
of my Ivy League school and my father afraid
to walk into the cafeteria because he said he
was wrong the wrong age the wrong skin the wrong
gender identity and he was paying my tuition and
before that
it was my father saying I was wrong saying that
I should have been a boy because he wanted one / a
boy and that I should have been lighter skinned and
that I should have had straighter hair and that
I shouldn't be so boy crazy but instead I should
just be one / a boy and before that
it was my mother pleading plastic surgery for
my nose and braces for my teeth and telling me
to let the books loose to let them loose in other
words

I am very familiar with the problems of the C.I.A.
and the problems of South Africa and the problems
of Exxon Corporation and the problems of white
America in general and the problems of the teachers
and the preachers and the F.B.I. and the social
workers and my particular Mom and Dad / I am very
familiar with the problems because the problems
turn out to be
me
I am the history of rape
I am the history of the rejection of who I am
I am the history of the terrorized incarceration of
my self
I am the history of battery assault and limitless
armies against whatever I want to do with my mind
and my body and my soul and
whether its about walking out at night
or whether its about the love that I feel or
whether its about the sanctity of my vagina or
the sanctity of my leaders or the sanctity
of each and every desire
that I know from my personal and idiosyncratic
and undisputably single and singular heart
I have been raped
be-
cause I have been wrong the wrong sex the wrong age
the wrong skin the wrong nose the wrong hair the
wrong need the wrong dream the wrong geographic
the wrong sartorial I
I have been the meaning of rape
I have been the problem everyone seeks to
eliminate by forced
penetration with or without the evidence of slime and /
but let this be unmistakeable this poem
is not consent I do not consent
to my mother to my father to the teachers to
the F.B.I. to South Africa to Bedford-Stuy
to Park Avenue to the American Airlines to the hardon
idlers on the corners to the sneaky creeps in
cars
*I am not wrong: wrong is not my name*

My name is my own my own my own
and I can't tell you who the hell set things up like this
but I can tell you that from now on my resistance
my simple and daily and nightly self-determination
may very well cost you your life.[12]

This strong poem begins on a personal note, a situation, clearly and precisely framed. The problem here, 'even tonight', is the difficulty of going out safely for a walk. It begins reflectively and slowly accumulates iterations and reiterations, the possessive pronouns, the three alone's and the contradicting points, and the emphasis on wrong which falls at the end of this particular sense section. The conjunction at the end of line nine introduces a hypothetical situation, which itself contains new clusters of repetition which are drummed out in their turn; 'thinking' and 'could not' are each repeated three times and the introduction of the twice-repeated 'alone' sums up this section and the first sense together, moving them towards the rhetorical and angry question 'who in hell set things up / like this'. Each possible lyrical or liberating expression ('alone / as I need to be') or the expansion into the hypothetical, the beach, the woods and the stars, are denied by the drum-like insistence of such elements as 'wrong', or 'I could not' which effectively act as cage bars to the possibilities suggested. Even the line, 'alone because I can't do what I want with my own' negates the positive aspects of the previous aloneness. This is a loneliness and alienation brought on by fear. The lineation further assists in emphasising the need for space and as it slows and diminishes, it loses in articulation what it gains in space, slowing to almost total stasis, having difficulty in clearing its head, as the first lines suggest. The angry rhetorical question recuperates the energy by pointing the poem away into a new section, having made an effective rhetorical break, and the possibility of questing for a site of blame.

The context becomes wider, moving out to France, the

reason for the stasis and anger becomes particularised. It is both the threat of rape and the other aspect of patriarchal law and unreason, the laws on rape. The locus becomes at once more general (for example, the present tense used in 'In France they say') and more personal as it deals with the speaker and a rapist set in the past, with a series of participles to suggest the ongoing struggle, which operate with the accumulation of 'if after's' to accentuate the grimness of the situation, and operate with the two 'finally's' as a wall which hems the speaker in, so that only a return is possible, a return to the earlier refrain, placed in the imperfect tense: 'I was wrong'. The line lengths shorten again in 'to be who I am' but do not shorten and slow quite so drastically as in the first section. The private/public litany of wrongs (and by implication rights) has now been connected by a series of oratorical flourishes and accumulations, such as a public speaker might use, the lack of punctuation serving to suggest a speaking rather than a writing voice and breaks, sometimes with slashes in mid- or end-line, which serve as an extra beat or emphasis on the subsequent word.

The third sense section begins with a widening-out still further in this chain of association, in which the notions of rape and penetration are repeated in a different context, the parallel being made between fascism and sexual crime, white imperialism and violation of the freedoms of the Front Line States. White on black becomes a suggestion of ejaculation, with its phonic equivalent of jackboot, and all its unpleasant onanistic and tyrannical associations. Again the line shortens to 'and if'. The white of the stasis, the overwhelming by the white page of the Blackland of resisting language and creative anger, looks immanent in the face of such ugly imagery and such appalling realities. To gather momentum and to remind us of the process of association, the motif 'if after' of the French section is taken up again and the personal pronoun 'my' is introduced to once again link the private to the public, the personal to the political situation. This interconnection of personal struggle, personal rage, personal resistance and the personal experience of victimisation with the wider military and political victimisation in the Blackland of South Africa and the Front Line States is emphasised in the direct question, capitalised for added emphasis, 'Do You Follow Me'. The demand on the reader/audience to keep up with the argument then has all the strength and power of a rallying call, as well as the other implication, that where one falls, you the reader may be the next. In this line 'you', 'me' and 'we' are collocated and at this point, where the reader becomes implicated in the struggle, the reiteration of wrong is taken up in a global context. 'We' are suggested as a community under oppression and violation. Thus the following lines, in which the media are seen to be reasonable and rational, are placed on the side of the law-givers, dispassionate, because contrasted with the 'we' that the voice of the poem is speaking for. Again the poem moves between the public and historical and the private and personal. Individual history and African history are interconnected, the connecting motif of 'wrong skin, wrong gender' and so on now being associated with personal and family history. In this setting bad faith and gender discrimination appear. Mother and father kowtow to the notions of white enclaves and white ideals of beauty. Father reveals his antipathy to his daughter's 'wrongness' by wishing her a boy. Mother demonstrates bad faith by expecting the speaker to conform to stereotyping.

The poem pivots around the one-word line 'words'. What the papers said, what the parents said, what the CIA said, what the Law says and what the 'big boys' are likely to say. The 'I' of the following lines turns about and looks the words fully and ironically in the eye, and also in the 'I' which she has been alloted by these institutions and 'White/America in general'. This

identity has been constructed as a problem. 'Problems
. . . problems . . . problems . . .' are chanted, until the 'I'
stands as an accusing finger; 'I', the victim and the
wronged, locates herself as victim:

> I am the history of rape
> I am the history of the rejection of who I am
> I am the history of the terrorized incarceration of
> my self

'I' becomes the site where white guilt, black indifference
and male sexual assault converge, but 'I' also is defined
as the place of the heart, mind and soul, in particular the
heart – 'my personal and idiosyncratic and undisputably
single and singular heart'. 'I' becomes a positive and
iterated litany of qualities as well as oppressions, of
possibilities encapsulated in the repeated 'whether' and
'about' which then move into the emphasised 'sanctity',
'The sanctity of my vagina', 'the sanctity of each and
every desire'. Affirmation has entered; the statement 'I
have been raped' is in the perfect tense. The action is
accomplished, the state imposed on the victim (and by
association all other victims of obscenities like racism
and rape) is a past state. The projection of guilt onto the
victim, of emphasising the victim's wrongness, has
produced a collusion by the oppressors, a belief in
inferiority and wrongness. The isolation of the prefix
'be' as a single line suggests that this state continues, but
we learn that it is not consented to. This 'be', desiring to
stand alone but inevitably linked to its 'cause', is then a
transition state, free to realise the collusion, free to reject
it, and thus far can 'be', but not free until the resistance is
completed, the oppressors vanished. 'I do not consent'
raises its fist in the certainty of not being wrong. This
defiant autonomy rests on the rallying call to those it has
addressed in the line 'Do You Follow Me', the line being
a personal and public and collective declaration of
intent, stemming from the sense of being wronged singly

and collectively, stemming from the right to choose one's labels: 'My name is my own my own my own'. Following the litany of wrongs comes the declaration of intent, self-determination operating as perpetual public and private resistance to any diminution of human dignity. The poem is concluded and knitted together with the refrains and ironic plays on those refrains, and variation with all the skill of a jazz musician. It has the drum-like rhythms of the civil rights orator, even the echo of Martin Luther King's Dream in the line 'the wrong need the wrong dream', and as the affirmation builds, so the repetitions build, the 'I' becomes the drum or the raised fist of resistance, and as June Jordan says in 'Poem No. 2 for Inaugural Rose', 'Sometimes I had to write drums to overcome the Terrors.'[13]

Nevertheless, her poetry can also be simple, in this section of direct elegiac songs, as in her 'poem for Nana', which laments the fall of the native American:

> Crow Nose
> Little Bear
> Slim Girl
> Black Elk
> Fox Belly
> the people of the sacred trees
> and rivers precious to the stars that told
> old stories to the night
>
> how do we follow after you
>
> falling
> snow before the firelight
> and buffalo as brothers
> to the man
>
> how do we follow into that?[14]

The collective 'I' has given way here to the use of the pronoun 'we', as the section is neither long nor complex, its utterance based on an incantation of the names of Amerindians, an evocation of them, and then their attendant environment, using the animistic diction which can be found in native American Indian poetry and in Black Elk's own work *Black Elk Speaks*.[15] Significantly, however, the poem both identifies the collective voice 'we' with the Amerindians through this technique and yet also distances itself from them by the introduction of the notion of cultural difference, in its use of the two pronouns 'we' and 'you'. Thus appropriation, through using Amerindian shamanistic incantations and identification with the natural world, is avoided by setting this means of regarding organic non-human life forms as sacred and informative to human society (indeed, so integral to the maintenance of the quality of life as to be invoked in familial terms, e.g. buffalo as brothers) in the terms of role models, something to be followed on from, but also followed by repeating the previous pattern, 'How do we follow into that', suggesting return.

Whereas 'For My Rights' operates as a public rallying cry addressed to Black women on a global level, identifying 'I' and ' We', and 'poem for Nana' takes up an identification with other oppressed cultures in its own deictics, Maya Angelou's 'Still I Rise', operates on an oppositional model, challenging the 'You' of white supremacy with another voice, another 'I' of resistance. It begins with the steady rhythm and rhyme of ragtime music, with all its attendant 'sassiness' and colloquial diction, and amalgamates it with the defiant hope of the Church meetings and Southern Black Baptist spirituals, which is underlined by the Biblical associations of 'I Rise':

### Still I Rise

You may write me down in history
With your bitter, twisted lies,
You may trod me in the very dirt

But still, like dust, I'll rise.

Does my sassiness upset you?
Why are you beset with gloom?
'Cause I walk like I've got oil wells
Pumping in my living room.

Just like moons and like suns,
With the certainty of tides,
Just like hopes springing high,
Still I'll rise.

Did you want to see me broken?
Bowed head and lowered eyes?
Shoulders falling down like teardrops,
Weakened by my soulful cries.

Does my haughtiness offend you?
Don't you take it awful hard
'Cause I laugh like I've got gold mines
Diggin' in my own back yard.

You may shoot me with your words,
You may cut me with your eyes,
You may kill me with your hatefulness,
But still, like air, I'll rise.

Does my sexiness upset you?
Does it come as a surprise
That I dance like I've got diamonds
At the meeting of my thighs?

Out of the huts of history's shame
I rise
Up from a past that's rooted in pain
I rise
I'm black ocean, leaping and wide,
Welling and swelling I bear in the tide.

Leaving behind nights of terror and fear
I rise
Into a daybreak that's wondrously clear
I rise
Bringing the gifts that my ancestors
gave,

I am the dream and the hope of the slave.
I rise
I rise
I rise.[16]

Marrying this religious input to sexuality creates an energised autonomy which repudiates the myth of the Black Southerner as merely oppressed and a broken object of pity, a trap the liberal sympathiser can easily fall into, and whom 'haughtiness' might well offend, who might prefer to minister to a submissively grateful down-and-out racial grouping which amounts, in its patronage, to a subtler form of oppression and appropriation:

> Did you want to see me broken?
> Bowed head and lowered eyes?
> Shoulders falling down like teardrops,
> Weakened by my soulful cries.

This can be read as a two-fold address, a challenge both to the out-and-out racial supremacist and also to the patronage of the liberal do-gooder, akin to the fore-runner, the missionary. Soulful cries are rejected then as being as weakening as being 'trod' in the dirt.

By continuing the associations with the Blues tradition and sexuality the 'I' of the poem identifies herself as being specifically gendered, sexy and sassy, with 'diamonds at the meeting of my thighs', refusing to look over into the promised land, over the Jordan of the Spirituals, but places hope and defiance back on an earthly and earthed footing, celebrating the resurrection of the body, sexiness and all, as well as the resurrection of all 'the gifts' the ancestors have given, sassiness, haughtiness, laughter, the dance and hope. Self-esteem and racial pride in songs like this lie in a steadfast refusal of passive suffering and an affirmation of the spirit of hope as being rooted in the present, physical enjoyment and the 'Dream' of a better future. The poem also contains a change of rhythm as well as of address in stanzas eight and nine, which drop the oppositional mode of address often used in Blues numbers. The opposition constitutes a challenge to the lover in Blues as oppressor and wrongdoer[17] effectively singing rather than speaking bitterness. In the case of this poem that which challenges is sexuality itself, so that the blues rhythm takes on the more assertive word-play, verbal texture and innuendo more redolent of Bessie Smith: '. . . I walk like I've got oil wells/Pumping in my living room', for example. In the following stanza we find the crooning sounds of the first line, 'Just like moons and like suns', and we are reminded again of her salty love songs that she mentions in *The Heart of a Woman*.[18]

The final two stanzas then move away from the main rhythms of the Blues into the variation and syncopation that alter the four-beat bars and incorporate the whoop so familiar to Blues technique, which is derived from the slave holler used to uplift the spirits of slaves while labouring in the fields. The repetition and building to a crescendo of this whooping effect is also reminiscent of the repetition used in Black preaching to rouse the congregation, and this association is emphasised by the inclusion of archaic terms such as 'beset' in the Bluesy stanzas and 'wondrously' in the ultimate stanzas. The poem can be seen, then, to draw its techniques from the musical traditions of the Deep South, and creates a song of gendered Black resistance both in its language and in its musicality without losing its wider Black influences and inferences. It suggests redemption in its treatment of rising from oppression, but it is a physical redemption which is not only resistance but also sexual celebration. It situates this redemption firmly in its own roots, its own links with the gifts of the singers' ancestors. Hence the poem never becomes simplistically transcendent in its hope and affirmation, neither does it become teleological in its aspirations, but remains anchored to physicality and dailiness, sexuality and celebration sited in the backyard and the living room.

Hope then is the dominant note of the songs of the South that Maya Angelou builds on, hope built on the force of the collective dreams and wishes of people with an enslaved past; hope also built on the power to unsettle brittle white dominance by a steady imperturbability that draws on the knowledge of collective consciousness, strong cultural identity and 'sassiness'. This consciousness comprehends that despair and self-pity can be profoundly corrosive both for the many and for the individual. Thus she insists on the energetic motivation of musical performance to infuse and permeate the songs, drawing on Rhythm and Blues, Bar Room Stomps and Boogie rhythms.

When Alice Walker deals with song she tends to muse upon the subject rather than creating the more public, and hence more repetitive, song itself. Take, for example, 'Hymn':[19]

I well remember
A time when
'Amazing Grace' was
All the rage
In the South.
'Happy' black mothers arguing
Agreement with
Illiterate sweating preachers
Hemming and hawing blessedness
Meekness
Inheritance of earth, e.g.,
Mississippi cotton fields?

And in the North
Roy Hamilton singing
'What is America to me?'
Such a good question
From a nice slum
In North Philly.

My God! the songs and
The people and the lives
Started here –

Weaned on 'happy' tears
Black fingers clutching black teats
On Black Baptist benches –
Some mother's troubles that everybody's
Seen
And nobody wants to see.

I can remember the rocking of
The church
And embarrassment
At my mother's shouts
Like it was all – 'her happiness' –
Going to kill her.
My father's snores
Punctuating eulogies
His loud singing
Into fluffy grey caskets
A sleepy tear
In his eye

*Amazing Grace*
*How sweet the sound*
*That saved a wretch*
*Like me*
*I once was lost*
*But now I'm found*
*Was blind*
*But now*
*I see.*

Mahalia Jackson, Clara Ward, Fats Waller,
Ray Charles,
Sitting here embarrassed with me
Watching the birth
Hearing the cries
Bearing witness
To the child,
Music.

This double-edged and ironic musing on the cultural past and its presence in the present is both personal and more broadly historical. Alice Walker's chosen situations and subject matter are seldom presented as ideal, seldom perfect, but therein lies her particular and hopeful note in celebrating the daily, the particular, the vulnerable, and identities in process rather than the fixed, anachronistic notion of unified sensibility and character. She draws on the moment and all its implications or on the individual, concentrating on what flourishes in that particular situational soil, imperfections and all. What interests her, as she says, are those who are perceived as incorrect[20] and those who offer affection, courage or beauty despite the impossibility of their circumstances. In the poem the mothers are thus presented as central to the event, maybe colluding with the 'illiterate preachers' on one level, maybe deceived by the notion of 'happy' tears but nevertheless contributing to the storehouse of Black culture in a way that no Philadelphia Negro, who is the byword in bad faith, could ever do.

On the other hand, these songs and traditions are not presented as in any sense empowering in terms of the way the world wags. They will not assist anyone to inherit the earth and it is precisely this kind of ambiguous response, coupled with line breaks which emphasise the ambiguity, which renders Alice Walker a less public kind of poet.

The form of the poem differs from her most favoured form for poetry in that it is not short and thin. Nevertheless it also represents her interest in 'painting the eye of the tiger'.[21] That is to say, she is adept at capturing the notation of the moment with all its subtlety, ambiguity contradictions and complexity. Thus the birth of Southern music, suggested in the poem and the success of such singers as Mahalia Jackson, can grow as strategies out of such awkward moments as outlined in 'Hymn'.

If the freedom song is poetry formed from the rage for fair order in an unfair and unbalanced world, then Alice Walker's poetic musings are more like jazz improvisations.[22]

Similarly, vision is presented in her poetry as always

only partial. Thus in her African poems the seeming imperfections of Africa, seen as the lost paradisial homeland for so many members of the diaspora, may be treated with respect and understanding rather than disillusionment. She mocks the partial vision of visiting non-African Black people, as well as her own physical eye problem, in 'African Images, xiii':

> See! through the trees!
> A leopard in the branches –
> No, only a giraffe
> Munching his dinner.[23]

Her more reflective position as a poet then places differing demands on the poetry, less publicly declarative, more aware of contradictions and complexities within Black experience, and the position of women and also therefore of situational strategies for creativity. This position is one which also gives rise to meeting points and exchanges of opinion, as in 'Love', x:

> Explain to the
> Women
> In the village
> That you are
> Twenty
> And belong –
> To no one.[24]

The break in the line after 'belong' suggests both a felt sense of community with her African sisters, a sense of belonging, but also a difference which is experienced through their differing gender roles within culturally separate sets of expectations. When she does, however, express a feeling of shared identity, like June Jordan she extends this to include other racially dispossessed groups, and once again American Indian tribes with whom she feels a common heritage and history, having Indian forbears herself.

Like Alice Walker, Ntozake Shange acknowledges jazz influences. Indeed, she styles herself a jazz poet. She affirms the rhythmic complexities of Black music and repudiates wholeheartedly the notion that it is a lesser art simply because it is seen as widely popular by adherents of 'high' culture. Not only do her poems follow the movements of music but also of dance, and the result is that her structures and spellings appear on the page as radically different from standard spelling and poetic form. As she says:

> It bothers me . . . to look at poems where the first letters are capitalized. It's very boring to me. That's why I use the lower-case alphabet. Also, I like the idea that letters dance, not just that the words dance. I need some visual stimulation, so that reading becomes not just a passive act and more than an intellectual activity, but demands rigorous participation . . . The spellings result from the way I talk or . . . reflect the language as I hear it . . . [I] hear very particular rhythms underneath whatever I'm typing . . . if I'm hearing a rumba, you'll get a poem that looks like a rumba on the page.[25]

Though her subject matter is frequently harrowing and shocking, for example the Willie Beau sequence in *for colored girls*,[26] the very complexity of the language as well as its appearance on the page, or the performance-orientated structure on the stage, repetitions, choruses and rhythms, counterbalances the pain of the content. It is, in effect, another means of drawing creativity and song out of despair and conflict. Nevertheless she never shies away from confronting crucial social and political issues and the dreadful effects these have on personal lives. However, the creative will rises in song, which is defiance, challenge and pain. *for colored girls* moves through the cycles and wrecks of heterosexual relationships into disaster, and reaches its conclusion through the healing of sisterhood and self-discovery. After each successive and worsening emotional and physical disaster the women move closer together in their choruses and their affirmation of their own hard-won emotional articulacy. Identity is finally affirmed as gendered, as well as a coloured collective identity. The following pieces from the final section of the play demonstrate this:

*lady in blue*

we deal wit emotion too much
so why dont we go on ahead & be white then /
& make everythin dry & abstract wit no rhythm & no
reelin for sheer sensual pleasure / yes let's go on
& be white / we're right in the middle of it / no use
holdin out / holdin onto ourselves / lets think our
way outta feelin / lets abstract ourselves some families
& maybe maybe tonite / i'll find a way to make myself
come witout you / no fingers or other objects just thot
which isnt spiritual evolution cuz its empty & godliness
is plenty is ripe & fertile / thinkin wont do me a bit of
good tonite / i need to be loved / & havent the audacity
to say
where are you / & dont know who to say it to
. . . . . . . . . . . . . . . . . . . . . . . . . . . . . . . . .

*lady in red*

i sat up one nite walkin a boardin house
screaming / cryin / the ghost of another woman
who waz missin what i waz missin
i wanted to jump up outta my bones
& be done wit myself
leave me alone
& go on in the wind
it waz too much
i fell into numbness
til the only tree i cd see
took me up in her branches

held me in the breeze
made me dawn dew
that chill at daybreak
the sun wrapped me up swingin rose light everywhere
the sky laid over me like a million men
i waz cold / i waz burnin up / a child
& endlessly weavin garments for the moon
wit my tears

i found god in myself
& i loved her / i loved her fiercely

> *All of the ladies repeat to them-*
> *selves softly the lines 'i found god*
> *in myself and i loved her.' It soon*
> *becomes a song of joy . . .*[27]

These passages not only equate emotional and intellectual aridity with whiteness, challenging the white habit of separating the head and issues of the heart, it also poses a striking challenge to post-modernist writing, in the insistence of rhythm, rhyme and lyrical continuity and expression. Paradoxically it appears on the page as the most post-modernist of all the poetry that has so far been examined in this essay. Its influences, as has already been pointed out, are jazz orientated, and its choreography and choral structure are more classical than contemporary; thus the work constitutes an interesting fusion.

The whiteness of the page here is disrupted by black writing; a fitting analogy for black women's articulacy disrupting the blank uniformity of white cultural dominance. The white light of the stage lights is also refracted into the colours of the rainbow exemplified by the colours of the 'colored girls'. The emphasis on the spectrum also serves to allude to the many shades of being Black and the term 'colored' is reclaimed from liberal patronage and given a positive stress.

The final passages also reclaim the term 'god' from the fixed, unitary universal of white religion and used to signify the richly variable spirit of love and physical desire, variable as colour and as individuals, and fittingly expressed as 'her'. This again is radically different in emphasis from white avant-gardeism which, in rejecting aspiration and notions of spirituality, has contrived to throw out positive aspects of sacredness with the bath water, just as earlier white male culture threw out the physical and sexual in adopting concepts of transcendence. Immanence is what is celebrated here and expressed fully in the concluding sequences of the play. It is variable, dancing and rainbow-coloured rather than uniform and homogenised but nonetheless, despite the importance of the liberation of the women of individual colours, there is a collective realisation of interconnectedness which is as important and necessary as that of the rainbow.

Audre Lorde's means of affirming her gender, racial and sexual identity in *Black Unicorn* is to reshape Yoruba mythology into the imagery and topography of both creativity and her own experience. That experience has grown out of inhabiting a marginalised territory as a Black woman, a woman poet, a Lesbian and cancer patient. Through the myths of Dahomey she has reinstated a mythology that is both affirmative and woman-centred. Seboulisa the goddess and Mother of Us All is represented as having 'one breast eaten away', 'worms of sorrow and loss' in '125th St. and Abomey',[28] and again with the same image in 'Dahomey'.[29] This image resonates profoundly with the poet's own experience of breast cancer. Who then but the Black Mother of All, with her 'happy tears' like Alice Walker's mothers in the South, would be most likely to be riddled by the worms of sorrow? Seboulisa is also represented as Mawulisa, the male/female sky goddess/god. Mawu, as mother, is the creator of the universe, Lisa being her son or her twin. So, as with many figures in the Yoruba pantheon, these provide us with images of female creativity and also the flexibility of gender-roles, which suits well Audre

Lorde's refusal to be trapped in restrictive social notions
of gender. All of this is woven into 'A Woman Speaks':

> Moon marked and touched by sun
> my magic is unwritten
> but when the sea turns back
> it will leave my shape behind.
> I seek no favor
> untouched by blood
> unrelenting as the curse of love
> permanent as my errors
> or my pride
> I do not mix
> love with pity
> nor hate with scorn
> and if you would know me
> look into the entrails of Uranus
> where the restless oceans pound.
> I do not dwell
> within my birth nor my divinities
> who am ageless and half-grown
> and still seeking
> my sisters
> witches in Dahomey
> wear me inside their coiled cloths
> as our mother did
> mourning.
>
> I have been woman
> for a long time
> beware my smile
> I am treacherous with old magic
> and the noon's new fury
> with all your wide futures
> promised
> I am
> woman
> and not white.[30]

Here the definition of woman begins to slip away as
soon as it appears to begin to inscribe itself, and so we
read that the 'magic' is 'unwritten', the shape still

waiting to be revealed when the tide turns. She is defined not so much by what she is as by what she is not, or by what she refrains from doing. Though she is associated twice with love in the first part of the poem, this love is evoked in connection with strange unfamiliar associations such as 'curse' and disassociated from other weaker emotions such as pity. These warrior-like associations accumulate largely through the line breaks which without punctuation leave a fitting uncertainty about one simple reading of the poem, and also intensify the associations with blood and danger. In the first stanza the lines 'I seek no favor/ untouched by blood' leave us in doubt as to whether it is herself or the 'favor' that might be untouched, or even whether the 'favor' is desirable unless touched by blood. Strangely enough, despite the violent images conjured up by the poem, and these certainly are fitting for Dahomey, legendary home of the Amazons, the associations are also decidedly connected to the women, 'sisters/witches in Dahomey' and also 'our mother'. The accumulation of images of mutability coupled with the syntactic ambiguity operates with added emphasis from the negative definitions such as 'I do not dwell', 'I do not mix', 'unwritten', 'unrelenting' and so on. The impression is reinforced therefore that she is continuously veiled, hidden under cloths. This then is the source of her power, because impossible to fix into one set of images or definitions, and the old magic becomes treacherous, empowering precisely because it lies within the art of concealment despite the obvious associations with energy and power, such as the sun and verb 'coiled' for example. The poet sculpts the unsayable, shapes lack of definition into a series of precisely worded and yet unrealisable images, until we reach the only possible certainly, 'I am/ woman', and this embedded in another negative 'and not white'. This is yet again the poem triumphing in its black overprinting of the white page, the parallel to Black songs of defiance despite white uniformity.

This then is one of Audre Lorde's gifts, to shape myths
that evade the trap of stereotype, myths of process and
power that are yet to fully become. Another gift is her
ability to sing love songs that move beyond the trap of
heterosexual fixity into tenderness and expressions of
communion with women, Lesbian love songs that also
move towards the 'you' of the reader, whatever their own
sexual persuasion. On one level these poems enact and
celebrate the act of poetic creation as a shared erotic act.
To define this eroticism briefly, it is not end-directed or
rooted in any notion of possession of the object/other,
but becomes a gesture towards the complete equality of
loving, or reading/writing, of giving and taking
pleasure as a shared mutual activity. The poem 'Bridge
Through my Window' affirms the two-way flow of love
and warmth as the essential components of survival, and
formulates the answer to the pain caused by imbalances
of power and the denial of differences that so many of
her poems so tellingly lament. She sees the process of
creation as a crucial part of changing the world. She
expresses it this way:

> The question of social protest and art is inseparable for me.
> I can't say it is an either/or proposition. Art for art's sake
> doesn't really exist for me but then it never really did. What
> I saw was wrong, and I had to speak up. I loved poetry and I
> loved words. But what was beautiful had to serve the
> purpose of changing my life, or I would have died. If I
> cannot air this pain and alter it, I will surely die of it. That's
> the beginning of social protest.[31]

She also puts it this way:

> *For Each of You*
> Be who you are and will be
> learn to cherish
> that boisterous Black Angel that drives you
> up one day and down another
> protecting that place where your power rises

running like hot blood
from the same source
as your pain.[32]

Like her Black writing sisters Audre Lorde honestly
follows her own advice, singing back to source, that
source being her race, her gender and her sexuality, and
she sings with a clear voice, commitment and un-
flinching honesty.

I have tried not to follow a complex theoretical line
with the poets I have chosen except for the thematic
backdrop of song. I agree with Stephen Henderson's
tentative proposal in his introduction to *Black Women
Writers*, that 'the raw sociocultural urgency of the literature short-circuits preoccupation with abstractions that
do not resonate on the level of myth'.[33] If there is any
consistent approach to be made at present from our
situation as white Europeans it must come from an
attitude of attentive engagement in which we must
shelve our critical criteria which derive from a pale
culture in the throes of struggling with the nature of
meaning when meaning has become our own entrap-
ment. Our direction needs to be outwards towards a
shared celebration which we have hitherto arrogantly
ignored and to those cultures which can still direct us
towards action and also conscience, and not only towards these but towards celebration and mutual affection. As women have less reticence regarding these areas
of experience then it is less difficult for white women to
engage with Black writers. Furthermore we do share
certain experiences, albeit not always positive, and have
already a glimpse of mutuality, even if only at the school
gates. To superimpose any theoretical models from our
own cultural experience would be yet another act of
appropriation and colonial vandalism. But not to
engage with these writers would be an unpardonable
breach of courtesy in the deepest sense of the word, and
courtesy, respect and love are qualities which these

writers here explore and employ down to the very treatment of the textures of their words.

# Notes

1. The *Gaeltacht* is the Gaelic title for the Gaelic-speaking areas of Scotland. It can be used to include the corresponding regions in the Irish Republic.
2. 'For the Sake of People's Poetry; Walt Whitman and the rest of us', *On Call: Political Essays* (Boston, South End Press, 1985), 11.
3. *The Cancer Journals* (New York, Norton and Co., 1980).
4. 'My Words Will be There', *Arguments and Interviews with Black Women Writers*, ed. Mari Evans (London, Pluto Press, 1985), 263.
5. 'i talk to myself', *Ms Magazine*, December 1977, in *Nappy Edges* (London, Methuen, 1987), 24.
6. 'Shades and Slashes of Light', *Black Women Writers*, ed. Evans, 3-4.
7. For her comments, which may not be quoted here, see 'In Search of Our Mothers' Gardens', *In Search of Our Mothers' Gardens: Womanist Prose* (London, The Women's Press, 1984), 241-3.
8. 'takin a solo/ a poetic possibility/ a poetic imperative', National Afro-American Writers Conference, Howard University, May 1977, in *Nappy Edges*, 4.
9. *ibid.*, 4.
10. *The Heart of a Woman* (London, Virago, 1986), 66-7.
11. *Lyrical Campaigns: Selected Poems* (London, Virago, 1986), 93.
12. *ibid.*, 102-4.
13. 'Poem No. 2 for Inaugural Rose', *Passion* (Boston, Beacon Press, 1980), 85.
14. *ibid.*, 'poem for Nana', 1-5.
15. Black Elk, *Black Elk Speaks: Being the Life Story of a Holy Man of the Oglala Sioux*, as told through John G. Neihardt (New York, Washington Square, 1959).
16. 'Still I Rise', *And Still I Rise* (London, Virago, 1986), 41-2.

17. For example, Memphis Minnie, 'Mean Mistreater', *Memphis Minnie 1936-1949; Hot Stuff*, Magpie, record no. PV1806, 1977.
18. See note 10.
19. 'Hymn', *Once* (London, Women's Press, 1986), 41-2.
20. See 'From an Interview', *Our Mothers' Gardens*, 268.
21. See Alice Walker quoting Muriel Rukeyser, 'From an Interview', 271.
22. *ibid.*, 270-1.
23. 'African Images, Glimpses from a Tiger's Back', *Once*, 6.
24. *ibid.*, 'Love', 19.
25. Claudia Tate, 'Ntozake Shange', *Black Women Writers at Work*, ed. Claudia Tate (Harpenden, Oldcastle, 1985), 163-4.
26. *for colored girls who have considered suicide when the rainbow is enuf* (London, Methuen, 1978), 55-60.
27. *ibid.*, 44-5, 63.
28. '125th Street and Abomey', *The Black Unicorn* (New York, Norton and Co., 1978), 12-13.
29. 'Dahomey', *Unicorn*, 10-11.
30. *ibid.*, 'A Woman Speaks', 4-5.
31. 'My Words Will be There', Evans, 264.
32. 'For Each of You', *Chosen Poems: Old and New* (New York, Norton and Co., 1982), 42-43.
33. Stephen E. Henderson, 'Introduction,' Evans, xxvii.

# Chronological Table of Works
# Christina Stead

*Born Sydney, Australia, 1902*
*Died Sydney, Australia, 1983*

### Novels

1934   *The Salzburg Tales*
       *Seven Poor Men of Sydney*
1936   *The Beauties and the Furies*
1938   *House of All Nations*
1940   *The Man Who Loved Children*
1944   *For Love Alone*
1946   *Letty Fox: Her Luck*
1948   *A Little Tea, a Little Chat*
1952   *The People with the Dogs*
1966   *Dark Places of the Heart;* republished 1967 as *Cotter's England*
1967   *The Puzzleheaded Girl*
1973   *The Little Hotel*
1976   *Miss Herbert (The Suburban Wife)*
1986   *I'm Dying Laughing: The Humourist*

### Short Stories

1985   *Ocean of Story*, ed. R. G. Geering

### Essays

1935   'The Writer Takes Sides', *Left Review* 1 (1935)
1979   'On the Women's Movement', *Partisan Review*, **46** (1979)

# 6

# Christina Stead

## Writing Expatriation

### Kate Lilley

Born in Sydney in 1902, Christina Stead left Australia in 1928, not to return until 1974, nine years before her death. Before she left she had already written, and unsuccessfully tried to publish, a collection of short stories: Angus and Robertson 'rejected it, saying that she would have to be published in London first'.[1] This became the basis of Stead's first book, *The Salzburg Tale*, published in London by Peter Davies in 1934, partly through the encouragement and business acumen of her husband, William Blake, a European–American Marxist economist, banker and novelist. A few months later her first novel, *Seven Poor Men of Sydney*, was published under the same imprint. As well as an ill-fated stint writing film scripts for MGM, she went on to publish another eleven novels, a collection of novellas, some occasional political prose, three French translations and an anthology co-edited with her husband, *Modern Women in Love: Sixty Twentieth-Century Masterpieces of Fiction* (1945). Since her death in 1974 there have been several further publications, including a novel of the McCarthy era, *I'm Dying Laughing: The Humourist* (1986), which Stead had been writing and revising on and off since the late 1940s.

All Stead's novels were written 'abroad'. Expatriation seems to have been the precondition of her career as a publishing writer, as well as an explicit and repeated imperative within her writing. It was the guarantee of a prolific literary production which inscribes woman as alien, and alien as woman, often in the doubly alienated figure of the emergent or fully fledged woman writer. As Drusilla Modjeska comments of the 1920s in Australia: 'It was a hostile environment for the woman writer. There was little to encourage them to stay in Australia then or during any of the early years of this century. When Christina Stead left for Europe in 1928 she was following a long tradition among women writers,' including Henry Handel Richardson, Alice Henry, Barbara Baynton and Miles Franklin (Modjeska, 6).

Expatriation has both active and passive senses – to leave, or to be forced to leave – and both are relevant to Stead. Australia was slow to foster or recognise her achievement, and hardly quick to reclaim her even in distinguished but apparently straitened old age (she was finally awarded a modest life pension in the form of an Emeritus Fellowship from the Literature Board of the Australia Council in 1980). All the same, going away does not necessarily imply repudiation. In an interview given in 1982, the year before her death at the age of 80, Stead insisted: 'I've always felt an Australian. I never lost Australia.'[2] But 'feeling' is one thing, formal affiliation another, and Stead was very far from being a nationalist. When, as secretary to the English delegation, she reported on the first International Congress of Writers for the Defence of Culture held in Paris in June 1935, only Nettie Palmer and John Fisher were bracketed in her list of participants as '(Australian)'.[3]

Stead's favourable report is a plea for socialist internationalism ('Internationalism abolishes all question of Occident–Orient differences', 462) though she notes without any apparent irony that, due to over-

crowding at the Congress, 'Some of the minor natio-
nalities did not get in at all' (460). She also refers to 'the
writer' (and 'the worker'), not only in the masculine
gender, but in terms of a patriarchal narrative of inheritance:

> the armies of reaction are trampling into the very heart of
> his own country: like the most ignorant peasant, he rises to
> defend what has come to him from his father, is his and
> makes him one of a community . . . the frightful insistence
> of economic questions leaves the writer, whatever his origin,
> quite at sea. He is reduced to consultation with his brother-
> writers, young or old, for the experience, intuition or
> natural seamanship.
>
> (435)

Stead clearly regarded herself as a full member of this
semen-ship, strangely insisting that 'The hall was not
full of half-feminine masculine revolutionaries and half-
masculine feminine rebels. They were neat, had no
postures and poses. The air was clean and pure
intellectually . . .' (456).

It would seem that, as an expatriate, Stead was able to
feel that she had acceded to the desired position of full
political and creative agency – become one of the boys,
wiped 'clean' of gender and nationality. She goes on to
quote approvingly Proudhon's distinction between 'possession' and 'property': 'It is by possession that man puts
himself in communion with nature, while by property
he separates himself from it: in the same way that the
man and woman are in communion by domestic
habitude, while voluptuousness holds them apart' (456).
Her commitment to 'cohabiting with the future' (456)
entails rejecting a disturbing and inauthentic androgyny
(presumably this would be posturing and posing) or,
equally, genderlessness. Equal heterosexual 'communion' with each other's 'nature' emerges as the authenti-
cally progressive model of social and sexual organization
in an international context.[4]

More than 20 years later when Stead sent her open letter, 'On the Women's Movement', to *Partisan Review*, she began it, 'Dear Sirs' – despite a female executive editor and three female assistant editors – and went on with a revealing qualification: 'My experience is limited because of the wandering life I led, living in a number of countries of which I was not a citizen and for the better part meeting married couples of modern ideas in great cities.'[5] Gender oppression is, for her, somewhere and someone else, among 'ordinary women' in the 'outmoded one-man family . . . where the wife is the husband's only serf' (272). Locating herself in a progressive, international, cosmopolitan context among other enlightened heterosexual couples she recognizes only the economic exploitation of women. The question of sexuality cuts no ice with Stead: she deplores the fact as well as the agenda of lesbians, along with 'so-called gay liberation', in a classic example of the operations of what Monique Wittig called the 'straight mind'.[6]

Though she claims to 'hate any sort of segregation', (273) Stead's passionate belief in the naturally given complementarity of men and women and the utopian possibilities of heterosexuality obliges her to allow differences between them. These seem to be in part culturally constructed (she writes, for instance, of women's 'cultivated timidity', 273), in part a function of biology: 'I do not know if there is a "feminine consciousness". Our perceptions and deductions spring from education, experience and function . . .' (273). Although Stead rejected the inevitability of maternity, she identified women's 'function' as loving men – at worst, the wrong men – adding that lesbians 'rob [women] of one of the best and most momentous things in life, love of a man' (273).[7]

*For Love Alone* (1944) is the novel which most directly addresses the question of expatriation, in a narrative very close to that of Stead's own life.[8] The adolescent Australian heroine, Teresa Hawkins, receives a mysterious injunction in a letter from a woman she has barely met, a Mrs Percy who had 'been something as a girl' (44): 'Look on [the world] as from Mars - or Heaven - whence you came and tell your own soul whether or not you like and admire the things you see and lend your hand to' (103). Stead links this recognition of a woman's inevitable internal exile to contrastive narratives of women and men as expatriates, strangers in a strange land at least partly by design. It is women's double difference which forms the matrix of Stead's work - figured not simply as an impediment, but as a potentially empowering source of revisionary insight, which carries with it a double imperative: to write and to love.[9]

Mrs Percy also tells Teresa, 'Don't leave home. I did. It is a great mistake' (59), and it is the flouting of this negative wisdom (symptomatic of women's 'cultivated timidity') which becomes the motive force of the novel. In various ways *For Love Alone* charts the process by which Teresa comes to accept the virtues of estrangement and restlessness, changing her country, her job and her virgin status, in order to fulfil a triple vow: 'Love, learning, bread - myself - all three, I will get' (87). Before she leaves Teresa tells Erskine, the office boy who is in love with her: 'I have to go, it isn't my fault. I am forced to. If I stay here, I will be nobody. I'd just be taking the line of least resistance' (285). Both in fantasy and reality, expatriation represents for Teresa a reciprocal process of radical defamiliarisation, rendering herself and her past and present environments visible in a way which facilitates personal agency, choice and further movement.

*For Love Alone* is a kind of fictional justification of the choices Stead made in her own life. Like Teresa, Stead worked as a secretary in London and played out that old script, marrying the boss, though neither of them were naturals for the part: she, an Australian would-be writer and daughter of a Fabian socialist naturalist; Blake, an already married European American in England, some years older than her, citizen of the world and linguist, man of commerce, letters and politics. Through Blake as lover and patron, Stead adopted a life not divorced from the economic realities and masculine secrets of the market-place, not anchored to a single country, and shaped by a heterosexual relationship which she always presented as living up to her ideal of communion and mutual support. In *For Love Alone* Teresa struggles to find a way out of both the patriarchal family home (in which she must also act as surrogate mother) and Sydney in the Depression, into the wide world of men: 'a country from which she, a born citizen, was exiled' (85). All Stead's writing begins from this recognition of disenfranchisement: an exile which inheres not only in her body, that of a born woman, but in her nationality, a born Australian.

The opening sentence of *For Love Alone* addresses a non-Australian audience, refusing to locate the narration fully inside 'the water hemisphere': 'In the part of the world Teresa came from, winter is in July, spring brides marry in September, and Christmas is consummated with roast beef, suckling pig, and brandy-laced plum pudding at 100 degrees in the shade . . .' (1). 'The other world – the old world, the land hemisphere – is far above her as it is shown on maps drawn upside-down by old-world cartographers' (1), but Stead's narrator offers the possibility of comparing maps and measuring the differences between them, plotting a voyage between part one, 'The Island Continent', figured as feminine and other, and part two, 'Port of Registry: London', which is narratively aligned with the world of men and commerce. The 'sea people' of Australia are identified as already transplanted and re-contextualised:

From that world [the old world] and particularly from a scarcely noticeable island up toward the North Pole the people came. . . . And there they live round the many

thousand miles of seaboard, hugging the water and the
coastal rim. . . . There is nothing in the interior; so people
look toward the water, and above to the fixed stars and
constellations which first guided men there.

(1)


They are marked as always already voyagers and
navigators; and it is women within this framework who
have farthest to go and most to gain. They must break
not only the tyranny of geographical distance, but also
cultural interdiction: the marks of gender as well as
place.

It is not only Teresa's voyage out with which *For Love
Alone* is concerned, but the genesis of her desire to leave
in the desire to desire. Though it is true that Teresa (like
Stead) consistently idealises heterosexual love as the
greatest good, she specifically resists the logic of patriarchal exchange and commodification:

> Woman had a power to achieve happiness as well – but in
> what way? Only by having the right to love. In the old days,
> the girls were married without love, for property, and
> nowadays they were forced to marry, of themselves, without
> knowing love, for wages. It was easy to see how upsetting it
> would be if women began to love freely where love came to
> them. An abyss would open in the principal shopping street
> of every town. . . . she wanted to try men.

(464)


Stead figures a woman's body as her moveable home, the
dynamic site of response and heterosexual dialogue,
which she must seek to 'possess' and control herself; and
*For Love Alone* includes a number of brave, often florid
attempts to represent the potency of female heterosexual
desire and fantasy:

> she felt her flesh running into his and clinging to him, as if
> they had never been sundered. . . . There was honey in his
> thighs and new-pressed unfermented wine in all of him;

and, mad with love, she sucked them both into her eyes,
only then understanding love of man.

(468)

The repressed physicality of women is stressed from
the novel's opening as central to Teresa's emerging
analysis of women's exile, and recognised as a source of
untapped knowledge:

> she saw insistently, with the countless flaming eyes of her
> flesh, the inner life of these unfortunate women and girls,
> her acquaintance, a miserable mass writhing with desire
> and shame, grovelling before men, silent about the stew in
> which they boiled and bubbled, discontented, browbeaten,
> flouted, ridiculous and getting uglier each year.

(18)

Emily in *I'm Dying Laughing* tells her cerebral
husband: 'I know where my feelings spring from, not
only the brain but from everywhere, I am myself everywhere'.[10] The body is also the origin of women's
language, sometimes displaced into hysterical
symptoms: Henny's muteness, headaches and fits in *The
Man Who Loved Children*; Emily's illnesses, un-
controllable laughter and compulsive talking ('You
don't even understand my misery, my agony, my
hysteria. I know it's hysteria, but it's me; it's the only
way I can live', 114). Just as she sought to represent
female sexuality, so Stead attempted to notate the erup-
tions of the female body in sounds which resist transcrip-
tion: Henny's sobs are registered, 'Ugh ugh', and *I'm
Dying Laughing*, as its title implies, abounds with more
extended examples:

> She began to giggle, 'W-w-would you b-believe th-that? A g-
> girl c-c-c-oh, he-he-he, c-ca-he-he-he, c-ca – ho-ho-ho. Ida I-
> oph-oh-oh, I ha-ca-caN.'
> 'You're just a schoolgirl,' said Stephen smiling.
> She said emphatically, 'Ida Nass and another girl called –

oh-he-he-he. C-c-Car-Carlotta Katz, o-ho-ho, he-he-he, Ida-na-na-nass and Car-l-l-lot – oh-ho-hohunh-hunh-it's funny. Ida Nass and Carlotta Katz. Ha-ha-ha!'

She threw herself on the sofa, and laughed helplessly.

'For God's sake, stop giggling,' shouted Stephen, laughing.

'There was one called Hed-oh-oh-oh, oh dear, oh, dear, I'm dying. Help me, Ste-ph-phen. I can't he-help it. Oh, dear, I'm dying. I'll die; oh-oh-oh! There was one called -ha-ha-ha-ha, Hedda, Hedda! There! Hedda-Hedda-Meyer! Oh-ho-ho!' She rolled on her belly. 'Oh-ho-ho, I'll die, I'll die.'

(305)

Like Stead's erotic writing this may look old-fashioned now, but both are characteristic of her innovative attempts to let in not only many different varieties of discourse, but what ruptures discourse.[11] Emily's laughter signifies the unstable meaning of women's liminality with respect to the linguistic system: its negative potential as the threat of anarchic disorder and unintelligibility; its positive force as bravura, free association, generous inclusiveness and ludic comic genius. Emily might be thought of as sliding from one to the other, while the eccentric raconteur, Aunt Bea, in *For Love Alone* embodies women's accommodation without capitulation to patriarchal social order (and feminised poverty), through the possibility of linguistic intervention and brilliant comic subversion:

'Nothing to wear but clothes, nothing to eat but food, nowhere to sleep but bed, nothing to marry but men, nowhere to go but home,' mused Aunt Bea. 'Nothing to do but live. My poor feet! Now I know where the shoe pinches.'

(54)

Stead revalues women's association with 'lying' as a gift for improvisation and story-telling, liberties taken where they can be, and as a rebellion against the decorums women are expected to observe when they speak at all. Emily, for instance, is subjected to a blisteringly chauvinist 'straightening out' by the male spokesman of the Hollywood branch of the Communist Party in chapter six of *I'm Dying Laughing.* She is 'indicted' for 'verbal incontinence, detailed recitals of insignificant events, a general excitement, incoherencies of speech, unsuitable confidences in public' (101); a combination of 'false and ridiculous ideas' (101) and 'almost delirious monologues as if the words came out without any censorship' (103). In short, Emily suffers from 'a monstrous growth of inborn characteristics' (101) (despite 'the joy of motherhood . . . [which] has cured many a woman', 102), 'bear[ing] her off in all directions without compass and without destination' (106).

Conversely, through Sam Pollit in *The Man Who Loved Children* and Jonathan Crow in *For Love Alone,* Stead offers a critique of singular, goal-directed masculine 'truth' as monological and monomaniacal, partly through female analyses internal to the narration which show them as ideologues, incapable of genuine dialogue. In *For Love Alone,* Teresa submits her own and Crow's letters to a constant scrutiny, while Crow has no idea of a correspondence; he either does not open the letters sent to him or indiscriminately violates the intimate contract between sender and receiver by showing them to other people. Though the real dissection of Crow's evil is saved for later in the novel (where it is undertaken by the true law-giver, the just man, James Quirk) Stead gives us a premonition of feminine retaliation against the vain Crow when some of the women to whom he has written return *his* letters unopened.

Aunt Bea has only the margin of comedy to keep herself afloat, but *For Love Alone* also, and more centrally, offers a model of the multiply disenfranchised woman of a younger generation who slowly but surely undoes the chain of the father's domestic tyranny and of sexual commodification. Teresa passes through masochism and abjection to reach uncertain sexual and economic autonomy: 'Here where she stood no old wives' tale and no mother's sad sneer, no father's admonition, reached' (495). The last chapter ('I Am Thinking I Am Free') leaves Teresa living with a married man, contemplating her recent and future sexual adventures, the light falling on her ringless hand: 'I will know how to make myself a life apart' (496).

Stead's self-imposed exile, her expatriate life, by contrast with those exclusions which gender, class and nationality made her heir to, becomes in *For Love Alone* a recuperative figure for a woman's self-made freedom, releasing Teresa from the constraints of home and inside, the seductions of the familiar and the line of least resistance. The narrative of leaving becomes a productive strategy for making visible the transparent structures of oppression, opening up the possibility of resistance, critique and exploration, particularly of the interdicted territory of female desire and sexual experience. Characteristically, this critique is effected partly through third person narration, partly through conversation, but chiefly through the reflexive meditations of Teresa herself, figured as at once physical and mental, sexual and intellectual.

Stead has recourse in such instances to a filmic repertoire of erotic symbolisation and externalisation, as in this scene of wild night-thoughts:

> She abandoned herself and began to think, leaning on the window-sill. In a fissure in a cliff left by a crumbled dike, a spout of air blew up in new foam and spray, blue and white diamonds in the moon, and in between the surges the ashy sky filled the crack with invisible little stars. Hundreds of feet beneath, the sea bursting its skin began to gush up against the receding tide; with trumpet sounds, wild elephants rose in a herd from the surf and charged the cliffs; the ground trembled, water hissed in the cracks.
>
> (74)

Out of this auto-erotic fantasising, represented as a kind of intercourse between mind and body (nature as a dramatic exchange between masculine and feminine principles) a clear-sighted critique emerges in the displaced form of an allegory of the regulation of female sexuality:

> A woman is a hunter without a forest. There is a short open season and a long closed season, then she must have a gun-licence, signed and sealed by the state. There are game laws, she is a poacher, and in the closed season she must poach to live. A poor man, a serf say, clears himself a bit of land, but it's the lord's land. As soon as it's cleared, he grows a crop on it, but it isn't his crop, only partly, or perhaps not at all, it isn't in his name; and then there must be documents, legalities, he must swear eternal fealty to someone. A woman is obliged to produce her full quota on a little frontage of time; a man goes at it leisurely and he has allotments in other counties too. . . . But one thing is sure, I won't do it, they won't get me. . .
>
> In her bare room, ravished, trembling with ecstasy, blooming with a profound joy in this true, this hidden life, night after night, year after year, she reasoned with herself about the sensual life for which she was fitted.
>
> (75–6)[12]

Towards the end of the novel there is a complementary morning-after scene, again at a window, but this time in the broad daylight of sexual knowledge:

> She was in a strange state of ecstasy, she seemed to float upright, like a pillar of smoke, or flesh perhaps, some little way above the pavement. Down below flowed a great slaty river, smooth but covered with twisted threads of water, swollen with its great flow, and directly under the window was an immense dusk-white flower with drooping petals, surrounded by green and living leaves. This extraordinary flower, alive though shadowy, and living not as material things are, but with the genius of life, the interior breath of

living things, after moving uncertainly like a raft began to
float downstream to the left. . . .
    '*Today put on perfection and a woman's name,*' she
repeated several times, and still as if dreaming moved away
from the window and put her things together. She was
withdrawn into an inner room of herself and here she found
the oracle of her life, this secret deity which is usually sealed
from us.

(489–90)

Here, in a double allegory of the female body as both
strongly flowing river, with a single but multiple-lipped
centripetal flower (the raft by which Teresa is carried
away) and as a house with secret inner rooms, our
heroine comes into her inheritance, 'a woman's name'.
Through her one-night stand with Harry Girton (they
are 'like a bridal pair', 490) Teresa effectively marries
herself, mind to body, desire to practice, and becomes
whole through her knowledge of sexual difference.[13]
    Leaving as a rite of passage coincides with entry into
another arena of work and especially sex which is
potentially freer, or at least more negotiable, promising
not only escape but its own rewards. Teresa finds herself
'an unexpected heir of estates in distant lands' (460)
through the acquisition of mobility itself. To leave once
inaugurates the possibility of other departures, a pattern
of exploration: 'She thirsted after this track-making and
wandering of the man in the world, not after the man'
(492), 'she knew why she continued restless and why the
men, having so much in the hollow of their hands, kept
on striving' (494).
    In *I'm Dying Laughing*, Stead deals more disturbingly
with issues of displacement, identity and category as they
are inflected by politics, nationality, class, gender and
writing. The tragi-comic heroine, Emily Wilkes – a
commercially successful writer of journalism, comic
sketches and Hollywood screenplays – declares, 'I want
to live in the whole world' (234). Her husband, Stephen
Howard, a left-wing intellectual from an extremely

wealthy family, counters: 'I'm used to my country. It's perfect. I don't see what's wrong. I live there in a blue daze' (209). The double privilege of gender and class means not only that he cannot 'see what's wrong', but that he cannot relocate. He is lost in another country, relatively impoverished and unemployable, reduced to the outlawry of the black market: 'That's what Europe has brought me to, me the proud heir of the Howards!' (349). Emily, on the other hand, is already a veteran of displacement and relocation, as a professional writer in a man's world and again in her upwardly mobile marriage.

From the beginning of *I'm Dying Laughing* the debonair Stephen is haunted by a story he read as a child, *The Man Without A Country* (71), of which we are given only the title. After they move to Paris from Hollywood to escape the recriminations (from the left and the right) of the McCarthy era, he is always a displaced person. Emily, meanwhile, is trying to educate herself and the children in the French manner, and writing a Hollywood feature about Marie Antoinette and the French Revolution. Though the narration frames this project as ill-fated, it remains consistent with the calling of the woman writer as expatriate: to write herself in to places and histories which will never, by virtue of this labour, simply become hers. Again, it is a model of communion rather than ownership. The valorised position for the woman, especially the woman writer, is one of openness, responsiveness, sympathy, dialogue.

Women are persistently figured as malleable, more responsive to context: never lost (Stead's 'I never lost Australia') because never fully assimilated. Emily's comic sketches of 'ordinary life' for large-circulation American magazines sell because she reads the market right and because of her gift for sympathetic identification: the cult of female intuition is revealed as founded on the conceptual mobility required of women in a man's world. When Emily's work stops selling it is not

because she has lost her touch but because of external
political developments – the Howards become an Un-
American couple. In Stead's terms, only if women lose
their citizenship of the country of love, their relationship
to men, do they risk falling outside meaning and
identity. Of her own marriage Stead said, 'it wasn't
place, it was him, it was he . . . he was my home'
(Giuffré interview, 26). It is not political exile or even its
corollary, professional failure, which ruins Emily – these
things are regarded as temporary set-backs – but the
irreversible decline and eventual suicide of her displaced
husband. Women are saved by men or destroyed by them
– either way, their narrative destiny (or 'luck') is bound
up in heterosexual relations, as they are mediated
through the affiliations of politics and nationality.

In the end of *For Love Alone* the world is envisioned
as a kind of space without closure, filled with colour, i.e.
difference: 'beyond was the real world, red, gold, green,
white' (494). Here Stead repeats the final textual movement of *The Man Who Loved Children*: 'Everyone
looked strange. Everyone had an outline, and brilliant,
solid colours. Louie was surprised and realized that
when you run away, everything is at once very different.'[14] In both *The Man Who Loved Children* and *For
Love Alone* the narrative destination involves reaching
one of the thresholds of becoming-woman (blossoming)
and entering into the potentially liberatory sphere of the
heterosocial. Each offers a utopian figure of the female
citizen of the world as the antidote to the threat of male
narcissism and closure.[15] This threat is represented by
the father in both novels (Sam Pollit in *The Man Who
Loved Children* cannot hear anything but the sound of
his own voice, mapping out an imperialist and fascist
project for self-replication and purification of the line;
Teresa's father is 'the handsome man, the family god,
sitting at the head of the table', 13), and by the colour-
blind, loveless Crow in *For Love Alone*, 'a glittering,
humming, self-devoted wheel' (425), encountered finally

in a brief and speechless recognition scene on a crowded Charing Cross Road. Before she realises who he is, Teresa describes him as 'the bachelor sucked into himself like a sea anemone which suddenly sees something wrong and falls into itself' (500), while the narration tells us that she is 'bolder and warmer than he had ever seen her' (500) since her rescue by James Quirk, the worthy father-figure.

The discrediting of a masculine authority figure can only be survived if another steps in to fill that gap. Neither husband nor lover can provide a positive model for Henny in *The Man Who Loved Children*, which leads to her suicide; but Teresa is saved from suicide over the vampiric, scavenging Crow by the healing agency of the stranger/father, James Quick, benevolent teacher, employer, free-thinker, tutor in love, true reader and principle of fecundity: 'She was like a cornered animal before which, miraculously, an escape through rich flowering country is opened; she fled away down the flowering lanes of Quick's life. . .' (460). And the process is mutual: she releases in him 'a well of strength closed over', thought 'sealed forever' (366). The two fairy stories of the Sleeping Beauty and Beauty and the Beast are merged together in the unfolding of the romance ending in *For Love Alone*, governed by reciprocal passion and complementary knowledges in the meeting of strangers and exiles as lovers.

In the two earlier novels, *For Love Alone* and *The Man Who Loved Children*, we are led to the brink of a utopian possibility – the self-determining woman – but always with the caveat that this quest can only be undertaken in dialogue with, and in love with, masculine power and difference at its most benevolent. In the later and more ill-fated *I'm Dying Laughing*, it is as though the foregrounding of political problems, defeats and compromises in the face of schisms on the left, McCarthyism and the Cold War also sharpens the gender politics. The woman writer is left with her writing in shreds, without audience, husband, family, job, country, home or bed. Perched on the steps of the Forum Romanum, she waits on the margins of a ruined civilisation, acting out an ironic masque where the no-place of women's exclusion may be the safest place left: ' "I get my mail here. I send letters. This is the only good place" ' (447).

In *I'm Dying Laughing*, Stead abandoned her faith in Aunt Bea's constant, genial refrain in *For Love Alone* – 'All is for the best in this best of possible worlds' (26) – to engage Emily's darker vision of the 'cruel book' she would like to write:

> [']I ought to say how everything becomes its opposite not only outside the besieged fortress but in: how we mis-interpret the mission of America, the position in the unions, ourselves; and what our lives are, that are going so far astray. We sneer at Utopian communities; but we are trying to live in Utopia.'
>
> 'It might be an epitaph of American socialism: I'd like to see it,' sang out Stephen.
>
> (72)

Emily never writes the book; but Stead makes her the indomitable centre of just such a book – and its fate recalls Emily's question, 'But who would print it?' (72). *I'm Dying Laughing*, has a fully apocalyptic ending: Stephen sets fire to himself and goes up in flames; Emily will 'die laughing', as we know she must, in a kind of spontaneous combustion. The joke alternative title mooted by Emily within the book – 'Emily Wilkes, in *Double or Nothing*; by Emily Wilkes' (191) – like everything else turns out to be prophetic: if you want a perfect doubling, if you want at all, then what you may end up with is nothing at all. (Equally, the novel could have been called by that other floating title without a text to attach itself to, *The Man Without A Country*.) Again and again, Emily's earlier words come back to haunt us and her: ' "Oh, oh, I need everything so badly so much, Stephen. I can't do without anything" ' (112). When the promise of politics is too severely threatened, then the project of gender equality and its corollary, the good marriage, also fails.

Throughout Stead's work the negativity of the feminine has a radical creative potential and energy but its anarchic excess must be contained and matched by the masculine if it is to be recuperated as other than destructive and masochistic, or merely wild and comic: the feminine requires masculine ratification and endorsement. In *I'm Dying Laughing*, Emily writes and Stephen corrects what she writes over breakfast; he constantly supervises her otherwise indiscriminate production of half-finished or inappropriate texts. When Stephen becomes ill and abdicates from his throne as king of the castle, Emily mourns like a deposed queen. She moves into the dim basement – a servant's room – to write a prose epic on 'the last days of Marie Antoinette' (408), saying, ' "I need Stephen. I need a man. I need men. I cannot live this way. What shall I do?" ' (407). There at the bottom of the house Emily begins her movement towards the fully asocial realm of homelessness, paranoia and discursive chaos (beneath/outside), to the accompaniment of her own lucid commentary: 'I have passed the signpost. I cannot go back. . . . I am going downwards now' (417).

Stephen returns from hospital and has Emily carried back upstairs for a time but the apocalyptic, prophetic machinery is gathering momentum. All that is needed to satisfy the logic of the novel is a political corollary of the Howards' disintegrating marriage. Quite early in the novel Emily dreams of passing the point of no return:

'I know we're going to be blackballed. I know we've got our feet on a road from which there is no turning back. I don't know where this road is going,' she said sadly, 'but I know in the night, one night, we passed a signpost, I dreamed

about it and when I woke up I shuddered. I shivered all day
long, for we had passed the sign in the night, in our sleep
and there was no going back.'

(164)

Now, in a doomed attempt to be reintegrated, first Emily
and then Stephen capitulates, turning informant. Stephen says, 'I am not a man without a country. They have
written into my record: good citizen. . . . The renegade
husband and wife: the perfect American couple, loyal to
each other and to the country' (436-7). This attempt to
turn back like sleep-walkers is the act of bad faith or
'contempt' (447) from which neither they, as political
subjects, nor their marriage can recover.

Stephen's double bind – that he cannot be a man
without a country; yet, in order to be a 'good citizen', he
must choose to morally discredit himself – leaves him no
alternative according to the masculine, aristocratic code
of duty and honour but suicide: 'I decided to make a
clean break. . . . So I am taking a run-out powder. I am
not proud of myself: it is not brave. But then my whole
history shows that I am not brave' (441). After his death
Emily disappears and is last seen with the 'loose papers'
(446) of her final project (metamorphosed into 'The
Monster') 'strew[n] about the steps' (447) of the Forum.
She is waiting in vain for a man to save her; but this is a
different kind of book and there will be no romance
ending, only the echoing of 'endless laughter' (447).

In *For Love Alone* Teresa dissociates herself from any
identification with feminine writing, negatively figured
as inchoate and unintelligible:

her world existed and was recognized by men. But why not
by women? She found nothing in the few works of women
she could find that was what they must have felt . . . it was
either rigmarole or raving, whereas the poets and playwrights spoke the language she knew, and the satirists and
moralists wrote down with stern and marvellous precision

all that she knew in herself but kept hidden from family and friends.

(76)

Reading is a kind of secret communion, but only possible with respect to the 'marvellous precision' of the literature of men, graced with a benign gender-neutral availability – 'the poets and playwrights . . . the satirists and moralists' – while women bear the negative mark of gender. 'Rigmarole or raving' might be Teresa's patriarchalised description of Emily's seamless talk/writing which eventually observes no decorums or boundaries and cannot be recuperated; her descent into placelessness enacts a Kristevan model of the pure negativity of the feminine in isolation. Feminist readings have in general tried to stress the liberatory, utopian potential of Stead's work, concentrating on those novels which best suit such a practice: *The Man Who Loved Children* and *For Love Alone*. It may be that equally rich, if more disturbing, material for an analysis of politics, gender and figuration in Stead's writing is to be found in those novels, as in *I'm Dying Laughing*, and *Miss Herbert: The Suburban Wife*, which refuse to posit any triumphant way of exiting from the problematic of female exile in patriarchal culture or of overriding the negativity which attaches to the position of the 'woman writer'.

Rebecca West describes 'a curious *trompe l'oeil* effect' in Stead's writing, commenting of *The Beauties and Furies* (1936): 'these were the days of the invasion of Paris by American expatriates, seen here by a woman writing in English but who was Australian. It is a fantasy based on fragmentary impressions of a real country and fragmentary dreams of an imaginary country.'[16] Arac makes the political implications of this analysis explicit when he writes that Stead 'came from an imperial margin that knew the heart of western culture only at a painfully felt distance of symbolic mediation' (123). I would argue that Stead's career was governed by the attempt to heal or combat the literal and symbolic distances she inherited as an Australian woman writer, through her 'wandering life', her marriage to another alien, her left politics and the international scope of her writing (which is often geographically divided by critics into Australian, American, English and European pieces).

In her incorporation of, and attention to, diverse idioms and registers, Stead declared her commitment to specificities of time, place, social status and gender – scrupulous in a way which indicated her desire for multiple citizenship rather than an imperialist levelling of cultures. She was also profoundly committed to the textual exploration – at the level of genre, mode, narrative, representation of figuration – of women's engagement, as writers, readers and desiring subjects, with the male canon, the masculine world of commerce and the male body. Stead's writing eloquently testifies to her experience as an expatriate Australian woman writer – shaped by the double exile of gender and nationality and the twin imperatives of mobility and desire – in ways, direct and indirect, which make more complex sense of her remark: 'A number of people, publishers and so forth, have written to me to say would I write my autobiography, and I always write back and say I have written it' (Giuffré interview, 23).

Stead apparently refused to appear in expatriate anthologies.[17] She rejected the notion of a communal identity formed by the given of nationality, particularly one of negation (Australians abroad), in favour of a more fluid project of multiple citizenship, non-exploitative gender relations and socialist internationalism, emblematised in her long, peripatetic marriage. They were based in London and Paris for about ten years; her most productive writing period was spent in the United States (1937–46); from 1946–53 they lived in a number of different European cities – finally returning to Surbiton, outside London, from 1953 until Blake's death in 1973.

This move to Surbiton was made at Stead's request – afraid that the penalty of being such an internationalist would be the deterioration of her English (Brydon, 12).[18] After Blake's death Stead completed the cycle of return by moving back to Australia, initially to the suburban house of her brother in Sydney, for the last decade of her life. There is a novelistic symmetry and circularity in this story of the young girl's original home, scene of family and nation, which must be left in order to enter the world at large and the field of sexual relations with men (thereby enabling writing) and re-entered as an old woman and a widow, veteran of many campaigns and author of more than a dozen books. Writing and hetero-sexual knowledge were powerfully intertwined for Stead (and equally powerfully thematised in her writing) and the death of her husband was also more or less the death of her writing. When she lost the country of her marriage, she returned to her first, childish hemisphere to complete her 'walk round the world' (*The Man Who Loved Children*, 522) and to set the story straight – displaying a gift for narrative closure which, in her novels, she always resisted.[19]

# Notes

1. Drusilla Modjeska, *Exiles at Home: Australian Women Writers 1925–1945* (Sydney, Sirius-Angus and Robertson, 1981), 30.
2. Interview (30 April 1982) by Giulia Giuffré, *Stand*, **23** (4) (1982), 26.
3. 'The Writer Takes Sides', *Left Review*, 1 (11) (1935), 463. For an account of relations between Stead and Nettie Palmer at the Congress, and a comparison of their reports on it, see Modjeska, 63–4.
4. Jonathan Arac notes the 'routinely sexist' language of Stead's report and its 'normative, positivist biologism', arguing that it was not until the late 1930s, in *The Man*

*Who Loved Children*, that Stead undertook 'a serious feminist critique of domestic patriarchy and its larger ramifications'. 'The Struggle for the Cultural Heritage: Christina Stead Refunctions Charles Dickens and Mark Twain', *The New Historicism*, ed. H. Aram Veeser (New York, Routledge, 1989), 124–5. It seems to me that the sexual politics of Stead's fiction were always far more radical than her stated views, perhaps because of the distance permitted by the mediations of writing, character and narrative. For a sharp, socialist–feminist analysis of the position of women of her own (and Stead's) age on the left see Naomi Mitchison, 'The Reluctant Feminists', rev. of *Women*, by Winifred Holtby, *Left Review*, December (1934), 93–4.

5. 'On the Women's Movement', *Partisan Review*, **46** (2) (1979), 272.

6. As Susan Sheridan argues, Stead hygienically separates 'lesbians' from 'women'. *Christina Stead*, Harvester Key Women Writers Series (Hemel Hempstead: Harvester Wheatsheaf, 1988), 8. See Monique Wittig, 'The Straight Mind', *Feminist Issues*, 1 (1) (1980), 103–11.

7. In the Giuffré interview Stead said, 'My ambition was to love', 22. For the way in which daughter–father/lover relations dominate much of Stead's writing see Sheridan, Chapter 2, and Judith Kegan Gardiner, 'Male Narcissism, Capitalism, and the Daughter of *The Man Who Loved Children*', *Daughters and Fathers*, eds. Lynda E. Boose and Betty S. Flowers (Baltimore, Johns Hopkins University Press, 1989), 384–99.

8. *For Love Alone* (1944) (Sydney, Sirius-Angus and Robertson, 1987). For an interesting discussion of the temporal dislocation between the stories of Stead and Teresa see Sheridan, 61.

9. 'Writing is creative, loving is creative. It's exactly the same', Guiffré interview, 22.

10. *I'm Dying Laughing: The Humourist*, ed. with a preface by R. G. Geering (London, Virago, 1986), 187. Stead tried to publish this novel in the 1960s without success.

11. Sheridan invokes Bakhtin's work on dialogism and the carnivalesque briefly in her discussion of *I'm Dying*

*Laughing*, while stressing the importance of a gender analysis of Stead's 'disorderly women', 133.

12. cf. *I'm Dying Laughing*, 154, 'We grow up longing for men, we slowly and with what miseries get to know them; and then just when we know them, we must never know them again. . . . But how can [men and women] know each other except by sex or divination, and I'm no mindreader. Sex is easier and surer.'

13. In an interview Stead said: 'the man's power is evident; the woman's is stranger. Behind the concept of woman's strangeness is the idea that a woman may do anything – she is below society, not bound by its law, unpredictable – an attribute given to every member of the league of the unfortunate. To make a small payment for their disability, we endow the slave, the woman, with unusual interior vision.' 'Christina Stead: An Interview,' by Joan Lidoff, in Joan Lidoff, *Christina Stead* (New York, Ungar, 1982), 226. The concealed power of women, for Stead, does not I think depend only on this compensatory explanation; it inheres in a woman's absorption with and dependence on the life of her body.

14. *The Man Who Loved Children*, Penguin Modern Classics, 1940 (Harmondsworth, Penguin, 1970), 523.

15. Sheridan argues that Louie's fantasy of a walk round the world is 'lyrically utopian', 'a closing figure which seems, paradoxically, to open out onto a whole new world' (54).

16. Rebecca West, 'Christina Stead – A Tribute', *Stand*, 23 (4) (1982), 33. In the same special issue of *Stand*, Lorna Sage writes, 'Her idiom seems often as alien as it is impressive' ('Inheriting the Future: *For Love Alone*', 35). Sage also writes tellingly of women's 'love as migration' in *For Love Alone*. Jonathan Arac argues that Samuel Clemens Pollit in *The Man Who Loved Children* represents Stead's critical 'refunctioning' of 'the masculine comic philistine humanist genius' of Charles Dickens and Mark Twain (Samuel Clemens) for America in the late 1930s (128). He adds, 'Perhaps only an Australian, and a woman at that, could have sufficient distance to allow the images of Dickens and Twain thus to superimpose . . .' (118).

17. Diana Brydon, *Christina Stead* (London, Macmillan, 1987), 172. I rely on Brydon for biographical details.

18. In *For Love Alone* 'a ticket to Surbiton' conjures up 'a semi-detached villa with a black rusty-browed wife and two dirty-skinned children', 500-1.
19. For a perceptive discussion of the way in which Stead sought to foreclose certain kinds of analysis, particularly feminist, by providing authorized readings of her life and writing through interviews, see Sheridan, 14-20.

# Chronological Table of Works
# Eudora Welty

*Born Mississippi, USA, 1909*

*Short Stories*
1941 *A Curtain of Green*
1943 *The Wide Net and Other Stories*
1946 *The Golden Apples*
1955 *The Bride of the Inisfallen and Other Stories*
1980 *The Collected Stories of Eudora Welty*

*Novels*
1942 *The Robber Bridegroom*
1946 *Delta Wedding*
1954 *The Ponder Heart*
1970 *Losing Battles*
1972 *The Optimist's Daughter*

*Non-fiction*
1978 *The Eye of the Story: Selected Essays and Reviews*
1984 *One Writer's Beginnings*

*Photography*
1971 *One Time, One Place: Mississippi in the Depression*

# 7

# The Rapist Bridegroom
## Sexual Violence in
## the Fiction of Eudora Welty

### Diane Roberts

Rape is an assertion of power, male over female. If, as
Lacan says, the phallus is the signifier of male power in
culture, then the use of the phallus as a weapon, forcibly
penetrating the body of a woman, is the most basic
manifestation of that power, upholding the symbolic
order. Violation of women's bodies in fiction has served
many thematic purposes. Hardy's Tess is a force of
nature victimised by exploitative man. She is deflowered
but organically intact, a 'pure woman' despite the
appropriation of her body. Faulkner's Temple Drake is a
*demivièrge* whose innate corruption transforms her
'desecration' into a radical rebellion against the Southern upper classes.

   In Eudora Welty's fiction rape takes on multiple
meanings. It can be an attack of male/culture on female/
nature; it can be an act of class defiance; it is often a *rite
de passage* which 'awakens' women simultaneously to
their sexuality and to their submissive role in the
symbolic order. As many readers have noted, Welty's
stories follow a fairy tale structure and use fairy tale or
mythic elements; her first novel, *The Robber Bridegroom*,[1] *is* a fairy tale. And in fairy tales the goal is often

the reanimation of the heroine, the awakening of the Sleeping Beauty, a story which Hélène Cixous finds illustrative of rape-initiation:[2]

> Sleeping Beauty is lifted from her bed by a man, because as we all know, women don't wake up by themselves: a man has to intervene, you understand. She is lifted up by the man who will lay her in her next bed so that she may be confined to bed ever after, just as the fairy tales say.
>
> And so, her trajectory is from bed to bed . . .

Or, we might say, from rape to rape. The impressive number of rapes in Welty's work is surprising, given Welty's public insistence that she is not concerned with gender, that writing is an activity 'outside sex', and that she is not interested in any kind of feminist discourse – what she calls 'feminine repartee'.[3,4]

Yet Welty's fiction is concentrated on the problems of gender as the focus on rape, particularly in the early part of her career, shows. Welty's female characters must negotiate in an atmosphere of sexual violence: rape is a threat that her women must be aware of every time they step outside the bounds of the home or community. To readers seeking to recover Welty for feminism, however, her attitude to rape is troubling; some prefer not to examine it too closely or even to find it somehow positive. Louise Westling, one of Welty's most astute readers, says that rape in Welty is linked to 'women's essential sexual wholeness': it

> appears to be a natural, if sometimes inconvenient, sexual encounter from which women, like slightly annoyed hens, pick themselves up, shake their feathers and go on about their business. The roosters strut away to further conquests.
> (99–100)

Westling correctly points to Welty's celebration of female sexuality, the location of a good deal of female strength. It is true that violated women in Welty usually seem to go on with their lives without histrionics or romantic tragedy, perhaps because Welty rejects the (white, male) Southern code of 'ladyhood' and its privileging of virginity and chastity. Yet Westling's barnyard analogy obscures the more serious results of rape in Welty. Violence against the female body leads to a loss of autonomy, as we see with Jenny in 'At the Landing',[5] and Easter in 'Moon Lake';[5] it leads to temporary or permanent madness, as we see with Rosamond in *The Robber Bridegroom* and Miss Eckhart in 'June Recital';[5] and it leads to death, as we see with the Indian Girl in *The Robber Bridegroom* and Maideen in 'The Whole World Knows'.[5] Though the *incident* of rape in Welty is often disposed of in a sentence, even a phrase, reminiscent of Tess Durbeyfield's offstage deflowering, the *effect* is always a loss of female independence to male dominance which women's wholeness and strength cannot always mitigate. In this essay I should like to consider how rape inscribes on women's bodies their subordination. Women in Welty's fiction protest this subordination in a number of ways, perhaps by becoming the heroines of their own stories, like Rosamond Musgrove, or by rejecting the community, like Virgie Rainey. But they are nonetheless subject to male power. Welty's women do find strength and solace in the feminised nature as well as their own sexuality, but such comfort is fragile and often short-lived.

Eudora Welty depicted rape as a defining female experience early in her career. Her first novel, *The Robber Bridegroom* (1942), is a gently satirical fairy story about the connection between capitalism, marriage and sexual violence set in the late eighteenth-century Mississippi frontier. The novel's relationship with the Grimm tale of the same name is simultaneously faithful and subversive: Welty is more explicit in her robberies, rapes and murders, emphasising the historical dangers of pioneering.[6] Yet where the Grimm heroine escapes

rape and defeats the wicked robber bridegroom who
wants to murder her, Welty's Rosamond is an increasingly willing victim of Jamie Lockhart, the smooth-
talking bandit.

One reading of this could be that the Grimm heroine
flees her own sexuality while Rosamond embraces physical love and its accompanying ambiguities. Some critics
see Rosamond's defloration under the plum trees as a
'consummation' of her and Jamie's 'love', a 'natural
fulfillment' of their desire in the Edenic New World
woods, asserting that the 'freedom of the Mississippi
forest parallels the freedom of the young man and
woman to enjoy each other'.[7,8] This is a curious way to
talk of a robbery and subsequent rape resulting in a
common-law marriage where the rape is re-enacted
nightly. Perhaps the process which turns Rosamond
from comparatively free virgin roaming the forest into
confined, sexually submissive *hausfrau*, cooking, clean-
ing and sewing for her husband's band of robbers like
Snow White with her dwarfs, appears to male readers to
be the 'natural' initiation of a woman into her traditional role. Perhaps the setting of the novel in the myth-
ologised American past reinforces this. Welty is aware of
the ironies attendant on Jamie's change from robber
bridegroom to robber baron – 'for him, the outward
transfer from bandit to merchant had been almost too
easy to count it a change at all' – commenting sardoni-
cally on the gentrification of the American frontier; she
is also critical of the process by which a girl becomes a
wife and mother in a world where physical strength is
the badge of power and gender roles are rigidly enforced.
As in Angela Carter's tales of young women's sexual
awakening, violence is part of the process.[9]

Welty employs conventional language in her description of Rosamond, a Mississippi Cinderella 'as beautiful
as the day', while her stepmother Salome is 'as ugly as
the night'. Salome is Rosamond's opposite, dark where
she is fair, cruel where she is kind, greedy where she is

generous, assertive where she is passive. As in a fairy tale, the wicked queen is destroyed and the princess marries: both movements exhibit the disabling of both women.

Sent away from the plantation house each day by her jealous stepmother, Rosamond meets the bandit Jamie Lockhart, the proverbial wolf in sheep's clothing, while looking for herbs in the forest. At their initial encounter, he strips her of her fine green silk dress, a first defloration (or defoliation), a symbolic rape. He offers her the choice of walking home naked or dying by his dagger: death through a penetration preferable to the kind of penetration deemed a fate *worse* than death. But, like Welty heroines after her, Rosamond is not concerned with the pieties of ladyhood which place death before 'dishonour'. The next day when they meet, however, she is raped in earnest: Jamie 'robs her of that which he had left her before'(65).

This is the first of the two rapes which galvanise the novel: the second is the attack on the nameless Indian girl by Little Harp the outlaw. While the Indian girl is raped, mutilated and killed, Rosamond recovers from her rape to marry a kind of successful businessman.

Rosamond's rape is presented lyrically, with none of the overt brutality of the assault on the Indian girl. Jamie carries her through a bower of trees dropping ripe plums to the riverside. The Edenic imagery, as well as a tradition in literature of romanticised (therefore disguised) violence against women, doubtless contributes to the reluctance of readers to see the rape for what it is. But Welty makes it quite clear: Jamie, his face disguised with berry juice, 'robs' Rosamond: 'His motto was "Take first and ask afterward" '. After he finishes with her, Rosamond wanders home in a confused state. She will not wash herself or comb her hair (a reaction common among rape victims in real life), she submits to beatings from her stepmother (who realises she has been raped) and does not recognise her 'dark lover' in the polished Jamie Lockhart who comes to dinner as her unwitting father's guest. He, in turn, does not recognise the 'little piece of sugar cane' he, like the Big Bad Wolf, had just eaten up in the woods (73).

Rosamond's addled wits are partly a result of the gap between her romantic fantasies and the brutal truth about gender relations. Her magic locket, emblem of maternal love, preserves her from certain harms – panthers and bears perhaps – yet has no talismanic power over rapacious men. Rosamond sings a ballad of chaste love well-met by moonlight which hardly prepares her for her actual meeting with a man who wants to rape her, not sing to her.

Yet Rosamond loses little time in trying to mould her relations with Jamie into a middle-class vision of love: 'as soon as Jamie had truly dishonored her, Rosamond began to feel a growing pity for him' (76). She seeks out his bachelor robber's hut in the woods, comically 'masculine' in its dirt and disorder, and tidies it. Rosamond becomes a parody-mother to the robbers, packing lunches for them to take on their daily raids, as well as a wife to Jamie. He still appears before her only at night and only in his berry juice disguise. Moreover, he nightly repeats the original rape, for while he 'spoke as kind and sweet words as anyone ever could between the hours of sunset and sunrise' his sexuality is rooted in violence:

> But when she tried to lead him to his bed with a candle, he would knock her down and out of her senses and drag her there. However, if Jamie was a thief after Rosamond's love, she was his first assistant in the deed and rejoiced equally in his good success.
>
> (84)

Abused by Salome in her father's house, Rosamond prefers abuse in her lover's hut. A woman's choice is between violence and violence, between paternal and sexual bondage.

A telling contrast is set up between Salome, the energetic Wicked Queen, and Rosamond, the willing captive princess. Where Rosamond is passive, submitting to her stepmother's domestic tyranny as readily as she submits to rape, Salome is a driven, ambitious woman. Her qualities are 'masculine'; it is she, not her husband, who is the American empire builder, the true capitalist. He wants simply to live off the land; she wants to exploit it, getting ' "twice as much of everything" ' (99). Even the Indians fear her. Salome defies her gender role even in the face of death, declaring her power to the Indians who have captured her, demanding in her sexual vanity that she, not Rosamond, be declared the fairest of them all: ' "No one is to have power over me!" ' she cries, ' "I am by myself in the world" ' (160-1). She boldly asserts her selfhood, dancing, like the original Salome, to usurp male power. Unlike the original Salome, however, she fails; her frenzied version of the Dance of the Seven Veils leaves her naked and dead: impotent. The true gender order reveals itself when the Indian Chief asks what man 'owns' her body; Clement steps forward to say ' "I own her body" ' (164). Dead, Salome is merely another of her husband's possessions. As there are two rapes in the novel, there are also two naked women, made vulnerable to the truth of masculine power. Where Rosamond's acquiesence saves her life if not her maidenhead, Salome's aggression kills her.

Can Welty's vision of woman's lot truly be as bleak as *The Robber Bridegroom* indicates? Affirmative possibilities for women seem few and far between. Yet Welty does not leave even her accommodating Snow White in a state of total bondage. Rosamond insists on telling her own story her own way: she is a noted liar. Even though her rape shocks her into telling the truth, she has control over how she presents events to others. More importantly, she insists on her moral authority. Goaded as much by her own curiosity as by Salome, one night she washes the berry juice off the sleeping Jamie's face, committing the sin of Psyche. She recognises her demon lover as a robber king, but he upbraids her for her 'faithlessness' and runs off: in this Eden, too, knowledge is a woman's downfall. Rosamond in turn chastises him for his violence:

> My husband was a robber and not a bridegroom . . . kept all the truth hidden from me, and never called anything by its true name, even his name or mine, and what I would have given him he liked better to steal. And if I had no faith, he little honor to deprive a woman of giving her love freely.
>
> (146)

Despite her indignation at being treated as stealable goods by Jamie, Rosamond has nonetheless hit on the truth about gender and property: her body, like Salome's, is 'owned' by a man. Women are identified not only with moveable property but with the land itself. Welty underlines the relationship between genders as between property and owners. The rape of the Indian girl by a white man is an extension of the conquest of the wilderness by colonial exploitation. The rape of Rosamond is an assault against her father's territory as well as her body.

Welty's association of women's bodies with land, with nature itself, follows a tradition in Southern writing. Most rapes in Welty's fiction takes place in the woods, away from the order and protection of the plantation house or town. There is a great deal of interplay between the forest as *terra incognita* and the mysterious territory of the female body: both invite penetration. Annette Kolodny[10] has shown that constructing the Southern landscape in terms of the female body goes back to the first Virginia colonists who wrote of the 'Virgin Beauties' and 'the womb of the land', a female space to be 'taken' by men (4, 10ff.). The perceived contrast between women and men, constructing the feminine as passive, receptive, a body to be 'used' (still a term for sexual exploitation), and the masculine as active, aggressive, dominant, defines the relationship between the colonists and the sexualised landscape, gendered feminine and thus created as simultaneously virginal and fertile, a space to be 'ravished'. Like Jamie Lockhart, European colonists took first and asked later, 'deflowering' (a term they often used) the land then developing sentimental and pious attitudes towards it – much like Jamie who rapes Rosamond but eventually marries her. The erotic creation of Southern nature does not change much from the early male colonists who looked on the new land with voyeuristic eyes, 'ravished with the Beauties of Naked Nature' to Ike McCaslin's lament for his beloved delta raped by entrepreneurial men in Faulkner's fiction. With the integrity of the land and the sexual 'ownership' of women equated in the white Southern male mind it is no wonder that rape, or the threat of rape, is a dominant image for the South.

But does Welty simply adopt this masculine equivalence of land and the female body? *The Robber Bridegroom* presents a relatively unproblematised vision of the rape of women echoing the 'penetration' of the frontier. As female sexuality must be 'tamed' and contained in marriage (or in Salome's case, death) the land must bow to the property-hungry lusts of white men. But in some of Welty's later fiction nature becomes a more complex entity, not simply an extended symbol of the passive female body but the signifier of a powerful female sexuality.

The dynamics of nature and the act of rape are overtly intertwined in 'At the Landing', a story in *The Wide Net* (1943).[5] If Rosamond in *The Robber Bridegroom* is Psyche or Snow White, Jenny in 'At the Landing' is surely Sleeping Beauty. She suffers explicitly what the princess in the fairy tale experiences symbolically, that is, the rape that, in Cixous's formula, introduces her to a life spent horizontal, sexually subservient.

Like Rosamond, Jenny is the beloved child of the big house, sheltered and unworldly. This big house is a shrine to fragile, genteel arts, with prisms hung in the windows, spilling borrowed colour into Jenny's distanced life. The house is furnished with needlework and paintings made by Jenny's mother; it is a female place, full of things made by, used by or associated with, women, culture and domesticity, an emblem of Jenny's virginity. Her innocence is as vulnerable to destruction as its fragile *objets d'art*. Emphasising her lack of contact with the rough world outside, Jenny's life in the house is backward-looking. Her grandfather is an old recluse; Jenny ventures out only to visit her mother's grave: she is entrapped in an infantile space, a regressive, yet nurturing maternal space. At one point, the house is explicitly compared to a womb (253). The flood that rises and rushes through the house with Jenny's rape expresses her 'birth' into womanhood (the world outside) and the destruction of the linked integrity of the house and her body.

Water signifies Jenny's sexuality. The river, three miles from the big house, is hidden until it floods; Jenny's desires are dormant until she meets Billy Floyd. Conventionally masculine qualities - violence, rugged individualism, physical strength - are exaggerated in him as conventionally feminine traits such as stasis and smallness are exaggerated in her. She is passive in the extreme:

> Jenny was obedient to her grandfather and would have been obedient to anybody, to a stranger in the street if there could be one. She never performed any act, even a small act, for herself, she would not touch the prisms. It seemed that nothing began in her own heart.
>
> (242-3)

But on a trip to her mother's grave she sees Billy Floyd, an itinerant young man who exists not in any domesticating house but in the frighteningly exposed world of nature. Now something begins in her heart. The rise of the flood coincides with the deepening of her obsession with him. The entombing (and enwombing) past which distanced her from the organic world is destroyed: her grandfather is dead, her mother's grave is drowned, the big house is filled with water. She is left symbolically naked to Billy Floyd's businesslike rape, a parody of the prince rousing the Sleeping Beauty with a kiss:

> After a time that could have been long or short, she thought she heard him say, 'Wake up.'
>     When her eyes were open and clear upon him he violated her and still he was without care or demand and as gay as if he were still clanging the bucket at the well. With the same thoughtlessness of motion, that was a kind of grace, he next speared a side of wild meat from an animal he had killed . . . .
>
> (251)

Welty could hardly be more explicit in identifying Jenny with Billy Floyd's dinner: like Jamie Lockhart and his 'sugar cane' Rosamond, a woman is something to be consumed and discarded. Indeed, Welty deliberately connects Billy Floyd with Jamie Lockhart: Billy Floyd rides a 'rusty-red horse that belonged to the Lockharts' (243): Jamie Lockhart's horse in *The Robber Bridegroom* is 'red as blood' (64). Jenny is herself half a Lockhart – her mother married one – heir to a hidden passion; her mother's life was ruled by a 'wild desire' to get to Natchez, to get out of that big mausoleum-like, prism-lit house. A Lickhartian lust for freedom lurks in Jenny as her sexuality lies in wait inside her like the great river waiting to flood.

The fairy-tale structure of *The Robber Bridegroom* is preserved in 'At the Landing'. Once again, a young woman ventures out into the wide world to find 'romance' and finds instead rape: the landscape is hostile and threatening. Billy Floyd abandons Jenny who then returns to the big house, to the setting of her former innocence which seems, as Jenny does herself, 'crouched like a child going backwards to the womb' (253). But the mother is dead; just as Rosamond's dead mother could not protect her daughter, Jenny's dead mother cannot restore her.

Jenny behaves as disorientatedly after her rape as Rosamond after hers and like Rosamond, her first act is to clean the house. But 'the shock of love brought a trembling to her fingers that made her drop whatever she touched' (253). Even cleared of its flood damage, the house is no longer a refuge, her childhood is gone: 'there was no place to hide in it, not one room' (253). As Billy Floyd violated her, the flood waters penetrated the house. Like Rosamond she leaves her home to search for the man who raped her, the one human being she feels connected to.

Jenny does not live happily ever after. During her search she is gang-raped by a group of fishermen. Her tenuous hold on a self disappears, her estrangement from her own body is complete: she does not even resist, her face bears an 'original smile'. Awakened to the powerlessness of adult womanhood by rape, she is rendered senseless by rape. ' "Is she asleep? Is she in a spell? Or is she dead" ' asks an old woman. Her attackers answer ' "She's waiting for Billy Floyd" ' (258). Outside the grounded houseboat where she lies, young boys throw knives at a tree in imitation of Jenny's multiple rapes, an attack on nature paralleling the attack on a woman. If the grandeur of the flood holds any hope for the feminine principle it is necessarily small: Jenny's body is no longer her own, her consciousness no longer her own: she is Sleeping Beauty once more.

Water is also an important signifier of sexuality in *Delta Wedding* (1946),[11] Welty's second novel. The delta

of the title is a semi-magical Mississippi region inhabited by the Fairchild family who, like the 'fair folk'
in Celtic mythology, lead charmed lives seemingly outside of time. Presided over by Ellen Fairchild, 'the
mother of them all', the Delta is a new Eden and Ellen an
unfallen Eve.

As the delta-shape itself is female, the Fairchilds' Delta
plantation, Shellmound, has an erotic character. There
are rich fields and luxurious waters as befits the setting
of an epithalamion. The impetus of the novel is toward
consummation; Shellmound is a female space, a matriarchal garden: 'In the Delta the land belonged to the
women – they only let the men have it and sometimes
they tried to take it back and give it to someone else'
(145). The name, Shellmound, evokes the *mons veneris*
as well as Venus Anadyomene floating ashore on her
shell. The Yazoo, River of Death in Choctaw, is also the
river of life-giving, a birth canal for the Delta. The novel
resonates with strong images of female sexuality displayed in the river. Paramount among them is the
whirlpool: Dabney, the bride, bravely gazes into it
though her brothers have always been afraid:

> She parted the thonged vines of the wild grapes, thick as
> legs, and looked in. There it was. She gazed feasting her fear
> on the dark, vaguely stirring water. . . . She saw how the
> snakes were turning and moving in the water, passing
> across each other just below the surface, and now and then a
> head horridly sticking up. The vines and the cypress roots
> twisted and grew together on the shore and in the water
> more thickly than any roots should grow, gray and red, and
> some roots too moved and floated like hair.
>
> (123)

No wonder the Fairchild boys fear the whirlpool: it is
female genitalia writ large in nature. The vines are like
'legs' and 'hair', the dark water suggests a vagina, the
swimming snakes are sperm as well as penises, dwarfed
by the magisterial female progenitive space. Dabney is

looking in a mirror (a speculum?), confronting her own femaleness. Like a woman Narcissus the water threatens to draw her in yet, tentative as she is, facing the mystery of her own body emboldens her. She rides to her fiancé's house to sing a taunting song under his window, courting behaviour more usually the province of the conventionally more sexually confident male. Fired by her sexual excitement, she gallops home for breakfast: 'How hungry she was!' Indeed she is hungry – for consummation. More and more, Dabney embraces her desire, rejecting the role of passive girl-victim: 'Draw me in, she whispered, draw me in – open the window like my window, I am still only looking in where it is dark' (90).

Dabney is not the only Fairchild to rejoice in her sexuality: her pregnant mother Ellen affirms the fecundity of the Delta; her uncle George and his wife Robbie, though they have quarrelled, form part of the erotic history of Shellmound. Ellen recalls their 'dalliance, pure play' when George, roughhousing with Robbie in the Yazoo, pulls her dress off and flings 'her down thrashing and laughing on a bed of their darling sweet peas, pulling vines and all down on her' (25). The water and the vines that excited Dabney are again evocative of joyous sexuality in George and Robbie as they enact a mock ravishment. Like a couple of Olympians they allow little India Fairchild to sprinkle them with grass and pomegranate flowers in homage to their desire. As if the fertile alluvial Delta soil heated their blood, the Fairchilds' sexual history creates their present life.

It is specifically a female history. Shellmound and the Grove are houses, like the house in 'At the Landing', furnished with women's creations and rich with women's stories. Unlike that carefully guarded emblem of the virgin womb, however, Fairchild houses are pregnant with life: past, present and future. There are Great-Aunt Mashula's rather suggestive paintings of 'full-blown yellow roses and a watermelon split to the heart by a jacknife'. 'Great-grandmother's cherished things', Dabney and Shelley's dancing dresses and silk stockings, the children's dolls, a kitchen always warm with food and portraits of their pioneer ancestress Mary Shannon, compared with the evening star. Mary Shannon as Venus is another reminder of women's erotic dominance of the Delta.

Yet in the midst of this celebration of female sexuality sound ominous notes, signalling that even in this pastoral haven sexual violence exists alongside fecundity and joy. Dabney's burgeoning sexuality inspires a rebellion against her class. She chooses to marry Troy Flavin, her father's overseer, a man outside the Delta landowning gentry. His status as outsider, as interloper, appeals to the side of Dabney which constructs sexuality as violent and disruptive. She devoutly wishes for consummation, she longs to tear down the limits of genteel behaviour. She tells her maiden aunts, '–"I hope I have a baby right away" ', to shock and hurt them (48). Suddenly she envisions smashing all the little fragile things in their over-precious parlour, destroying their prim order with her anarchic lust.

It is around Troy that most of the violence is situated. Returning from her aunts' house with their wedding present (a glass night-light) Dabney's attention is on him, appearing as a 'black wedge in the lighted window' of Shellmound (53). Running to him in her desire, she breaks the night-light, a Fairchild relic used by Fairchild women awaiting their men in the Civil War. Heedless of the shattered glass, Dabney rejects the class-bound past for a subsuming erotic present, exchanging decorous light for the mysteries of the dark. Troy, the 'black wedge' obscuring the perpetual illumination of Shellmound, is a menace to Fairchild harmony. There are hints of the rapist in Troy's pursuit of Dabney:

Troy treated her like a Fairchild – sometimes he was so

standoffish, gentle-like, other times he laughed and mocked
her, and shook her and played like fighting – once he had
really hurt her. How sorry it had made him!

(33)

Troy's rough treatment of Dabney is half-apologetic
aggression against her as a woman and a member of a
more elevated class. He is constructed as a potential
destroyer. His arm looks like 'a gun against the sky' (30).
Ellen does not want him to touch the glass wedding
presents (any more than she wants him to touch Dabney)
before the wedding. Unlike the Fairchilds, Troy is at
home with danger. The night before the wedding,
Shelley finds Troy pointing a gun at a knife-wielding
field hand. 'Nobody could marry a man with blood on
his door', she thinks (196). At the same time she realises
he will have his way. The violence in him does not lead
to full-fledged rape as it does with Jamie Lockhart and
Billy Floyd; nonetheless it assures him of complete
control. He violates Fairchild decorum, calmly discussing sleeping with Dabney under his mother's quilts in
front of Ellen, he treats Shelley with a kind of amused
contempt. He does not need to rape Dabney: she is eager
for him. Dabney, like Jenny and Rosamond, perversely
craves the dangerous union with the outsider. Still, one
wonders what would have become of her had he worked
at another plantation and found her one day wandering
in the woods.

The actual rape – or is it seduction? – in the novel is
committed by George, the beloved uncle of the Fairchild
children. Abandoned by his wife, George comes back to
the nurturing Delta, unhappy and angry. As his sister-
in-law Ellen tells him about a girl she meets in the
woods, he smiles with 'gratification and regret', pre-
empting her story: ' "I took her over to the old Argyle
gin and slept with her, Ellen" ' (79).

Ellen meets the girl walking in the eroticised Shellmound woods full of 'trumpet vines and passion flow-

ers'; she is 'a beautiful girl, fair and nourished, round-armed. Not long ago she had been laughing or crying' (70). Her skirt is torn. While there is no direct evidence that George has forced her, her ripped clothing and emotional state speak of some charged encounter. They have an enigmatic conversation, full of sexual metaphor. Ellen mentions that she has lost a brooch, a courting present from Battle, but the girl repeats, ' "Nobody can say I stole *no pin*. I haven't seen *no pin*" ' (71). The pin represents Battle and Ellen's youthful courtship, made of garnets in the shape of a rose; it, too, is a traditional emblem of female sexuality. But this girl has no connection with such affirmitive sexuality – she has seen no pin but has been pricked by a conquering penis.

The sexual violence in Welty's fiction we have looked at so far involves a man of lower or outlaw status and an upper class woman. Sexual congress between classes is always problematic in the South; when Jamie Lockhart rapes Rosamond or Billy Floyd rapes Jenny, women's bodies become representative of the rich, the aristocratic and therefore unattainable. These men attack not only the woman's forbidden body but the integrity of the big house. This can be related to the Southern paranoia about 'black rape'; the violation of a white woman by a black man is an assault on white male hegemony.[12] Troy Flavin's troubling marriage to Dabney Fairchild is a similar attack, though a class threat replaces the sensational racial threat. But George's encounter with the girl in the woods (like his marriage and, indeed, the marriage of Denis Fairchild to the madwoman Virgie Lee) reverses the class positions. Upper class men are capable of mounting their own revolt against gentility and Southern 'chivalry'. George has been, in a way, the model for Dabney's rebellion. She sees him – and herself – as separate from the mass of Fairchilds: 'It was actually Uncle George who had shown her that there was another way to be – something else . . .' (33). What George has shown Dabney is the rule of desire, of sexual gratifica-

tion. Ellen Fairchild's self-abnegating maternalism is in
direct contrast to this search for sexual fulfilment. Obsession with desire can be exploitative, particularly of the
lower class women involved. George is unfaithful to
Robbie without a thought: the girl in the woods does not
occupy his mind for long: he sends her off in the
direction of Memphis, 'the old Delta synonym for
pleasure, trouble, and shame', and returns to Shellmound. Ellen's warning to her, ' "You'll bring mistakes
on yourself that way" ', a lone motherless girl in the
forest, the traditional scene of rape, is too late. Finally
Ellen herself acknowledges that the pin is a metaphor for
penis: ' "I wasn't speaking about any little possession to
you. I suppose I was speaking about good and bad,
maybe. I was speaking about men – men, our lives" '
(71).

Welty makes the point that in the midst of life, the
celebration of sexuality, we are also in death, the danger
of sexuality. The mysterious girl George slept with so
casually is killed by a train; Dabney, having consummated her marriage with Troy, is limp and still as 'a
drowned girl'. She is in thrall to the desire she has seen as
'both banks of a river and the river rushing between'
(244). This is a much different image from Dabney's
earlier vision of the vaginal whirlpool, a more *male*
image in a more phallic shape: the pervasive female
sexuality has been subsumed into the dominant male;
Dabney has become a deferential wife. There is still a
touch of violence and illicitness in Troy's sexual deal-
ings with her: kissing her he has to 'set her up straight
again like something he had knocked over and was
putting back so no one would tell the difference' (244).

It is difficult to tell at the end of *Delta Wedding*
whether the rapaciousness of men has truly violated the
Delta Garden of Adonis. Dabney 'belongs' to Troy yet
she has removed him to her world: her plantation house,
Marmion. The Delta is still gendered feminine: in nature
there is still a feminised *jouissance*; in culture, however,

women are absorbed into social roles that divorce them from the freedom of nature – they become wives. Even the sexually honest Robbie may be pregnant: it seems Welty sees the positive direction for female sexuality in maternity. Not only is Ellen the mother of them all, she is an exemplar of affirmative female sexuality.

There is not a story in *The Golden Apples* (1949)[13] that does not vibrate with sexual menace towards women. The erotic feminised nature so dominant in *Delta Wedding* is here subdued by the constant threat of male violation. Morgana, the name of the town where most of the stories take place, implies both an illusory world, a *fata morgana*, as Welty herself has pointed out, and Morgan le Fée, the powerful woman magician in the Arthurian myth whose name comes from *Morrigan* or 'Great Queen', a Celtic mother and moon goddess. As is often the case in Welty's fiction, nature is the background for the trial of strength between genders. The dance of rival sexual sensibilities in Morgana is finally inconclusive; Welty is once again ambivalent about women's sexuality and women's role in the community.

In 'Shower of Gold', the first story in the volume, male sexuality is made divine in the Olympian person of King MacLain, married to the albino Miss Snowdie Hudson. As in *The Robber Bridegroom*, 'At the Landing' and *Delta Wedding*, Welty contrasts the hero and heroine as extremes of masculinity and femininity. King is large, tall, sexually confident, an outlaw. Snowdie is small and pale, confined to their dim house to protect her weak eyes from the blaze of the sun. Their encounter in Morgan's Woods, under an oak tree, is not a rape except perhaps in the classical sense of the rape of Danaë. But it has a clandestine air to it. King insists on preserving his freedom and his sexual power from the feminine world of home and community. Snowdie is left pregnant with twins; an imperial male sexuality has impressed itself upon her, inscribing his will on her body.

'Sir Rabbit' is another story about King MacLain's

vaunting sexuality and the mythologisation it undergoes in the mind of Morgana. There is some question as to whether the crux of the story – Mattie Will's rape by King MacLain in the woods – is 'real' or Mattie's fantasy. While most readers have taken the rape as actual, Patricia Yaeger argues convincingly that it is a daydream Mattie has while churning on the porch.[14] In the mind of Morgana King MacLain is the designated rapist about whom the women tell half-admiring, half-cautionary tales, the embodiment of masculine sexuality unfettered by culture, lurking in Morgan's Woods waiting for female prey. Like the fertility figure 'Sir Rabbit' who dances in the woods at night, King MacLain is outside domesticity. Given the dullness, predictability and petty violence of Morgana men it is no wonder that the women identify with the anarchic but self-determining sexual bogeyman.

The impetus for Mattie's fantasy comes from her remembrance of being frightened by King MacLain's twin sons in the woods. She thinks it is King himself come to 'carry her off'; instead, it is his sons who assault her, sitting on her and kissing her. Later married to the prosaic Junior Holifield, a man inclined to 'give her a licking' for her stories, she fantasises what it might be like to really be 'carried off' by their father. She imagines Junior's insistence that she not even look at him, this seducer of maidens, nor he at her:

> 'Show yourself and I'll brain you directly, Mattie Will,' Junior said. 'You heard who he said he was and you done heard what he was, all your life, or you ain't a girl. . . . And don't nobody know how many children he has.'

Junior gets himself laid out unconscious, frightened by the sound of King MacLain's gun, easily read as fear of MacLain's overwhelming virility. Maggie is then raped by MacLain, 'with the affront of his body, the affront of his sense too. No pleasure in that! She had to put on what he knew with what he did –' (95).

In her dextrous reading of 'Sir Rabbit', Patricia Yaeger
has shown how the story is a parody of Yeats's 'Leda and
the Swan' (the whole of *The Golden Apples* is a reworking of Yeats's poetry of desire and inspiration from
a woman's viewpoint) which poses the question 'Did she
put on knowledge with his power?'. Welty's answer is
clearly yes – Mattie's social, Morgana-defined identity is
transformed:

> she was Mr MacLain's Doom, or Mr MacLain's Weakness,
> like the rest, and neither Mrs Junior Holifield nor Mattie
> Will Sojourner; now she was something she had always
> heard of.
>
> (95)

What is the thing she has always heard of that Mattie has
become? A fallen woman? A free woman? A raped
woman? Mattie has temporarily shared in King
MacLain's strength; she has circumvented the strictures
of her husband, defied the wisdom of her community
and come face to face with power.

The question arises as to why a rape is the means by
which Mattie can imagine gaining power and selfhood.
Why is the outlaw sexual menace King MacLain the
Jovian force that endows the town Ledas with divine
liberty? The answer must be that Mattie feels herself
someone else's property, a Sojourner or a Holifield, a
daughter or a wife. Therefore the rape is an attack
against *a man's* property. Thus would Mattie revenge
herself on Junior and his narrow vision of a woman's
place in the world.

Welty's divided attitude towards rape is revealed in
other stories in *The Golden Apples*. An encounter with
King MacLain is creative and empowering, but other
sexual attacks are just the opposite: destructive and
enervating. 'The Whole World Knows', a story about
King MacLain's son Ran, deals with sexual betrayal,
anger and a rape that ends in suicide.

Ran MacLain seems much more his church-going mother's son than his free-wheeling father's: he has left his wife Jinny Love Stark because of her infidelity. Upper-class Jinny is a self-assured, almost masculine woman who underscores this threatening (to Ran) demeanour by sawing off her hair and wearing boy's shorts. In contrast, country girl Maideen Sumrall is conventionally feminine down to her white gloves, her precious manners and, as her name implies, her virginity. Once again, the poles of masculinity and femininity set the scene for sexual disaster. Ran's pain over Jinny's 'inappropriate' behaviour leads him to take up with her opposite in class, appearance and sexual politics. Ran participates in the male fantasy of purity for women. As his mother (whom Maideen resembles in her deferential attitude toward men), accepting victim of King MacLain's promiscuity for years, says, ' *"It's different from when it's the man"* ' (157).

Ran is in a rage against women. He appropriates his father's pistol – as if he could absorb his father's sexual confidence – wanting to penetrate women's bodies with bullets. He fantasises about killing Jinny in a combination of pornographic enjoyment and anger: 'I was watching Jinny and I saw her pouting childish breasts, excuses for breasts, sprung full of bright holes where my bullets had gone' (151). Later, he points the pistol at Maideen and envisions her 'with blood on her, blood and disgrace' (159). This imagined violence has a specifically sexual content – the holes in Jinny's breasts are an attack on the sexuality that betrayed him; the blood and disgrace on Maideen project her lost purity.

Acting the nurturer, Maideen tries to save Ran from his intended suicide. When the pistol he has stuck in his mouth fails to go off (an image of his sexual inadequacy) she takes it from him. His response is to 'have' her, making actual the blood and disgrace he fantasised before. He is emotionally detached, alienated from her body and his; Maideen is just something to possess, then turn away from. While not precisely in the forest, their sexual encounter happens in a wild spot far from the female structures that have protected her in the past. The name of the place is Sunset Oaks, an ironic reference to the big oak Ran was conceived under and the west with which King MacLain is associated in the collective mind of Morgana.

After being 'taken' by Ran, Maideen's sense of self is utterly destroyed. She shoots herself, sacrifice to his need to feel powerful, another victim of the sexual violence that seems to surround women in Welty's Mississippi.

That rapacious atmosphere teaches women early on that their role is to be passive and receptive. In 'Moon Lake', the symbolic rape of the orphan Easter (another motherless girl) by Loch Morrison (he is actually resuscitating her after she falls in the lake) displays the power struggle between genders in its most terrifying light.[15] Rape saves a woman's life! It is no wonder that Nina Carmichael and Jinny Love Stark vow at the end of the story to remain unmarried and uncompromised by violent male sexuality.

The camp at Moon Lake is a training ground in gender conventions. The girls are a sort of parody-harem for the misogynist Loch Morrison, the bugling 'Boy Scout and Life Saver', the only white boy at the camp who pours out his hatred for females in the spit that goes into his playing of 'Reveille'. Every morning the girls parade before him, stripping off their robes before taking a swim. Nature is as contemptuous of the girls as Loch is: the mosquitoes enact their own symbolic ravishment on the girls' bodies:

> as they walked out of their kimonos and dropped them like the petals of one big scattered flower on the bank behind them, and exposing themselves felt in a hundred places at once the little pangs.
>
> (101)

Despite the name of the lake, suggesting a feminine

entity, the water is dreaded by the girls who must swim in it every morning; they characterise it as masculine, singing their daily song to 'Mr. Dip' whose touch is cold and whose mud sucks at their feet. Where water in other fictions by Welty is a positive image of female sexuality, here it is hostile. Easter almost drowns and is brought back to life only by Loch Morrison's 'driving' up and down on her:

> He lifted up, screwed his toes, and with a groan of his own fell upon her and drove up and down upon her, into her, gouging the heels of his hands into her ribs again and again. She did not alter except that she let a thin stream of water out of her mouth, a dark stain down the fixed cheek. The children drew together. Life-saving was much worse than they had dreamed.
>
> (129)

The image is of a rape, the 'dark stain' like the blood of a defloration. The women and girls mostly watch resigned but Miss Lizzie Stark, Jinny Love's mother, seems to realise the implications: ' "Loch Morrison, get off that table and shame on you"–' (130). Easter, the orphan who dared change her name from Esther, who was brave and independent, is virtually destroyed: her body 'lay up on the table, ready to receive anything that was done to it' (129). When it is over she acts like a violated girl, pushing Loch off her and pulling her skirt down. She has become truly feminine: ' "Carry me" ', she says (135).

In a final display of machismo and disdain Loch, the 'hero' of the day, undresses with his tent open, displaying his genitals to the world and specifically to Jinny Love and Nina who are not impressed with his 'little tickling thing' (137). Though his penis seems more mock-heroic than threatening, the girls realise that violation is woman's lot. Loch's penis is just a junior version of what is to come. Jinny Love would rather remain free. She says, ' "You and I will always be old maids" ' (138).

Such hope as there can be for women in a world of rape is expressed in Virgie Rainey, a character justly praised as Welty's great expression and celebration of female sexuality. In 'June Recital', Morgana is again full of sexual menace for women: Mr Voight, who lives upstairs in the house where the Morgana girls get their piano lessons is an exhibitionist and Miss Eckhart, the piano teacher, is raped by a nameless black man. Yet Virgie is untouched by all this, her desire somehow liberates her. She trysts with a sailor with the same passion that she plays Beethoven: sweatily, earthily. Later, in 'The Wanderers', she arrived at some mythic understanding of the perpetual struggle of sexuality against community. She recalls a picture of Perseus cutting off the head of the Medusa that Miss Eckhart used to have. This representation of the male attempting to contain and destroy female sexuality expresses the infinity of male violence against women. Like the figures on Keats's Grecian Urn, the struggle is forever: 'Endless the Medusa, and Perseus endless' (243).

Yet Virgie embraces her independence and her desire: unlike Dabney she does not direct it at any one man but at the glory of sexuality itself. Sitting in the rain with an old black woman (some hope of sisterhood, perhaps?), Virgie has a vision not only of King MacLain, the legendary rapist of Morgana, but of the beasts of myth, horse and bear, leopard and dragon, and finally swan. But Virgie is no Leda. She does not need the Jovian rape to put on power or knowledge; her body has its own language. Perhaps this language could be read as the expression of a specifically feminine desire. Julia Kristeva[16] has said that women writers can try to 'break the code, to shatter language, to find a specific discourse closer to the body and emotions, to the unnameable repressed . . .' (24–5). Perhaps this language of sexuality, of the mythic beasts, is the only mitigation in the world of rape women necessarily inhabit. With the speech of their bodies, they can redress their bodies' wrongs.

# Notes

1. *The Robber Bridegroom* (London, Virago, 1982).
2. Hélène Cixous, 'Castration or Decapitation?', trans. Annette Kuhn, *Signs*, 7 (1) (Autumn, 1981), 41–55.
3. *Conversations with Eudora Welty*, ed. Peggy Whitman Prenshaw (Jackson, Miss., University Press of Mississippi, 1984), 36.
4. Louise Westling, *Sacred Groves and Ravaged Gardens: The Fiction of Eudora Welty, Carson McCullers and Flannery O'Connor* (Athens, University of Georgia Press, 1985), 67.
5. *The Collected Stories of Eudora Welty* (New York, Harcourt Brace Jovanovich, 1980).
6. *The Robber Bridegroom* also has elements of *The Brown Bear of Norway, The Goose Girl, Cinderella, Snow White and the Seven Dwarfs, Little Red Riding Hood, Beauty and the Beast* and *Cupid and Psyche.*
7. *Welty: A Life in Literature*, ed. Albert J. Devlin (Jackson, Miss., University Press of Mississippi, 1987), 110, 112.
8. Paul Binding, Introduction to *The Robber Bridegroom* (London, Virago, 1982), v–xiv.
9. See especially *The Company of Wolves* and 'The Bloody Chamber'.
10. Annette Kolodny, *The Lady of the Land: Metaphor as Experience and History in American Life and Letters* (Chapel Hill, University of North Carolina Press, 1975).
11. *Delta Wedding* (New York, Harcourt Brace Jovanovich, 1974).
12. It is interesting how few black man/white woman rapes there are in Welty. In Southern white male writers, Faulkner and Allen Tate for example, fear of the black rapist appears far more often.
13. *The Golden Apples* (New York, Harcourt Brace Jovanovich, 1949).
14. See Patricia S. Yaeger, ' "Because a Fire Was in my Head"

*Eudora Welty and the Dialogic Imagination', Welty: a Life in Literature*, 159-67. While I disagree with some of her optimistic conclusions regarding women's efficacy in Welty's fiction, Yaeger's feminist readings of *The Golden Apples* (see below) have greatly contributed to this essay.

15. I am again indebted to Patricia S. Yaeger; in her essay 'The Case of the Dangling Signifier: Phallic Imagery in Eudora Welty's "Moon Lake" ', in *Faith of a Woman Writer*, eds. Alice Kessler-Harris and William McBrien, *Contributions in Women's Studies* **86** (Westport, Conn., Greenwood Press, 1989), 253-72, is the first as far as I know to point out that the description of Loch's reviving of Easter could be the description of a rape.

16. Julia Kristeva, 'Women's Time', trans. Alice Jardine and Harry Blake, *Signs*, **7** (1), (Autumn, 1981), 13-35.

# Chronological Table of Works

## Bessie Head

*Born South Africa, 1937;*
*lived in Botswana*
*Died Botswana, 1986*

### Novels

1969 *When Rain Clouds Gather*
1971 *Maru*
1974 *A Question of Power*

### Short Stories

1977 *The Collector of Treasures and other Botswana Village Tales*
1989 *Tales of Love and Tenderness*

### Non-Fiction

1981 *Serowe: Village of the Rain Wind*
1984 *A Bewitched Crossroad: An African Saga*
1989 *Tales of Love and Tenderness*

## Ama Ata Aidoo

*Born Ghana, 1942*

### Plays

1965 *The Dilemma of A Ghost* and *Anowa*

### Short Stories

1970 *No Sweetness Here*

### Novels

1977 *Our Sister Killjoy: or Reflections from a Black-Eyed Squint*

### Poetry

1985 *Someone Talking to Sometime*
Ama Ata Aidoo has also published children's stories in Zimbabwe

# 8

# Are We in the Company of Feminists?

## A Preface for Bessie Head and Ama Ata Aidoo

### Caroline Rooney

The question asked in the title of this essay might be heard to be saying: 'What are we, writers from different parts of Africa, doing here in this collection where white women critics - feminists? - write on predominantly white women writers?'

In an anthology whose binding thread is 'diverse voices' it could be said that there is a need for at least one African woman/writer. But one is not enough: one would either abolish the 'African' in its individualistic emphasis or would take that one to be representative of an entire continent. But then, if there is a demand for African women writers in an anthology in which individual white writers from the same or different countries are singled out, privileged perhaps, this would not only be suspect but impossible - Africa being so many countries. For pragmatic reasons, at least, I will be concerned with Bessie Head and Ama Ata Aidoo.

The question - 'Are we in the company of feminists?' - raises questions of inclusion/exclusion. One appropriation of the question might be to ask to what extent can these writers and their concerns be included among feminists and their concerns, which would evaluate or measure them in terms of some standard(s) of feminism. That is not my interest. It is rather one of the politics of textual, as well as topographical, borderlines and discourse relations as they affect writers from Africa, and in particular women writers.

To begin, I am interested in the construction of this titular question, which calls into question the possibilities of answering it. Although it is asked of, it is not yet addressed to, the company of feminists who are thus not invited to reply. They may attend, listen and furthermore be prompted to ask themselves, in an aside: 'Are we . . . feminists?' One question which may be heard to murmur at times in this essay is: what motivates 'us' to place black writers on the agenda of feminism or women's writing? For instance, is it the need for diversity, for extra sites, broader or simply more bases? Is it the need to protect against dispersal through enlisting more same-sex allies? Or is it the need to diversify from interests that are too narrow or self-contained? This is not necessarily to discredit the gesture of hospitality, which need not be suspect, although one cannot know this without some inspection or self-examination.[1]

Leaving these asides to return to the question asked – 'Are we in the company of feminists?' – it can be said that the question is to be answered by the ones who ask it, albeit as a speculation, that which yet holds on to the question. While they, African women writers, may be invited into a company where the line has been drawn along sexual lines, they may yet address questions and interests of their own. Invited, they may still invite themselves to speak and the issues they give rise to may go beyond any lines drawn up for discussion. The inclusion of two African women writers might incidentally serve to identify a certain homogenisation of interests – as in, why women? women only? – at the same time that they bring with them their own diverse interests which I would not like to and could not contain. The question, 'Are we . . .', was once asked by Bessie Head.[2]

When she asked it, she at once differentiated herself among others from 'the company' while at the same time expressing a willingness to address the interests of others.

If I ask myself questions pertaining to the interests of the writers to be considered here, this is to provide a speculative reading, while remembering that these texts ask/answer themselves. Given the latter point it can be said that these texts are not addressed to 'us', and cannot be made to answer back to 'us'. I wish to avoid the enclosure of these texts in a foreign frame of reference; I also wish to avoid an exclusivist position which would foreclose the possibility of outsiders engaging with them.[3] While one can point out the inadequacy of certain, say, foreign or culturally limited readings of the texts in question, it is also necessary to go beyond this dis-location to a re-location of possible discussions. This is not simply to propose new grounds for discussion but to consider the grounds for discussion already there in the texts and their contexts. A close reading of the texts is important in so far as they serve to suggest the specific models for reading them.

In what follows, I hope to show how the texts under consideration revise 'us' without necessarily addressing us, as they speak for themselves.

## ` The Message´ and Broken Lines

Frederic Jameson writes of the western reader confronted with a so-called 'third world' text: 'We sense, between ourselves and this alien text, the presence of another reader, of the Other reader, for whom a narrative, which strikes us as unconventional or naive, has a freshness of information and a social interest that we cannot share.'[4] He goes on to explain the 'fear and resistance' in the face of this 'alien' text in terms of the fact that to read adequately, 'we would have to give up a great deal that is individually precious to us. . .'. There is, of course, another side to this. That is, it could be that the text of the Other is not merely that which is resisted but that which resists, cognitively or with deliberate disregard, readings which are alien to it or which would penetrate its 'mystery'. Zora Neale Hurston writes of the tactics of Negro people faced with white questioners: 'We smile and tell him or her something that satisfies the white person because, knowing so little about us, he doesn't know what he is missing.'[5] In 'Drapaudi', a story by Mahasweta Devi, the comrades are able to elude the army despite the army's skills in 'deciphering', because: 'The clue will be such that the opposition won't see it, won't understand it even if they do.'[6] Even when the signs are quite visible, they may remain impenetrable to eyes for whom they are not meant.

It is with the above considerations in mind that I would like to show how Ama Ata Aidoo's story 'The Message'[7] serves to dramatise the 'decoy' of the possibility of an educated misreading, while it offers revisions of that reading at the same time as it tells itself. The supposedly educated western/northern reading of 'The Message' would probably be to construe the story in terms of an illiterate village woman's inability to understand a message she received concerning her daughter, on whom a Caesarean operation has been performed. The scholar who reads what she calls 'this tengram thing' informs her that her daughter has been 'cut open' and the 'baby removed'. Hearing this, the woman fears that her daughter and the baby must be dead and she undertakes a journey to the metropolitan hospital. When she arrives the nurse identifies the daughter as 'the Caesarean case' but the village woman still does not understand. When taken through to her daughter, lying 'in state', she believes her to be dead until the daughter speaks, revealing herself to be alive and well. The western or westernised reader, familiar with the operations and terms of modern medicine, would read the story with a certain superior knowledge, seeing the tale as an ironic dramatisation of the old woman's ignorance and fears, perhaps especially since it is science that saves and not kills her daughter.[8] However, such a reading would eclipse the other message, 'The Message', that a less informed or, in a certain sense, naïve reader would receive. The old woman, it would seem, is too hasty to jump to the conclusion that her daughter is dead. But to jump to the conclusion that this is a misunderstanding, and that all is well, is even more hasty.

A reader open to the, in Jameson's phrase, 'freshness of information' would, in the place of the illiterate woman perhaps, find a horror, or more closely, terror, in the graphic reality of the words: 'opened her up', 'stomach . . . open to the winds' (38). Medical science then presents itself not in terms of what it says it does, not in terms of an ideology of saving lives nor in its scientific, latinised terms, but in terms of what it actually does: cut open bodies. In this respect, stripped of its licence of professionalism it can seem sinister or barbaric: 'Horrible things I have heard done to people's bodies. Cutting them up and using them for instructions' (39). What is brought 'home' – but to whom? – is the vulnerability of the body operated upon, the violence of operations on the body, and so on. Perhaps. At any rate, it can be said that the language of knowledge/ knowledge of language of the medical profession constitutes a sterilisation; a sanitising and sublimating operation which distances both theory and its practice from the reality of what is performed and from the immediate effects of fear and suffering. The ready identification: 'It's the Caesarean case' is a sterile and dehumanising abstraction which in a sense loses the life of the daughter, as it ignores the human reality of the mother, humiliating or *mortifying* her. What for an educated audience might be a farce of misunderstandings – and Africa serves as but a site of such a farce in some western narratives[9] – is for the supposedly 'ignorant' woman a potential tragedy.

Scrappy nurse-under-training, Jessy Treeson, second-gener-ation-Cape-Coaster-her-grandmother-still-remembered-at-Egyaa No. 7 said, 'As for these villagers,' and giggled.

(46)

As suggested by the above, the resistance to an empathy with the old woman is based on a fear of slipping 'back' into 'ignorance' or fear of lack of knowledge. It could be said that the will-to-ignore of the educated is not only a question of insensitivity but one of a systematic de-sensitisation that enables a supposedly sophisticated culture to deal with the unknown, especially the unknowns of a sophisticated as opposed to primitive culture. That is, 'we' educated/western(ised) people learn to use certain languages, in the wider sense too, in order to adapt to or operate in a world we do not ultimately understand; we can confidently speak of telegrams and Caesareans without knowing how a Caesarean is executed precisely or how tele-communications operate exactly. And 'we' may know how to use words with perfect correctness while for-getting or being ignorant of the reality they refer to.

The above discussion concerning the deconstruction of a discourse of knowledge in terms of what it hides or fears to confront still refers back to that discourse which is to recapitulate the error in 'the message', that failure of the '*tene*gram' thing to communicate over a distance. For example, if one puts oneself in the place of the woman and goes on to register the frightening vulner-ability of the body operated upon, this supposed insight might accord more with a possible feminist perception or insight than with what the woman character might specifically fear herself. It is a question of an empathy which displaces or eclipses.

The title of the story is 'The Message'. It is not

elaborated further. There is no message in that sense. It could be said that the message, as a trigger for debates, readings or misreadings, is a decoy. The misunderstood message is, in fact, a vehicle of suspense. It grants the delay, time or space that the narrative needs, and what the narrative is most concerned with is the importance of the child. That is, the misunderstood message as vehicle of suspense allows a realisation to develop of what the child means to the woman of the village. This realisation or message is not something that is stated as such. Rather, perhaps, the clues are so obvious or self-evident as to be overlooked by those who can and would read and decipher. 'Our' readings get in the way of our reading.

> 'They do not say, my sister.'
> 'Have you heard it? '
> 'What? '
> 'This and this and that . . .'
> 'A-a-ah! that is it . . .'
> '*Meeewuo*! '.
>
> (38)

The story begins with the transmission of and reactions to the news by the people of the village, but the words are used not so much to spell out or literally phrase this news and its effects, as to build up a dramatic picture. The picture is one of a flurry of exchanges whose meaning is, say, commotion. What is thus communicated, or passed on, is the mutually felt emotional impact of the news concerning the child and this indicates the importance accorded to children by the whole community. Furthermore this importance is not something that needs to be made explicit, for everyone *concerned* knows about it. By not making the point explicit, Aidoo is actively not crafting her story for western consumption, which would be at the expense of the local or contextual verity of the event, where explanations would be superfluous. It is not that the meaning is between the lines, nor that it is eclipsed by the villagers who get between 'us' and the message. The message is in the lines, which do not elaborate, and so are expressive of the assumptions in everything that is expressed; and the meaning is in the coming together or affiliation of the villagers. It can be said that the importance of children in the community is a value that cannot be extracted from the community. Children are communally important: more than simply a case of maternal instincts, it is a matter of cultural and social values. Paradoxically, this is what serves to isolate the childless woman from the community, even as they share her fears and suffering. The woman who fears her daughter dead, having lost all her other children, reflects: 'Now they are coming to . . . "*poo* pity" me' while their children and grandchildren, she ruefully notes, all survive and thrive (39).

An interesting feature of the narrative is that while the speech of all the characters in the tale is enclosed within quotation marks, the words of the old woman are not. Among various imports that could be attributed to this, it might be that it marks the withdrawal of the woman from society. She goes alone to the hospital and on the journey she addresses her own feared plight of childlessness, that which distinguishes her from the community. This misunderstood message/telegram is a device necessary for allowing the space to emphasise the value ascribed to having children and the concomitant desolation of being childless. The final delivery of the 'true' message is not the final sight or apocalyptic revelation of the daughter, presumed dead, alive and well. The relief of this ending is rather where the story about the value of children loses its crisis impetus and so ends, although the impetus for narrating 'The Message' continues, as I will elaborate.

It can be said that it is precisely the values of the village society that the modern, scientifically progressive metropolitan culture, here instanced in the locus of the hospital, cannot read. It is constitutively unable to recognise these values in so far as the colonially derived

advent of this modern society marks a rupture with the
social and economic organisations which preceded it
and which are ignored, and this ignorance projected.
The village is then naturalised as the site of this ignorance, an 'unrecorded' pre-history, which cannot be read.
The child that leaves home for the city and its modern-
western ways joins that culture at the expense of
remembering its past, its mother, its collective identity,
its history; in short, where it comes from. In 'The
Message' this amnesia is portrayed in the characterisa-
tion of Nurse Jessy Treeson. While the old woman is
called 'our grandmother' by the villagers, Treeson –
treason? – cannot or refuses to recognise her as such or
even see her own grandmother or mother in the old
woman, despite the fact that her grandmother is still
remembered by others. That is, while she cannot read or
recognise her past, the people of her past can read,
recognise or remember her. This relates to the story's
concern with the condition of childlessness. In a sense,
the city kidnaps children from their villages, thus induc-
ing an artificial childlessness. In the hospital, the nurse
and the daughter have western names and when the old
woman asks for her daughter by her birth-name or
'native' name, there is no record of such a person.
Significantly, the daughter's original name is the same
as that of her mother, Esi Amfoa, and so it might be
inferred that as the daughter is interpellated into a
westernised culture, not only is the tie between mother
and daughter cut, but a whole lineage of descent, this
history, is terminated. In this respect the Caesarean
operation of violent severance does paradoxically
become a metaphor for child loss or the rupture of a
child from its birthplace, its society and history.

   The old woman's reading is then legitimated in or by
the story. One might then say that the writer of it is the
'good daughter', the one who 'returns', or who preserves
and does not betray the village woman's culture and
history. It is possible to arrive at this interpretation

through reading the text. It can be tangentially noted that the text might be referring to a historical matrilineal culture. Cheik Anta Diop, among others, has drawn attention to matrilineal descent and matriarchal culture in Ghana.[10] However, I cannot say whether this text, 'The Message', is specifically referring to or 'all about' a matrilineal society. I would not want to offer a self-satisfied anthropological reading that would detract from the telling of the story; from feeling the value of the child to the mother and in the community and from registering the story's legitimation of a culture that pre-dates and is not erased by colonial founding fathers, who are not then an originating point of reference. What interests me is the line between the educated writer and the woman character, the grandmother; which is perhaps why the woman's words are not enclosed within quotation marks.

## 'Maru' and 'Bewitched Crossroads'

It has been argued, by Frederic Jameson and Stephen Slemon respectively, that 'third world' or 'post-colonial' texts 'necessarily project a political dimension'[11] or 'reinstate the sphere of the political as paramount over the individual or private'.[12]

One of the major projects of feminism has been and is an undoing of the opposition between the private and the public or political.[13]

Bessie Head is commonly regarded as having shunned a political role in her writings and her first three novels, especially *Maru*, are said to be about the abdication of political power. I wish first to situate *Maru* in relation to the above assertions and then to consider the adequacy of the terms – 'private', 'political' – in any attempt to define the nature or project of this text, at least.[14]

*Maru*[15] can be read as a love story in which Maru, a paramount chief-elect, marries Margaret, a woman of the reviled Masarwa [Bushmen]. Read in this way, the story might appear to be a romantic fairytale in which a poor Cinderella gets to marry a Prince Charming. However, it cannot simply be read as a romantic story of the individual social betterment of Margaret, an orphan of an outcast tribe, since the royal heir necessarily abdicates to marry her. Given an emphasis on the latter, the story might seem to uphold love between individuals as supreme and 'the world well lost'. However, again, it might be said that Maru does not abdicate to marry Margaret but that he marries her in order to abdicate, since he resents being 'public property' (67) and wishes to assert his individual freedom. In this respect he might be regarded as rejecting the 'male' world of power for the 'female' world of love. Or it may be argued that Maru renounces his inherited position and marries Margaret as a step towards realising his dream of a better society.

One can read *Maru* as a political fable. As such, the story could be reconstructed in terms of the undoing of a racial–tribal prejudice. In this respect it would be Margaret's identity as a Masarwa, rather than a woman, that would feature most prominently. It is given in the text that her mission is to disprove the notion that the Masarwa is an inferior being (17). However, it is also indicated that she cannot 'uplift' the oppressed Masarwa on her own since their oppression is embedded in the structures of the society, psychological, ideological and economic, since the Masarwa are both projected as inhuman others and exploited as slaves. It is Maru who both understands and condemns the elitism and greed of his society and who calculates a way of countering it through an alliance with Margaret. In marrying a Masarwa and giving up the chieftancy he not only flaunts his entire inheritance, its power and entrenchment, but sets in motion the liberation of a people. The novel ends with the words: 'It would no longer be possible to treat Masarwa people in an inhuman way without getting killed yourself.'

While, if one reads the book as a love story, this is to ignore its political import, if one reads it as a political trace this is to ignore the individuality – and to a large extent, the sexual status – of the protagonists. In the political text Margaret, for instance, would seem to be but a pawn in Maru's schemes, or the author's plot, or in a political reading of the story she would function as but a trope for a despised people.

The perhaps obvious point is that the 'private' and 'individualistic' spheres in the text are inextricably bound up with the 'public' and 'political' ones, so that one cannot privilege one dimension over the other. As one indication of this, 'individuality' is a political issue for Margaret since it is as a Masarwa that she is granted none, but is instead at times treated like an animal, as a member of a species (17, 45). Nonetheless, this fate is that of her tribe as a whole, and so what is at stake is a collective individuality. As for Maru, his personal liberation or renunciation of power is at once a denunciation of a corrupt society – his abdication from politics is political – and the occasion of the liberation, the regained self-esteem and awakened will to resist subjugation, of those his society has oppressed. The point I wish to make at this stage is that the political liberation of the individual is an *instance* of a wider political liberation of others. In other words, the supposed individual–private liberation is not a symbol or allegory, in that representative sense, of the political liberation of a group, a tribe, a nation. It is itself one instance or happening of that happening. In Head's portrait of the village of Serowe, she writes: 'Great gestures have an oceanic effect on society – they flood a whole town.' [16] The great gesture is greater than itself. It is not a case of the individual acting on society, nor of the converse, as if one were cause and the other effect; it is rather a case of the individual social act itself spreading, continuing or being repeated throughout the society.

In the above paragraph it is possible to notice

slippages and re-combinations of terms such as 'individual' and 'political'. The inability of these terms to retain their definitive hold and clarity indicates a certain rejection of them by the text, like a graft that does not quite take. I therefore wish to consider what incompatible assumptions or alien motivations might be involved in attempting to explain the text in the above terms as well as to show how *Maru* serves to dispel or question such assumptions and motives.

If the so-called 'third world' text is 'necessarily political', to what necessity is this due? It might be said that one assumption of this definition is that the 'Third World', or as I would say, African society, is a naturally, automatically or predictably political one in so far as the capitalist-induced split between the private and political is foreign to it. The motivation in this formulation might be the desire or need to posit an ideally political society. With respect to the special case of *Maru*, it can be pointed out that the text does not represent a naturally political society. For a start, it is questionable whether the text does reflect a pre-given historical society, as opposed to being a fictional reconstruction. In a footnote to her story, 'The Deep River: A Story of Ancient Tribal Migration', Head writes: 'The story is an entirely romanticized and fictionalized version of the history of the Botalaote tribe . . . A re-construction was made in my own imagination.'¹⁷ Later I will say more about such revisions and about the writer's place in society as leading to romantic or fictional or political revisions. At this point, it can merely be said that while the identities and destinies of Maru and Margaret are bound up with those of their respective peoples, this situation is not ineluctable. Margaret, for instance, has the opportunity of passing as Coloured, because of her light skin, and of thus avoiding the abuses suffered by the Masarwa (24). However, she *decides* to affirm her identity as Masarwa and so share their misfortunes. More extremely, Maru chooses to link his destiny with the

Masarwa using his public status in a politically transgressive way. Margaret and Maru are necessarily political, deliberately and atypically, given a far from ideal
society, one prejudiced against individual deviation and
tribal heterogeneity. I will briefly suspend the question
of the historical political nature of Botswana society. It
can broadly be suggested that the 'idealisation' of an
other society – as naturally political, or naturally
creative, or naturally deconstructive – testifies to what
the culture, from which such ideal naturalisations come,
lacks and so seeks in the other.

Another assumption in the formulation of the
necessarily political nature of the Third World/post-
colonial text might be that the mutual material experience of colonial and neo-colonial oppression serves to
provoke homogenous, national, even multi-national
political response. Aijaz Ahmad, in his critique of
Jameson, discounts the assumption of a homogeneous
political response and asserts: 'Literary texts are produced in highly differentiated, usually very overdetermined contexts of competing ideological and
cultural clusters. . . .'[18] *Maru* is set in and based on
Botswana, a British Protectorate from 1885 to 1963.
However, Head's perspective of this society and her
preoccupations are, at least to some extent, determined
by her own origins and experience as a Coloured person
in South Africa. It is as a refugee from South Africa that
she perhaps chooses to explore and expose the tribal-
racial prejudices of the Batswana. It is perhaps as a
South African refugee and as a Coloured person, unable
to place herself easily in relation to a tribe and a tribal
heritage, that she is sensitive to and critical of tribal
elitism. It is for such reasons perhaps that she is interested in the Masarwa, 'Masarwa' being a Tswana word
for 'a person from the uninhabited country'. Furthermore, Head's protagonist, Margaret, is an orphan cut off
from her cut-off tribe. *Maru* then does not arise from a
common or unitary experience of oppression. It is a

strange crossroads, where the possible 'inter-mixing' of Coloured and Masarwa exists in the realms of analogy and the sympathetic imagination rather than in the text-book history.

In both issues I have addressed so far – the naturally political society/text and the homogeneously political society/text – it would seem that the African text is being made to answer to or refer back to a western/northern/colonialist/pre-colonialist/First World. While Head might bring to her novel concerns that might refer back to the apartheid regime coloniser/colonised polarisation – her novel is very much concerned with moving away from the enclosures of that world. An identification with the Masarwa, from the position of the Coloured, is also a step *away* from the society which constructs, in order to contain and subjugate, the identity of the Coloured group and is a movement across racial barriers towards . . . the unprecedented. Head is concerned with the moving away from the world of the white-man-in-the-first-place and even more concerned with moving to-wards or into a society which is its own First World.

Although a British Protectorate, Botswana was hardly colonised at all: 'The most notable characteristic of British rule during this time can be summarized in one word – neglect!'[19]

In *Maru* we are shown a society that is locally con-cerned and, in particular, two negative aspects of this village society, both relating to the will to dominate, are highlighted. One aspect is the power-mongering intrigues of the village elite, this pertaining to Bots-wana's own history of conflict within tribes for seces-sion.[20] The other aspect of the society is the subjugation of the Masarwa by the Batswana. Of the racist attitudes of the Batswana, Head writes: '*Before the white man* became universally disliked for his outlook, it was there' (11; my italics). Thus the white man is not the source of all, good or evil.

However, Head does not set up an Afrocentrism in

reaction to white ethnocentricism. The thrust of her work is rather that before attacking/emulating foreign others, one must first examine one's local condition; one begins to undo oppression not through reaction to an other but through self-examination. This is how Head addresses the issue in *Maru*: 'Something they liked as Africans to believe themselves incapable of was being exposed to oppression and prejudice. They always knew it was there but no oppressor believes in his oppression. He always says he treats his slaves nicely. He never says that there ought not to be slaves' (48).

*Maru* sets out to revise a whole history of conquest and domination, of ever-perpetuated resentment, through the revisionary eradication of prejudices. The novel begins with the outcome of a new society, a new history taking root (6–7), but one cannot simply begin with the new beginning. As it is said in Head's novel prior to *Maru*: 'Things could start in a small way . . .'[21] and in *Maru* we move from the opening 'new beginning' to the events which made it possible. These events consist of a series of magic coincidences or unpredictable encounters.

The 'first' encounter is that of the missionary woman, Margaret Cadmore, after whom Margaret is named, with Margaret's dead mother. The missionary woman, 'quite unconscious of the oddness of her behaviour', makes a sketch of the dead woman and finally scrawls on the sketch: 'She looks like a goddess' (15). This vision opens her eyes still further and she observes the miserable state of the woman – 'thin stick legs of malnutrition' – as well as the reactions of other people present towards the dead woman: 'the hatred of the fortunate' (15). In this strange meeting the missionary woman unexpectedly sees in the Masarwa woman what prejudices prevent people from seeing: 'a goddess'. This unprecedented recognition is one which breaks with her Christian frame of reference and constitutes a self-transforming receptivity towards and feeling for the other. She adopts a 'part of the woman', her child. This is not so much a logical effect of her vision as a continuation of it: a ripple effect. Far from being self-contained, this incident or such an incident has the power to revise the history of conquest and domination, for it presents a cross-cultural contact that is not destructive but creative in that preconceptions and biases are 'swallowed', with compassion and humility appearing in their stead.[22]

A repetition of sorts of this initial unprecedented encounter occurs between Margaret and Moleka, a son of a chief, during their first meeting. 'How was it? Something had gone "bang!" inside his chest, and the woman had raised her hand to her heart at the same time' (32). Moleka is transformed from his habitual arrogance by this contact with a 'goddess' (67), as he perceives her, and one of the 'ripple effect' continuances of his transformation occurs when he invites his Masarwa slaves to dine with him. As for Margaret, she receives an inner continuous support from this momentous moment – 'He seemed to have said silently: "Now there are two of you" ' (31) – and it is this that gives her a sense of belonging in a hitherto and otherwise hostile society.

Maru is given to us from the start as a visionary, as one possessed with the vision of a transformed society (7, 68). Like the author, he plots or arranges the unexpected and plans or 'plants' explosive situations. As in an experiment, in the novel different personalities and cultures are thrown together and events constructed to go off like 'bombs' (115), producing new compounds or incalculable re-configurations. I use the word 'experiment' since it is used in the novel. Margaret is said to be the missionary woman's 'experiment' (15); she is said to be part of Maru's 'experiment' (70); she is given art materials to 'experiment' with (100). It could be said, too, that *Maru* is Head's experiment. The term 'experiment' is linked with creativity; 'She had a real living object for her experiment. Who knew what wonder would be created? ' (15). Of Maru it is said: 'He knew true purpose and direction are creative. Creative imagination he had in over-abundance' (58). It is he who gives the art materials to Margaret to 'experiment' with and the drawings she does are hijacked by Maru, who recognises his intuitions and intimate predictions in them: 'He'd stare wistfully at those three beautiful pictures . . . and question himself: "If we have the same dreams, perhaps that means something" ' (67). It means, at any rate, that Margaret is not his pawn, but accomplice. The paintings speak other messages to Maru's heart:

> Look! Don't you see! We are the people who have the strength to build a new world!
>
> (108)
>
> You see, it is I and my tribe who possess the vitality of this country . . .
>
> (109)

It is as if the originating epiphany and sketch of the Masarwa woman as goddess, this repetition of what has never been, this re-vision, continued to repeat itself with increasing realisation until the message reaches the Masarwa people at the end of the book: 'When people of the Masarwa tribe heard about Maru's marriage to one of their own, a door silently opened. . . . The wind of freedom, which was blowing throughout the world for all people turned and flowed into the room . . . their humanity awakened' (126).

'Great gestures have an oceanic effect on society . . .' It can be said that the novel breaks with a history of ever-perpetuated resentment, creating a new society through the 're-visionary' eradication of prejudices.

I would now like to say that *Maru* is a love story, but not in 'our' terms. '[S]omething . . . belonged to her in a way that triumphed over all barriers. Maybe it was not even love as people *usually think of it*. Maybe it was everything else; necessity, recognition, courage, friendship and strength' (99) (my italics). It can be said that the

marriage of Maru and Margaret is a partnership based
on the mutual recognition of the need to build a new
society. Their love is set up in contrast with the 'dog-
love' (28, 35) of other characters; it is rather a love which
includes others and whose desire is the realisation of a
shared vision. I would venture that its desire is, in a
sense, 'political', despite Head's caution over the term. It
is said of Makhaya in Head's *When Rain Clouds Gather*:
'You so easily fell prey to all the hate-making ideologies
. . . these hate-making ideologies in turn gave rise to a
whole set of retrogressive ideas and retrogressive
pride. . . . Yet the very real misery was still there' (80).

I would say that *Maru* is a political text, but not in
'our' terms. Perhaps Head's supposed hatred of 'politics'
is best spoken of as a politics of love: 'That was the
essential nature of their love for each other. It had
included all mankind, and so many things could be said
about it, but the most important was that it equalized all
men and all things.'[23] It might be said that Head's
resistance to 'politics' is to an extent based on a western/
northern implementation and usage of the term. That is,
in her writing she opposes exclusive systems of power
which promote the interests of a race, a nation, at the
expense of concern for and the concerns of the ordinary
man.[24] In Head's books the 'political' is 'down-to-earth'
and 'home-grown': 'Things could start in a small way
with crops like millet, with talks, with simple lectures,
and with some practical work done on the land' (*When
Rain Clouds Gather*, 43). A recurrent topic – with the
senses of both issue and locality – in her works is the
working of a vegetable garden or plot of land. The
itinerary of *Maru* leads to this, where we are shown Maru
in his new beginning as involved in the construction of
vegetable beds with friends: 'Every new and unaccept-
able idea had to be put abruptly into practice, making no
allowance for prejudice' (6). '[D]id it end there? was that
only a beginning?' (7). *Maru* is not the last word. While
in *Maru* Head re-words and re-worlds in accordance

with (her) African experience and (political) vision, the process continues in her other works.[25]

The works of Aidoo and Head might be seen as standing in a revisionary relation to each other, to an extent. In Aidoo's play, *Anowa*,[26] the visionary Anowa leaves her village home with its set ways to marry the devil-may-care man of her choice. However, this marriage does not constitute a liberation as in *Maru*, but turns into a nightmare, for the husband becomes concerned only with making money and more money, taking slaves into his household to help him do so. Anowa, in contradiction to her will, is expected to become the idle, decorative wife, the private property of her patriarchal, capitalist husband who is in league with the forces of colonialism. Eventually the estranged Anowa discovers that her husband is impotent – given as the result of his profit-making efforts – and she exposes him publicly and he shoots himself. Anowa, who cannot go back to her village home, partly because she swore not to and also perhaps because she cannot return to that past and type of society, commits suicide.

Some might say that *Anowa* is pessimistic in a more realistic way than Head's optimistic and visionary *Maru*. However, the works deal with different historical realities. The visionary nature of Head's work has a material and historical basis. For instance, 'the vegetable garden' is not some African Garden of Eden. It is a reference to the cooperative farming Head was involved with in Botswana, where people worked together to find practical solutions to local environmental, social and economic problems for the common good.[27] Similarly, the move away from one tribal organisation to set up another society has a historical precedent in the migrationary history of tribes in the region.[28] The point is that there is a place for Head's vision, especially in so far as Botswana: 'eluded the colonial era . . . it remained black man's country. It was a bewitched crossroad.'[29]

As far as Ghana, Aidoo's birthplace, is concerned, the

corrupt and corrupting destructive forces of colonialism
have to be more directly reckoned with in any reconstruction of society. However, the story does not end
there. In *Anowa* Aidoo re-works traditional legends, as
Head might be said to re-work the fairy-tale, though
Aidoo is working with actual legends to produce a new
legend. As it is said in the play: 'This is the type of
happening out of which we get stories and legends'
(123). It is implied that Anowa will serve to inspire
current and future generations to transform their society,
revising the prejudices of village society and refusing
any marriage with capitalism. One could say that the
place of the visionary Anowa is a future post-colonial
Africa.

## A Country of One's Own?

Woolf's *Three Guineas*[30] examines at length the patriarchal conspiracy of the division of the world into private
and public spheres. As already mentioned, this division
is still the target of feminist critiques. In *Three Guineas*
Woolf presents a certain impasse for women: 'Behind us
lies the patrarchal system; the private house. . . . Before
us lies the public world . . . with its . . . pugnacity, its
greed. The one shuts us up like slaves in a harem; the
other forces us to circle . . . round . . . the sacred tree, of
property' (86). It would seem that women have no real
space, no material sphere, no room of their own, in
which to operate. Significantly, Woolf can only envisage
an engagement with the world at large when the word
'feminist' is burnt: 'The word "feminist" is destroyed;
the air is cleared; and in that clearer air what do we see?
Men and women working together for the same cause'
(117). However, she abandons this 'utopian vision' when
she reconsiders the fact that the public sphere is dominated by or owned by men so that, should women work

with men, women would merge their identities with them (121). This realisation leads to the famous assertion by the 'outsider': ' "As a woman my country is the whole world" ' (125). This assertion can be read as desperately rhetorical; that is, given that women have no sphere of their own, the statement might appear as the gesture of an impossible desire, without a material and historical referent. From a perspective of 'our' times, it might read as a postmodernist fallacy or imaginary of a-historical scattering or placelessness: my here (country) is nowhere ('I have no country'), is everywhere ('. . . is the whole world'). One can strategically tease the statement out further, without specific attention to Woolf's probable intentions. One might see in it the Englishwoman's, or the disinherited outsider's, quest for a home elsewhere, an outside base from which to attack and reclaim her home-which-is-not-*her*-home country. In this respect, the 'whole world' with all its differences would be nothing but a needed site for an 'alterity' *for woman*. This might include the assumption that the whole world is affected by the sexual differential which all-powerfully affects Englishwomen. The claim – 'as a woman my country is the whole world' – would certainly sound suspiciously arrogant or ambitious if addressed to women from, for instance, African countries. However, there is another way of hearing the words. They could indicate a desire to tackle issues of a global significance or problems that go beyond 'sexual difference'. It is this attitude that might strike some accord in African contexts. It is, very generally speaking, an attitude characteristic of some women characters in works by Bessie Head and Ama Ata Aidoo.

'I don't care to be shoved out of the scheme of things. Maybe in some other life I'll *just be a woman* cooking food and having babies, but just now Shylock is demanding his pound of flesh. I have to attend the trial . . .'
Bessie Head, *A Question of Power* (192)

We have been scattered. We wander too far. We are in danger of getting completely lost. We must not allow this to happen. You are saying, 'There goes Sissie again. Forever carrying Africa's problems on her shoulders . . .'
                              Ama Ata Aidoo, *Our Sister Killjoy*[31]


# 'Womanism' and Sisterhoods


Chikwenye Okonjo Ogunyemi writes: 'More often than not, where a white woman writer may be a feminist, a black woman writer is likely to be a "womanist". That is, she will recognize that along with her consciousness of sexual issues, she must incorporate racial, cultural, national, economic and political considerations into her philosophy.' [32] Ogunyemi uses works of Bessie Head and Ama Ata Aidoo to illustrate the 'philosophy' of womanism.

While the distinction between feminism and womanism is a useful and broadly apt one, Ogunyemi's polarisation of the two positions in terms of 'white' and 'black' can be misleading.

Ogunyemi asserts a continuity of experience between Afro–American and African women on the basis of a common racial subjugation. Aidoo's play *The Dilemma of a Ghost*[33] stages a confrontation between a black American woman and the African family and culture she marries into. The woman's American consumerist and individualistic values clash disastrously with the customs and communal values of her African family. The play is about this ideological and cultural incompatibility but it is also about the 'dilemma of a ghost', the role of the cultural go-between, as I will elaborate later.

With regard to the unhappy confrontation between the white feminist and black womanist, Ogunyemi takes a section and an episode in Aidoo's *Our Sister Killjoy* where Marija attempts to befriend and then seduce the unwilling Sissie, as symptomatic. She writes: '[Sissie] rejects feminism as she moves towards womanism' (70). Certainly, the African Sissie does reject the German Marija, which is why I find two readings of Sissie in the light of this relationship bewildering. One is by Katherine Frank who sees Sissie as a proto-lesbian feminist separatist[34] . . . a 'developing' feminist? The other is by Oladele Taiwo who presents Sissie as having an affair with Marija – through editing out Sissie's rather violent reflex rejection of her – and goes on to say that the relationship does not work out because: 'it is an error to think that they (African women) can live a full life without men. This is the significance of the role that Sissie is made to play in the novel.'[35] For Frank, a feminist, Sissie is a feminist–separatist. For Taiwo, an (African) man, the (African) Sissie necessarily cannot live without men.

What the above critics ignore is the chronology of the text. Sissie leaves Marija and goes on to confront her African male compatriots abroad in the hope of persuading them to return home, unsuccessfully in so far as they are lost in dreams of making it in Europe. In my reading, this is precisely what Sissie does not want to do. Her rejection of Marija is not simply a sexual matter nor a matter of sexual politics – Marija can hardly be taken to represent a feminist – but rather an unwillingness to be complicit with the fantasies and desires of the European woman and consumed by a European consumerist amnesia.[36] It can be suggested that the above entities recapitulate the error of Marija, the error of appropriating Sissie in the expectation that she can be made to supply a need or a lack.

After referring to *Our Sister Killjoy* in terms of the conflict between white feminists and black womanists, Ogunyemi goes on to say: 'Similarly, in *A Question of Power* Head demonstrates, through the portrait of

Camilla, that the white woman yearns to control black men and women by humiliating them. She is stopped by an open confrontation' (70). What is not mentioned is that this open confrontation is instigated and carried out by another white woman, Birgitte, who tells Camilla she is a racist. As is typical of Head, there is a refusal to set up a stereotype of 'the white woman': Camilla is a patronising racist; Birgitte is a friend and ally of the autobiographically based Elizabeth.

From the above two instances in the texts by Aidoo and Head, it might seem that Aidoo indicates that a close bond with a European woman is impossible, while Head indicates that it is a possibility. However, their positions are not as polarised as that. In *A Question of Power* Birgitte, who has come out to teach in Botswana, is a sensitive, sympathetic person and is able to see eye to eye with Elizabeth on certain matters. That is, in some respects at least, they can share a vision. In *Our Sister Killjoy* Marija is ignorant, though curious, of African realities and she is oblivious of African history and seemingly of the imperialist and racist history of her own country. If there are crucial issues of political commitment which Sissie and her African brothers cannot see eye to eye on, Marija is at a much further remove, lost in her own empty marital nest.

What is this 'company of feminists'? One way of avoiding the binary opposition of white–feminist and black–womanist would be to say that feminism is not 'only white'. It is not just some multi-national company; it is not just a sort of imported commodity. It is not something that white women introduce like new missionaries. It is those things; but not only. The danger of saying that feminism is foreign is that this can lead to the oppositional formulation of a traditional African womanhood: a constructed or invented traditionalism that may be used against the independence of African women.[37]

# Brotherhoods?

One might begin to concentrate on concerns of specific importance to women in the works of Ama Ata Aidoo and Bessie Head through a consideration of their respective depictions and critiques of different forms of irresponsibility or faithlessness in African men.

In Bessie Head's work there is a recurrent critique of the promiscuous man, whose portrait she gives in *Serowe*: 'a gay, dizzy character on a permanent round of drink and women, full of shoddy values and without any sense of responsibility for the children he so haphazardly procreates' (60). He, this type, is not only the perpetuator of the breakdown of family life, but a product of this in the first place. Head notes in *Serowe* that when Christianity was introduced and imposed: 'the discipline which people now had to impose on themselves was internal and private. People might not have realised this, and this might account for the almost complete breakdown of family life in Bamangwato country, which under traditional custom was essential for the survival of the tribe' (xiv–xv). In her story 'The Collector of Treasures'[38] Head gives another portrait and further analysis of the promiscuous male. She explains that: 'The colonial era and the period of migratory mining labour to South Africa . . . broke the old, traditional form of family life and for long periods a man was separated from his wife and children . . . he then becomes "the boy" of the white man and a machine-tool of the South African mines' (92). She goes on to explain that while Independence with its new localisation programme provided the opportunity for a new family life it also brought jobs with high salaries. The African man without the inner resources to build a new family and social order lost himself further in a dizzy round of dissipation.

First detached from communal discipline, the man behaves as an individual 'free' to take on responsibility *or not*; he is then further detached from family responsibilities through the institution of migrant labour and moreover degraded by his South African employers, by which time he lacks a sense of self-respect, respect for others and a sense of collective responsibility. This African problem can be said to be a colonially induced one and an almost exclusively male phenomenon. That is, women, generally speaking, were less ravaged by colonialism, not being a migrant labour force and not being the recipients of the new high-salaried jobs. This, by the way, explains the womanist position from a local perspective rather than in relation to white feminism. For, it could be said, the women of the villages continued and took upon themselves the responsibility of the survival of family and community.[39]

It is in 'The Collector of Treasures' especially, as well as in other stories in the volume of that title, that we are given portraits of such village women alongside the portraits of fickle and sometimes vicious – in so far as they recuperate their esteem through degrading others – men.

> They had asked me –
>
> a worthy friend and
> a loving brother –
>
> to 'stop shouldering
> the world's troubles.'
> – one meaning Africa
> the other woman –
>
> Ama Ata Aidoo, 'Routine Drugs' I[40]

Ama Ata Aidoo offers portraits of brothers who are politically fickle or faithless to Africa or who fail to involve themselves in the needs of their countries. It is particularly in *Our Sister Killjoy* that the diaspora of the educated African elite is addressed, where the protagonist, Sissie, indicates that participation of her brothers in some crazy notion of a 'universal brotherhood' is tantamount to forgetting who they are, where they came from, and so the tie with their true families and peoples. The problem is not confined to men – sisters are also part of the educated elite and its diaspora – but it is mainly men to whom the situation pertains. This is so in so far as educational systems and the stratification of the job market – both as set up in colonial Ghana and as existing in the West – serve to privilege the male individual.

Sissie addresses the problem in 'A Love Letter', a letter which is in context addressed specifically to one man. In this letter she considers the reasons why she cannot sustain a relationship with him: 'Now it is quite clear even to me that having political quarrels with a man or insisting that once he has finished his political studies abroad he should go home, are not any of the more recognised ways to enchant him' (118). It can be suggested that for Sissie the relationship is not viable because love has to include or be included by shared 'political' priorities and commitments, as indicated in my analysis of *Maru*. More generally, the picture we are given is of men who do not expect women to be so politically insistent: 'No, My Darling: it seems as if so much of the meekness you and all the brothers expect of me and all the sisters is that which is really western' (117). In something of an over-simplification, but for the sake of a general statement, it can be said that the 'error' of the errant men is that they would live as private individuals, unencumbered with urgent commitments beyond their careers, whereas it is Our Sister Killjoy who would refuse them this licence and ease of conscience. While they 'improve' themselves, little is done for those back home, especially the people in the villages, especially the Mothers for whom they say they are making money (123).

But there are other versions. In 'A Collector of Treasures' we have, beside the portrait of the degenerate

Garesego, a portrait of the wonderfully caring Paul Thebolo. In Aidoo's story, entitled 'Other Versions', a son who has gone to study in America has it brought home to him that good intentions towards his Mother are not enough; he realises that a wider and stronger commitment is needed.

Earlier I spoke of the line or affiliation between the educated woman and the village woman in Aidoo's work. Also, I promised to take up further issues of *A Dilemma of a Ghost*. In this play, the ghost is Ato who has studied in America and who returns with his black American wife. I have spoken of the clash between cultures, but not of Ato's role as a go-between. He is in the position of the interpreter,[41] possessed of different languages, conversant in different cultural discourses. As such, he has the responsibility of explaining his and his family's culture to his wife and his wife's culture to his family. More than this, he has the responsibility of not setting up western knowledge as 'more knowing' or knowing more, and he has the responsibility of preserving the knowledge and ways of knowing of his own culture, as opposed to translating it into the language of the Other. Ato fails in his role because he is torn between the two cultures, as if he no longer had a country of his own. His mother upbraids him:

> ESI: You do not even tell us about anything and we assemble our medicines together. While all the time your wife laughs at us because we do not understand about such things . . .
>
> (51)

With Ato's failure as interpreter, his mother brings his wife –who has been seeking her lost Mother country – home to her: 'Come, my child' (52).

Now, Aidoo and Head, in their own ways and to an extent, are engaged in the role of the interpreter. They record their respective African cultures, with particular concern for the concerns of the women within those cultures. They record the social and cultural upheavals as well as the continuities, the aspirations as well as the traditions, and in doing so, they inform the present and future with the past, and the past with a 'knowledge gained since', in a phrase of *Our Sister Killjoy*. While these two women writers do this, they must and do resist the danger of their works being translated into the language of the Other.[42] english literature is not English. The uncapitalised 'e' is not a grammatical or typographical error. I will leave the rest for you, and you to revise.

# Notes

1. Gayatri Spivak has repeatedly spoken of the need for such self-awareness. See e.g. *In Other Worlds: Essays in Cultural Politics* (New York, Methuen, 1987).
2. This was at an informal gathering in Zimbabwe.
3. See Edward Said's critique of exclusivism in 'Orientalism Reconsidered', *Race and Class*, **27** (2) (Autumn, 1985), 15.
4. Frederic Jameson, 'Third World Literature in the Age of Multinational Capitalism', *Social Text*, **15** (Fall, 1985), 66. For an important discussion of this essay, see Aijaz Ahmad, 'Jameson's Rhetoric of Otherness and the 'National Allegory', *Social Text*, **17** (Fall, 1987).
5. Zora Neale Hurston, *Mules and Men* (1935; Bloomington, Indiana University Press, 1978), 4.
6. Mahasweta Devi, 'Drapuadi', trans. and ed. Gayatri Spivak, in *In Other Worlds*, 194.
7. Ama Ata Aidoo, 'The Message', in *No Sweetness Here*, 1970 (Harlow, Longman, 1988).
8. This point is made by Sara Chetin in her paper, 'The Use of Story-Telling Techniques: A Comparative Study of Bessie Head and Ama Ata Aidoo' (ACLALS Silver Jubilee Conference, August, 1989).
9. I am thinking of Evelyn Waugh's *Black Mischief*, Joyce Cary's *Mister Johnson* and William Boyd's *A Good Man In Africa*.

10. Cheik Anta Diop, *The Cultural Unity of Negro Africa*, 1959 (Paris, Presence Africaine, 1962), 71. He speaks of the Ashanti. Chikwenye Okonjo Ogunyemi, writing of another text by Aidoo, notes that Aidoo is an Akan by birth and sees her as embracing Akan matrilineal culture. See Ogunyemi, 'Womanism: The Dynamics of the Black Female Novel in English', *Signs*, 11 (1) (Autumn, 1985), 75.
11. Jameson, 69.
12. Stephen Slemon, 'Monuments of Empire: Allegory/Counter-Discourse/Post-Colonial Writing', *Kunapipi*, **IX** (3) (1987), 13. I cannot enter here into the respective thought-provoking debates of Jameson and Slemon or present Ahmad's detailed critique of Jameson. However, a few of the issues these critics and theorists serve to raise will be indirectly and strategically addressed in my following arguments.
13. See Spivak, 'Explanation and Culture: Marginalia', in *In Other Worlds*, 103.
14. Head's work, in particular *Maru* and perhaps particularly in the context of South African literature, is sometimes read in terms of a retreat from politics. See e.g. Odalele Taiwo, *Female Novelists of Modern Africa* (London, Macmillan, 1984), 190.
15. Bessie Head, *Maru*, 1971 (Harare, Zimbabwe Publishing House, 1985).
16. Bessie Head, *Serowe: Village of the Rain Wind*, 1981 (London, Heinemann, 1988), xv.
17. Bessie Head, 'The Deep River: A Story of Ancient Tribal Migration', in *The Collector of Treasures* (London, Heinemann, 1977).
18. Aijaz Ahmad, 'Jameson's Rhetoric of Otherness and the "National Allegory" ', *Social Text*, 17 (Fall, 1987), 23.
19. Christine Qunta, *Women in South Africa*, ed. Qunta (London, Allison and Busby, 1987), 190.
20. See Bessie Head, *A Bewitched Crossroad: An African Saga* (Cape, SA, A. D. Donker, 1984).
21. Bessie Head, *When Rain Clouds Gather*, 1969 (London, Heinemann, 1985), 202.
22. My reading here of Bessie Head is obliquely informed by the poetics and views of Wilson Harris. See, e.g. Wilson

Harris, 'Adversarial Contexts and Creativity', *New Left Review*, 154 (November–December 1985).

23. Bessie Head, *A Question of Power*, 1974 (London, Heinemann, 1985), 202.

24. In the works preceding and following after *Maru*, the local 'grassroots socialism' is also shown to be transnational in so far as people from other countries are involved.

25. For instance, in *A Question of Power* the female protagonist is given as but the pawn in a power contest between two men; and then, Head's story 'The Deep River' is a more romantic version of *Maru*, while an historical and political version of the story is given in *A Bewitched Crossroads*. In broader terms, I would suggest that Head goes on to treat tribal societies more sympathetically and, in a sense, less subjectively, as she ceases to conflate the narrative of self-redemption with the representation of other constituencies.

26. Ama Ata Aidoo. *Anowa and The Dilemma of a Ghost*, 1965 (Harlow, Longman, 1985).

27. See the autobiographical *A Question of Power* and the historical *Serowe*.

28. See Head, *A Bewitched Crossroad.*

29. *ibid.*, 196.

30. Virginia Woolf, *Three Guineas*, introd. Hermione Lee (London, Hogarth, 1986).

31. Ama Ata Aidoo, *Our Sister Killjoy*, 1977 (Harlow, Longman, 1982), 118.

32. Chikwenye Okonjo Ogunyemi, 'Womanism: The Dynamics of the Black Female Novel in English', *Signs*, 11 (1) (Autumn, 1985).

33. In Aidoo, *Anowa and The Dilemma of a Ghost.*

34. Katherine Frank, 'Women Without Men: The Feminist Novel in Africa', in *Women in African Literature Today* (London, James Currey and Africa World Press, 1987).

35. Oladele Taiwo, *Female Novelists of Modern Africa* (London, Macmillan, 1984), 26.

36. For my reading of the text in question, see ' "Dangerous Knowledge" and The Poetics of Survival: A Reading of *Our Sister Killjoy* and *A Question of Power*', in *Motherlands*, ed. Susheila Nasta (London, The Women's Press, 1990).

37. See Terence Ranger, 'The Invention of Tradition in Colonial Africa', in *The Invention of Tradition,* eds. Eric Hobsbawm and Terence Ranger (Cambridge, Cambridge University Press, 1983).

38. Head, 'The Collector of Treasures', in *The Collector of Treasures.*

39. As a cross-reference, Vandana Shiva in her book *Staying Alive: Women, Ecology and Development* (London, Zed Books, 1988), writes: 'Women of the Third World have conserved those categories of thought and action which make survival possible. . . . Ecology movements, women's movements and peace movements across the world can draw inspiration from these categories of opposition and challenge to the dominant categories of western patriarchy . . .' (xx).

40. Aidoo, 'Routine Drugs' I, in *Someone Talking to Some-time* (Harare, The College Press, 1985).

41. This discussion of the role of the interpreter draws on *The Empire Writes Back,* eds. Bill Ashcroft *et al.* (London, Routledge, 1989), 80.

42. For a further discussion of these and related issues, see my essay ' "Dangerous Knowledge" and the Poetics of Survival' and other essays in the collection, *Motherlands.*

# Chronological Table of Works
## Eavan Boland
*Born 1944*

### Poetry

1967  *New Territory*
1975  *The War Horse*
1980  *In Her Own Image*
1982  *Night Feed*
1986  *The Journey and Other Poems*

### Essays

1987  'The Woman Poet: Her Dilemma', *American Poetry Review*
1987  'The Woman Poet in a National Tradition', *Studies*

## Medbh McGuckian
*Born 1950*

1980  *Portrait of Joanna*
1980  *Single Ladies*
1982  *The Flower Master*
1984  *Venus and the Rain*
1988  *On Ballycastle Beach*

### Essays

1981  'Medbh McGuckian', *Trio Poetry 2*
1988  'Medbh McGuckian', *Map-Makers Colours: New Poets of Northern Ireland*

# 9

# Contemporary Irish Women Poets

## The Privatisation of Myth

### Clair Wills

The ruined maid complains in Irish
Ocean has scattered her dream of fleets,
The Spanish prince has spilled his gold

And failed her. Iambic drums
Of English beat the woods where her poets
Sink like Onan. Rush-light, mushroom-flesh,

She fades from their somnolent clasp
Into ringlet breath and dew,
The ground possessed and repossessed.[1]

Possession, dispossession and repossession, in the context of literature by contemporary Irish women, are not only powerful reminders of Ireland's colonial and post-colonial history but also image a way of approaching women poets' relation to tradition. When the nation is represented as one version of femininity, the mother-land, when the dispossession of the Irish is figured in terms of exile from the mother's body, the mother's tongue, what access to legitimating roles, what means of 'possessing' a history or a tradition do Irish women have? The desire to legitimise oneself, to legalise one's position, to submit to an authority (that of the father) in order to accede to it, presupposes acceptance of the supremacy of tradition. The process of legitimation asks us to fit ourselves into a family narrative in which goods, and the authority to own them, pass from father to son. But the daughter's inheritance requires not simply a diversion of familial chattels; it necessitates a disruption (an evolution) of tradition. In the literary system it performs a mutation of genre. This essay focuses on the generic 'disruption' effected in work by contemporary Irish women poets (specifically Eavan Boland and Medbh McGuckian) and examines poetry which questions current definitions of cultural and national identity in Ireland, in particular the repeated association of the use of myth and dialect and the writer's attempt to link herself with, to repossess, a history and a community.[2]

It is now a commonplace that the inherited tradition constitutes a difficulty for women poets. As Margaret Homans points out in *Women Writers and Poetic Identity*, where the major literary tradition normatively identifies the figure of the poet as masculine, and voice as masculine property, women writers 'cannot see their minds as androgynous, or as sexless, but must take part in a self-definition by contraries'.[3] For Homans there are two main difficulties facing the woman poet: her association with nature and her exclusion from the traditional identification of the speaking subject as male. Within the Irish tradition, however, the woman writer must also inevitably come to terms with the Catholic representations of the female as virgin handmaiden or equally desexualised mother, and with the nationalist trope of Ireland as the motherland. In an important sense this trope derives from the colonial moment in Ireland, whose legacy thus poses certain problems for the Irish woman writer. For the feminisation of Ireland and the Irish as a whole in colonial discourse has shaped post-colonial attempts to redefine Irish identity. The traditionally nationalist post-col-

onial 're-naming' of Ireland serves only to reconfirm the
mythology of woman – through Catholic representations of the female as virgin handmaiden or equally
desexualised mother, and through the nationalist trope
of Ireland as the motherland.

In a recent essay entitled 'The Floozie in the Jacuzzi'
Irish feminist Ailbhe Smyth ponders the particular
problematics of culture and identity for Irish women,
and specifically the difficulty of finding a place from
which to 'rename' themselves. Where femininity stands
as symbol of the nation, how can woman 'consume' the
symbol without 'erasing' herself?[4] She points out that,
long denied the power to name, naming in post-colonial
Irish culture has achieved an overdetermined status.
Smyth draws a parallel between the colonisation of
Ireland and the patriarchal definition of woman but
maintains that women experience dispossession differently – because doubly colonised they do not have access
to the naming process by which definitions of Irish
identity are promulgated. Delineations of the lost
motherland take place through the metaphor of woman
and 'we are lured into a belief in the *significance* of the
representation. But the message carried is paradoxically
(?) one of our in/non-significance. Woman-as-image and
woman-as-spectator participate in the reproduction of
our own *meaninglessness* in culture.'[5] Moreover, already
'inhabited' by meanings, what strategies are open to
women whereby they may define their own meanings
without thereby feeding into the existing mythology?
Smyth approaches the issue in terms of the possible
strategic defence positions available to women; she advocates a type of *écriture feminine*, an oblique discourse
from women's marginalised position which will disrupt
spurious notions of Irish unity of culture and identity.
And indeed, this analysis of the role or mask the woman
writer should adopt as a shield against the public female
stereotype does correspond to the writers' own understanding of their projects.

All the poets under discussion are concerned with the possibilities of using woman as a metaphor without merely reducing her to a figure for something else. The motherland trope is rejected not simply because it is an abstraction, but also because it legitimises a particular version of historical and political rhetoric. Moreover, despite their many differences, both political and aesthetic, these poets have tried to find ways in which they can work to some extent within the Gaelic or native Irish tradition, rather than simply rejecting it outright, since to reject it would involve accepting some sort of place within an English tradition – more particularly the English tradition of the well-made Movement lyric, with its aesthetic of 'privacy'. Particularly for McGuckian, as for the Irish language poet Nuala Ni Dhomnhaill, this process has involved an attempt to invest an older figure of femininity with a positive meaning for women.[6] Proinsias MacCana argues that what occurs as colonisation progresses is a desexualisation, through the twin pressures of catholicism and celticism, of the more positive and powerful Gaelic figure of the land of Ireland as sovereignty goddess.[7] Since in eighteenth- and nineteenth-century Irish literature the available roles for women seem to be polarised into virgin daughter on one hand, or equally chaste mother on the other, the poets have attempted to reach further back into the Gaelic tradition and to retrieve from the mythic and early Irish past an image of woman as sexually and socially active, desiring and powerful.

Yet, a number of theoretical problems are posed by this reading of contemporary work in terms of re-configuration of tradition. To interpret the 're-writing' of the myth of the motherland by poets such as Boland and McGuckian in terms of an attempt to negotiate a place in a retroactively created Irish literary tradition obscures the radical redefinition of the role of poet in Ireland which their work necessitates. The acknowledged desire on the part of these poets to legitimise their work by deferring to the authority of their literary heritage (a practice Jurij Tynyanov terms 'traditionalism') obscures their poetry's disruption of the very basis of the tradition itself.[8]

As I will argue, the poets are engaged in a tropological 'privatisation' of the myths of Mother Ireland, but once this strategy is defined as an attempt to undermine the existing stereotype of Irish femininity by the 'truths' of women's personal experience, it becomes all too easy to fault them for simply creating new stereotypes. For example, along with the turn to archaic sexualised femininity marked in Ni Dhomnhaill and McGuckian's work come new problems of stereotyping, which bear on the ability of the woman to take an active role in the history of the nation. There is a danger, more or less present in all these writers, that they will simply replace a passive female figure waiting for her sons to fight for her, with a sexually, but not politically, active earth mother, again dependent on her sons for a link with 'actual' history. For the figure of the sovereignty goddess is one which confers power and kingship on the men who sleep with her, rather than retaining it for herself. Furthermore, a more general difficulty with an analysis which concentrates on the 'personalisation' of early Irish 'female' myth and folklore is that the use of such personae may merely serve to reinforce a concept of the 'eternal' feminine. The body of the myth thus acts as a 'container' for the body of the woman. If definitions of femininity and nationhood are to be questioned the process of 'raiding' the past must involve an interrogation, not simply a reconfirmation, of existing symbols; but recent interpretations of the poets' work have tended to stress their continuity with rather than their difference from 'tradition'. So, for example, in an examination of modern Irish poetry's 're-use' of folkloric themes Gearoid Denvir notes how Ni Dhomnhiall's recourse to ancient Irish female 'archetypes' such as the goddesses Mor-Rion, Badb and Macha enables her to express the 'most genuine voice of the female experience', and he comes close to a dangerous equation between the two.[9] The theoretical distortion involved in such interpretations lies in their acceptance of the myth as 'origin', compromising any alternative message the contemporary utterance may carry by denying that historical and individual articulations of myths have bearing not only on their meaning, but also on their function in contemporary writing.

## Mother Irelands

Recent discussion of the relationship between myth or tradition in Ireland, and the future, has tried to suggest ways in which the past can be 'raided' in order to create a utopian vision of Ireland which differs from both traditional and modernist conceptions (so, for example, Richard Kearney argues forcibly not for a transposition of myths of the past into the future but for a continual interrogation of myths in order to *create* myths for the future, along the lines of Walter Benjamin's concept of 'revolutionary nostalgia').[10] Women poets, however, are characteristically ignored in studies of the re-reading of tradition, despite an awareness, notably in Cairns and Richards' work, that questions of national identity are intimately bound up with questions of sexuality.[11]

Two main issues arise from the particular mythic paradigm of Ireland as a woman, as critics such as Elizabeth Cullingford and Richard Kearney have argued.[12] The progressive idealisation of Irish womanhood can be traced in the literature from the seventeenth century, and it is connected, among other things, to the fact of English colonialism in Ireland. As Cullingford points out, historically the allegorical identification of Ireland with a woman, variously personified as the Shan Van Vocht (the poor old woman), Kathleen Ni

Houlihan or Mother Eire, 'has served two distinct ideological purposes: as applied by Irish men it has helped to
imprison Irish women in a straitjacket of purity and
passivity; and as applied by well-meaning English
cultural imperialists it has imprisoned the whole Irish
race in a debilitating stereotype, or in a fruitless
inversion of that stereotype'.[13] The motherland trope,
then, in all its guises, is like a pin which connects sexual
stereotyping with political and cultural domination of
the Irish – thus the ways in which the poets are radical in
terms of sexual and gender politics bear on issues of
imperialism and definitions of national identity.

As a consequence, merely to assume the role and
function of poet depends on a certain stance in relation
to this trope of the motherland. For the representation of
the Irish land as a woman stolen, raped, possessed by the
alien invader is not merely one mythic narrative among
many but, in a literary context, it is *the* myth, its
permutations so various and ubiquitous that it can be
hard to recognise them for what they are. The trope
functions not only as the means by which the poet can
lament the loss of the land but also, through his
linguistic embodiment of it, the means by which he may
'repossess' it. The structure through which the poet
obtains this mandate is complex, but its critical ingredi-
ent is an already poeticised (mythic) political discourse
of the nation which enables the poet to act as spokesperson for his community – 'public voice' of his mute
and beleaguered rural 'tribe'. Since 1975 (in other words
since the publication of Heaney's *North*) discussion of
the use of myth in contemporary poetry has centred to a
remarkable extent on a single set of concerns, which
might be summarised as the 'humanism v. atavism'
debate.[14] Briefly, either myth constitutes the means of
access to the primitive, atavistic, barbarian and of course
feminine, part of Irish society and the Irish psyche; or
else the use of myth is a corruption of pure poetic
imaginative discourse and an aestheticisation of politics

which leads inexorably to fascism, or at least to militant republicanism. The interesting fact about this second view is that it believes like the first that myth is a door into archaic atavistic tribalism; the only difference is that it would rather that door remained closed. It is through myth that the artist as spokesperson can symbolise the 'atavistic' thought of his people, without which any understanding of Ireland's political situation remains merely rationalist and therefore impartial. So Heaney can describe his poetry without embarrassment as 'a kind of slow, obstinate papish burn, emanating from the ground I was brought up on', implying that it is continuous with, almost an extension of, the 'mythos' of his dispossessed community.[15] The nationalist poet's role is to bear witness, thus enabling 'a restoration of the culture to itself', a restoration which like all restorations opposes itself to modernity, losing itself in a nostalgic celebration of a pure, organic and monocultural society.

Thus the motherland trope poses a very specific problem for the Irish woman writer. For the writer who rejects the association of woman and land thereby questions the relationship between poet and community, and the *type* of community it posits – one which excludes women. In her essay 'The Woman Poet in a National Tradition' Eavan Boland points out that the question of her relationship to the English tradition is complicated by a femaleness which sets her apart from 'the sense of community which came early and easily to male contemporaries'.[16] Put crudely, the problem is that not all members of the community can relate to the received public and universal myth successfully.[17]

I wanted to relocate myself within the Irish poetic tradition. A woman poet is rarely regarded as an automatic part of a national poetic tradition. There has been a growing tendency, in the past few years, for academics and critics to discuss woman's poetry as a sub-culture within a larger tradition, thereby depriving both of a possible enrichment. I felt it vital that women poets such as myself should establish a discourse with the idea of a nation, should bring to it a sense of the emblematic relationship between the feminine experience and the national past.

The truths of womanhood and the defeats of a nation. An impossible intersection? At first sight perhaps. Yet the more I thought of it, the more it seemed to me that if I could find the poetic truth of the first then, by virtue of that alone, I would repossess the second. If so, then Irishness and womanhood, those tormenting fragments of my youth, would at last become metaphors for one another.[18]

To gain a place in the construction of an idea of a nation Boland turns to experiential testimony. The linkage of femininity and the idea of the nation is accepted, and her objections turn on the simplifications which both have undergone in male writing. Her alternative is summed up in a poem such as 'Mise Eire'.

'Mise Eire' ('I am Ireland') was the normal response of the beautiful and radiant maidens of the eighteenth- and nineteenth-century Aisling ('Vision') poems on interrogation concerning their ideneity. After a series of questions had been put to them by the male poet, such as 'Are you Venus, or Aphrodite, or Helen fair? Are you Aurora, or the goddess Flora?,' the maiden would reply, 'I am Ireland and I am sick because I have no true and manly husband' (since the men in Ireland had been cowed into submission by the force of English imperialism). Boland replaces the generalised, idealised Aisling figure whose function is to remind her menfolk that they must fight the English for her (or await Jacobite forces) if they are to repossess their homeland, with the imagined history of a single emigrant woman. Her deprivation and prostitution in England or America, Boland implies, stand as an historical corrective to mythic representations of the nation:

No. I won't go back.
My roots are brutal:

I am the woman –
a sloven's mix
of silk at the wrists,
a sort of dove-strut
in the precincts of the garrison –

who practises
the quick frictions,
the rictus of delight
and gets cambric for it,
rice-coloured silks.

I am the woman
in the gansy-coat
on board the 'Mary Belle',
in the huddling cold.
holding her half-dead baby to her
as the wind shifts East
and North over the dirty
water of the wharf

mingling the immigrant
guttural with the vowels
of homesickness who neither
knows nor cares that

a new language
is a kind of scar
and heals after a while
into a passable imitation
of what went before.[19]

Rather than draw a metaphorical parallel between one woman's personal history, her loss of national 'heritage', and the breach in the presumed continuity of Irish history caused by English colonial rule, the poem insists on the radical disjuncture between the histories of the emigrant woman and her nation. It is impossible to use the woman as a symbol for the fate of the land because she has left it; unlike the deserted maidens of the traditional Aisling she is not there 'at home' to be repossessed.[20] Hence, for Boland, the 'real story' of Irish women will combat the falsification and abstraction of the motherland myth. Her argument could be summed up as a version of 'No taxation without representation'; Boland, in effect, is a suffragette. She seeks not to challenge the basis of the poet's authority, but to widen the political constituency, adding women to the electoral rolls. But of course poetry cannot simply add the 'private' or 'personal' experience of women to its dominant structures, and Boland herself does not so much represent female experience as trope it.

This desire to celebrate 'personal truths' arises out of a confusion regarding the status of privacy and the domestic in relation to the 'public' national image of femininity. For the domestic image has a legal as well as a poetic expression. In post-colonial Ireland it stands alongside the legal construction by the Irish Free State of a sphere of private domesticity, and De Valera's insistence on a constitutional definition of a woman's place as in the home (or as he put it, the comely maiden's place in the cosy homestead).[21] Paradoxically, it is because of the construction of such a sphere that the concept of 'mothering' can continue to stand as ideological confirmation of the representation of the Irish nation as a traditional rural community. To investigate the 'personal dimension' of the motherland myth is thus a contradiction in terms, not merely because a myth cannot be 'undone' by reality, but because that personal experience is already 'public'. Privacy, defined as the domestic, is not the residence of the unique and individual, the non-communicable. It is a social institution with genres, codes and a semantics. Moreover 'Mise Eire' knows this. For all that we seem to be offered a woman's 'private' thoughts on her 'personal' situation, what the poem in fact stresses is that her sexuality is publicly owned (through prostitution), her personal story *is* a public narrative. So even though one might want to reject the symbolisation of the dispossession of the nation through a woman's rape, any attempt to be possessive in one's turn, even self-possessed, is doomed to failure. In this sense the slogan 'the personal is political' carries not the liberal message that the lot of individual women should be added into the account, but that the personal as individual is a chimera.

What is actually at stake in these arguments is not a modification of tradition to fit changing social circumstances, as Boland suggests, but following Tynyanov, a 'mutation' of the literary system in which the semantics of domesticity takes on a particular literary function. A trope of privacy appears in place of the motherland trope, the function of which is to allow women to accede to the role of poet.

Of course, if woman as national monument is all too public a figure, women's traditional confinement in the 'private' sphere of the home is mirrored by a tendency to read women's writing in terms of its personal significance, for what it has to say about love, marriage and the condition of being female, rather than for its insights into the world of work and politics.[22] The difficulty of analysing privacy as a code for the domestic is compounded by the traditional habit of the reading of women's texts through an autobiographical grid. Nevertheless, despite the dangers of a reading which would merely serve to reconfirm notions of women's concerns as primarily personal, it is important to be aware of the ways in which a seemingly 'personal' or confessional poet such as McGuckian is radical precisely in her attempts to talk about public and political events through the medium of 'private' symbolism. The recontextualisation or re-accentation of myths of womanhood can be read as a 'personalisation' or 'privatisation' of the myths of Mother Ireland, but it is for its consequences for the relationship between poet and community, rather than for its 'truthfulness', that we can read in this gesture of 'privatisation', that beacon of Thatcherite values, the mark of political responsibility.

Medbh McGuckian is generally read as a poet

obsessively concerned with femininity, with her personal life, even with the dimensions of her house, to the exclusion of 'wider', more 'public', concerns. She characteristically reads public and political events through the changes occurring in the contours of her body, and her experience of sex and childbirth. This is perhaps precisely because as a woman writer she lies outside the tradition of poetry as public statement – she does not have access to the language of poetic 'responsibility'. Indeed, her only 'public' discourse is one about women, but it is inevitably read in terms of its private significance (i.e. as confessional, rather than as an intervention in Ireland's public or civic discourses about sexuality and nationhood).

However, it is odd that she should be read as a confessional poet, as in fact it is impossible to glean much about her life from the typically enigmatic, veiled style the poems employ. McGuckian seems to be looking for a way to speak about women's experience which avoids being 'investigated' – a riddling discourse which will be public and at the same time distinctively different, disruptive of the normative codes of literary discourse. She uses a repeated image of language as a veil which may be lifted only for the ideal reader who will not react by simplifying the complex nature of the 'life' which is being offered up for inspection. 'Openness' connotes betrayal; she wants to tell a personal narrative, the story of giving birth, or of a marriage, but she is wary of 'opening herself up' to be probed by a public readership. So she says, in discussing the difficulties of writing about a private life: 'I feel that you're going public – by writing the poem you're becoming a whore. You're selling your soul which is worse than any prostitution – in a sense you're vilifying your mind. I do feel that must be undertaken with the greatest possible fastidiousness.'[23] Such 'explanations' of her project naturally encourage readings of her work as concerned with individual female experience. A different reading would argue that the poems provide not veiled representations but allegories of privacy; the difficult style connotes or signals private meaning, through a play on the ambiguity of the term privacy. (Again what this equivalency suggests is the 'individuality' of the private sphere. Codes of domesticity mesh with codes of impenetrability to imply that rather than a social institution, a shared or typical life, domesticity is experienced *personally*, femininity is unique.)

However, the private and personal in her poems may act as another type of veil in McGuckian's work – a veil which obscures her political statements. Indeed, in part she comes across the problem of 'publicity' precisely because she wants to use the private narrative or experience as a metaphor for the public. Instances of private life in many of her poems 'stand for' public events – there is thus a metaphorical relationship between them, so that in some sense the experience becomes 'generalised' or 'typical'. For in fact she shares with Boland the belief that one of the functions of her writing is to 'speak for' the community of women, so that the personal recording of her everyday life becomes analogous to a type of history writing:

> I'm trying to make the dead women of Ireland, who I am the living memory of, I'm trying to give them articulation, if anything. In that sense I'm trying to make their lives not a total waste, that they didn't live in vain, that they have no record at all.[24]

But in addition personal history is used metaphorically to present national history – for example, the nationalist response to the Hunger Strikers of 1981 is examined through the metaphor of the female body and childbirth in 'Dovecote', as is the dispossession of the Catholics during the plantation of Ulster in 'The Heiress'. One is an analogue for the other.[25]

This type of metaphorical approach is strikingly

different from Eavan Boland's. Boland wants to use women's experience as an example of what has been erased from Irish history and literature. But for McGuckian it is not the *content* of women's histories and experiences which suggest a lack in the national ideal, for in a sense McGuckian's obscure and enigmatic private 'worlds' are *contentless*. Instead she presents women's experience as unknowable and therefore *useless*. Her project is the very opposite of Boland's; by figuring sex and childbirth in language which serves to veil rather than represent she takes sexuality *out* of the public sphere. Since sexuality is already publicly 'owned', specifically by the Catholic Church in alliance with the State in Ireland, to shroud the female in mystery may be the only way to resist her appropriation.[26]

## Privatisation and Historical Responsibility

If one problem with the repeated metaphor of woman-as-topography, the motherland, is the effacement of the materiality of the woman's body, the reduction of her sexuality to her status as the passive object of desire (what McGuckian calls 'all those poems about Ireland laid out as a passive woman in a bed and mounted'[27]), a more general difficulty is the elision of history which the use of such mythic metaphors demands. Heaney's poem 'Act of Union' describes sex with his wife as the rape of Ireland by the male English soldier: 'And I am still imperially/Male, leaving you with the pain,/The rending process in the colony,/The battering ram, the boom burst from within,/The act sprouted an obstinate fifth column/Whose stance is growing unilateral.'[28] The Act of Union becomes a struggle between primitive, landed, situated femininity and rational, social, organised masculinity which creates the inhabitants of the bastard province Northern Ireland.[29] In questioning the symbolism of such poems of dispossession, and linguistic repossession, I do not want to deny the traumatic effects of the plantation and the mass dispossession of Catholics in Gaelic Ulster and the rest of Ireland. Rather, my concern is with what is historically elided in the attempt to describe such events through the metaphor of the motherland. The desecration of the motherland signals a fall into history, into the discontinuities of modernity. The feminine becomes the sign of secure national identity, the body of the woman is both the site where a breach in national continuity and tradition has been effected (the result of the rape) but also the place where that breach may be healed, through a return 'home' from linguistic exile.

McGuckian's trope harbours a different politics; the mother is an extremely *unstable* guarantee of identity and patriarchal continuity. Her poetry repeatedly stresses women's dispossession and their *displaced* relation to the land, and therefore also the language – for there is a sexual as well as a racial element to dispossession. Continually and arbitrarily displaced, moved from one home, one piece of land to another, what kind of secure motherland can woman represent? Though the land may be represented as a woman, the woman herself has no rights over the land which is passed, along with her sexuality, from father to husband. But while authority and possession for women is always by chance 'slips', always second-hand, through motherhood the woman's relationship to the nation is supposed to be anything but secondary.[30] Women play a crucial role in the furtherance of the nation through their reproductive labour. As Gayatri Spivak points out in her essay on the short story 'Breast-giver', the term proletarian, defined as one who serves the state with no property but only with his offspring, carries an effaced mark of sexuality.[31] And specifically in the context of a national struggle mothering belongs to the sphere of politics and ideology, as rearing children becomes an investment in the future of the nation.

If the child in 'Act of Union' is symbolic of a bastard fifth column, the source of the trouble, in McGuckian's poem 'The Heiress' the male child is a way to regain land. In 'The Heiress' McGuckian allies the position of women to that of Gaelic Ulster – defeated by the plantation, dispossessed after the Flight of the Earls, they must retreat to higher, more barren ground. From her vantage point the woman addresses a man who reveals his 'good husbandry' in relation to her 'pinched grain'.[32] McGuckian has said that the genesis of the poem lies in the story of Mary Queen of Scots – denied her heritage in her own life, Mary's son became King James of England (during whose reign the major plantation of Ulster was carried out):

> But I am lighter of a son, through my slashed
> Sleeves the inner sleeves of purple keep remembering
> The moment exactly, remembering the birth
> Of an heiress means the gobbling of land.

Whereas her birth has led to the loss of land, the birth of a son through the 'slashed sleeves' of her Tudor dress and the torn body of the woman in childbirth, will regain the land (although Ulster will thereby be gobbled). So the heiress of the title is precisely the one who has been usurped; only through her children will she inherit. The final stanza implies that in order to regain her rightful position, the marginalised woman must place herself at the very limits of society – neither the hill nor the fields but the shore.

> I tell you dead leaves do not necessarily
> Fall; it is not coldness, but the tree itself
> That bids them go, preventing their destruction.
> So I walk along the beach, unruly, I drop
> Among my shrubbery of seaweed my black acorn buttons.

Here the sand is associated with fertility; the speaker

finds a place where she can plant the seed of her authority on the beach – which is without order and authority in itself (unruly).[33] The implication is that if the writer/woman is underrated, her poems/children may have citizenship, lend weight to her statement. Similarly, if Irish Catholics have been banished to barren ground, it is not by identification with the land that they will gain power. The intermediate realm between traditions, between land and sea, may be productive. In this way Ireland could be mother of a new history. But the problem with the poem is that by placing woman on the margin between history and flux, land and sea, the mother is reduced to a passage for history to pass through in the shape of her (male) child. Secondly, the poem does not offer an alternative to the use of the figure of the woman as a metaphor for the state of the nation. McGuckian seems to be simply reinflecting the identification of woman and land.

McGuckian's poem 'The Soil Map' may offer an alternative to the use of the figure of the woman as a metaphor for the nation. I read the poem as a parody of a 'place-name' or Dinnseanchas poem. Dinnseanchas was a major poetic genre in the Gaelic tradition, a celebration of rootedness, of knowing one's place through the etymological understanding of the roots of the place-name and the history that goes with it. In the typical scenario the poet's loving resurrection and exploration of the Irish or dialect name for the locality undoes the alien rape of the ruined maid, who can thus return to be 'possessed' by her rightful kin. McGuckian's poem is addressed to a house (biographically the large Victorian house where McGuckian lives in Belfast, in an area built for wealthy Anglo–Irish Protestants though now inhabited almost entirely by Catholic families). The soil map is of course the map of Ireland on which the house stands, but the house is also a woman: 'I am not a woman's man, but I can tell,/By the swinging of your two-leaf door,/You are never without one man in the shadow/Of another'. The woman in Irish myth who was 'never without one man in the shadow of another' was Queen Medhbh. Territorial goddess as well as legendary queen she conferred kingship on all those who slept with her. (She is self-possessed rather than possessive.) In contrast to the purity and chastity inscribed in the Aisling tradition the essence of the myth is sexual, and Medhbh is not a mother but a seductress. This woman/house has lifted her skirts to all comers. Irish and English, Protestant and Catholic. It is therefore not necessary to lay siege to the house, the woman does not need to take possession with the 'hardness' of a male, because the Anglo–Irish big house tradition has already failed: 'Anyone with patience can divine how your plaster work has lost key/The rendering about to come away'. So the house is 'open', but to ignore the tradition of previous inhabitants is foolhardy because the present includes the layer of Anglo–Irish history as it does the earlier pre-colonial era. Where Heaney's or Montague's place-name poems imply that it is possible to disinter from the land a piece of history that has remained untouched by subsequent events, as though the past could simply visit the present, McGuckian uses the metaphor of the mud on which Belfast is built, rather than bog. While the seepage and mud flats are the reason for the house not being well preserved, that wet soil has also caused all the historical traditions to become mixed up. The motherland is extremely unreliable:

> I appeal to the god who fashions edges
> Whether such turning points exist
> As these saltings we believe we move
> Away from, as if by simply shaking
> A cloak we could disbud ourselves,
> Dry out and cease to live there?

The saltings and movements of water have changed the lie of the land. The act of possession may give the

illusion of a break with previous history, but the poem
implies that the inhabitants of the North are rooted in a
contradictory position and it is useless to ignore any
strand of it.

So far woman and house again serve as allegorical
semes for the motherland; in opposition to the 'rape'
theory of colonisation the poem brings to the fore the
copulative as well as the reproductive body, stressing the
woman's active sexual desire. In fact McGuckian's self-
proclaimed 'modesty' of style veils a celebration of
sexual openness which itself stands as analogue for the
'opening up' of community. To combat the Catholic/
nationalist ideal of chaste, passive femininity, McGuckian foregrounds the unfaithfulness of both woman and
nation, thereby undercutting notions of racial purity.
But this identification fails to expand the thematics of
the woman's political body. The sexualisation of the
nationalist trope of the motherland is not going to help
transfer the woman from her status as ground of the
nationalist teleology to active participant in the nation's
history; but it is possible to focus on the figure of the
woman as gendered subject in the poem, rather than as a
metaphor for the nation. The place-names on this map,
which shows the contours of historical change, are
English women's Christian names - the only names
women tend to keep. Carrying women's identification
with the landscape to its logical conclusion, the Anglo-
Irish houses were built for women with English names,
and taking possession of the house should mean taking
on its female name:

> I have found the places on the soil map,
> Proving it possible once more to call
> Houses by their names, Annsgift or Mavisbank,
> Mount Juliet or Bettysgrove.

But the names are a joke since women, exchanged along
with the land, do not have the right to name it. It is

because of her economic dispossession rather than her sexual excess that woman is an unstable guarantee of the nationalist teleology. The land is not something she has lost along the way, something that has been usurped from her, but something she never owned.

Much of the force of the poem resides in what I have termed the characteristic 'personalisation' of public narratives engaged in by these poets. They aim to *disable* one aspect of myth's power – its claim to universality – introducing discontinuity into their version of the myths by privatising them, by taking them out of the public realm in which they are everybody's story and everybody knows their significance. But the poems in fact show that the woman's body is already public – thereby simultaneously calling into question public narratives of nationhood and community and the private (familial) narratives of traditional femininity on which they depend. At the same time, both Boland and McGuckian imply that one of the functions of their work is to 'speak for' the community of Irish women, though they differ radically in the strategies they adopt for such articulation. And yet this 'organicist' position, which assumes a continuity between the writer and her 'people', is denied by those very writing strategies which force a change in the relation between poet and community, and thus a structural alteration in the generic tradition.

# Notes

1. Seamus Heaney, 'Ocean's Love to Ireland', *North* (London, Faber and Faber, 1975), 46–7.
2. An essay of this length cannot hope to do justice to the diversity of women's poetry in Ireland. Indeed, it is through the differences between and among the poets discussed here and other writers such as Eilean Ni Chuilleanain, Nuala Ni Dhomnhaill and Rita Ann Higgins that notions of what constitutes the 'traditional'

Irish community are called into question. Two useful anthologies of Irish women's writing are *Pillars of the House: An anthology of verse by Irish women from 1690 to the present*, ed. A. A. Kelly (Dublin, Wolfhound, 1987) and *The Female Line: Northern Irish Women Writers*, ed. Ruth Hooley (Belfast, Northern Irish Women's Rights Movement, 1985).

3. Margaret Homans, *Women Writers and Poetic Identity* (Princeton, Princeton University Press, 1980), 11.

4. Ailbhe Smyth, 'The Floozie in the Jacuzzi', *The Irish Review*, 6 (Spring, 1989), 7-24.

5. *ibid.*, 9.

6. See Nuala Ni Dhomnhaill, *Selected Poems*, trans. Michael Hartnett (Dublin, Raven Arts, 1986).

7. See Proinsias MacCana, 'Women in Irish Mythology', *The Crane Bag*, 4 (1) (1980), 7-11, and Cullingford, 7-13 (see note 12).

8. See Jurij Tynyanov, 'On Literary Evolution', in *Readings in Russian Poetics*, eds. Ladislav Matejka and Krystyna Pomorska (Ann Arbor, Michigan Slavic Publications, 1978), 77.

9. Gearoid Denvir, 'Continuing the Link: an aspect of contemporary Irish poetry', *The Irish Review*, 3 40-54. In the same way Nic Dhiarmada claims that Ni Dhomnhaill's use of mythic personae enables her 'to explore what she considers to be the very essence of being female, especially the dark side of female nature'. As a counterbalance Anne O'Connor points out that such folkloric themes are not 'natural' or archetypal, but have ideological and propaganda value for contemporary definitions of femininity. See Nic Dhiarmada, 391-2 (see note 22), and Anne O'Connor, 'Images of the Evil Woman in Irish Folklore: A Preliminary Survey', *Feminism in Ireland*, 281-5.

10. Richard Kearney, *Transitions: Narratives in Modern Irish Culture* (Dublin, Wolfhound Press, 1988), 269-82. See also Seamus Deane 'Remembering the Irish Future', *The Crane Bag*, 8 (1) (1984), 81-92.

11. See David Cairns and Shaun Richards, *Writing Ireland: Colonialism, Nationalism and Culture* (Manchester, Manchester University Press, 1988).

12. See Elizabeth Cullingford, 'Thinking of her as Ireland', Paper presented at Yeats Annual Summer School, Sligo, 1988, and Kearney, 'Myth and Motherland', *Ireland's Field Day*, ed. Field Day Theatre Co. (London, Hutchinson, 1985), 61–80. See also David Lloyd, ' "Pap for the Dispossessed": Seamus Heaney and the Poetics of Identity', *Boundary 2* (Winter/Spring, 1985), 222–3.
13. Cullingford, 1 (see note 1).
14. See particularly the articles by Mark Patrick Hederman, Richard Kearney, Edna Longley and Conor Cruise O'Brien in *The Crane Bag*.
15. Seamus Heaney, 'Lost, Unhappy and at Home', Interview with Seamus Deane, *The Crane Bag*, 1 (1977), 66. It would of course be inaccurate to claim an uncritical celebration of the virtues of the organic society in contemporary Irish poetry – the vacillation between tradition and modernity in Heaney's poem 'Hercules and Antaeus' is a case in point. Nonetheless the very fact that the poem has achieved the status of a kind of text for our time and the fact that it is read as summing up the Irish dilemma goes some way to prove the strength of the rural, organicist nostalgia.
16. 'A Woman Poet in a National Tradition', *Studies*, **76** (Summer 1987), 152. See also Eavan Boland, 'The Woman Poet: Her Dilemma', *American Poetry Review* **16** (1) (January/February 1987), 17–20.
17. On a more general level, as Dillon Johnston points out in *Irish Poetry After Joyce*, much contemporary poetry reveals in its strategies of address an understanding of the breakdown of the putative 'unity of culture' of the Irish audience. In fact Johnston rightly intimates that such 'unity of culture' never existed, but was simply claimed as both result and evidence of Ireland's traditional communal identity. See Johnston, 'Toward a Broader and More Comprehensive Irish Identity', *Irish Poetry After Joyce* (Indiana, University of Notre Dame Press; Mountrath, The Dolmen Press, 1985), 247–72.
18. *Studies*, 156–7.
19. 'Mise Eire', *The Journey and Other Poems* (Manchester, Carcanet Press, 1987), 10.
20. In any case the woman's 'heritage' would not have been

the possession of land, a privilege reserved for eldest sons. Emigration, undertaken at a greater rate by women than men, though often a result of Ireland's disadvantaged economic relationship with Britain, was contributed to by the traditional system of land inheritance and marriage. See Beale, 33–40 (note 21). For a brilliant overall study of Irish emigration see Kerby A. Miller, *Emigrants and Exiles, Ireland and the Irish Exodus to North America* (Oxford, Oxford University Press, 1985).

21. For example, women's traditional familial role was institutionalised in the Republic by a marriage bar which forced women in certain jobs to give them up on marriage. For a general study of the ideology of femininity in the Irish Republic see Jenny Beale, *Women in Ireland: Voices of Change* (Basingstoke, Macmillan, 1986).

22. In the Gaelic poetic tradition this traditional division is encapsulated in the generic separation of the (male) role of professional poet from 'feminine' modes of love and grieving poetry. Briona Nic Dhiarmada points out that 'The professional poet or 'file' with his socially integrated status generally spoke through conventions and on behalf of the tribe rather than personally'. See 'Tradition and the Female Voice in Contemporary Gaelic Poetry', *Women's Studies International Forum: Feminism in Ireland*, ed. Ailbhe Smyth (New York, Pergamon Press, 1988). Nic Dhiarmada notes that a fusion of 'traditional' and 'personal' modes has a precedent in the Danta Gra of the late seventeenth century. See also Eilean Ni Chuilleanain, 'Women as Writers: Danta Gra to Maria Edgeworth', *Irish Women: Image and Achievement*, ed. Ni Chuilleanain (Dublin, Arien House, 1985) 111–26.

23. Personal interview, November 1986.

24. Personal interview, November 1986.

25. See *Venus and the Rain* (Oxford, Oxford University Press, 1984) and *The Flower Master* (Oxford, Oxford University Press, 1982).

26. This strategy of 'resistance' has similar ties with Luce Iragaray's advocation of 'riddling' enigmatic discourse to women as a way of undoing their objectivication, although there are obviously important differences between Irigaray's radical feminist deconstruction of

representation and McGuickian's stated wish to 'educate' a male audience in the complexities of femininity.

27. Personal interview, January 1986.
28. Seamus Heaney, 'Act of Union', *North*, 49–50.
29. Witness Heaney's description of the roots of the troubles: 'To some extent the enmity can be viewed as a struggle between the cults and devotees of a god and a goddess. There is an indigenous territorial numen, a tutelar of the whole island, call her Mother Ireland, Kathleen ni Houlihan, the poor old woman, the Shan Van Vocht, whatever; and her sovereignty has been temporarily usurped or infringed by a new male cult whose founding fathers were Cromwell, William of Orange, Edward Carson, and whose godhead is incarnate in a Rex or Caesar resident in a palace in London. What we have is the tail end of a struggle in a province between territorial piety and imperial power', *Preoccupations, Selected Prose 1968–78* (London, Faber and Faber, 1979), 57. On this opposition between a mythic motherland and a historical masculinity see David Trotter, *The Making of the Reader: Language and Subjectivity in Modern American, English and Irish Poetry* (Basingstoke, Macmillan, 1984), 188.
30. See McGuckian's poem 'Slips' in *The Flower Master*.
31. Gayatri Chakravorty Spivak, 'A Literary Representation of the Subaltern: A Woman's Text from the Third World', *In Other Worlds* (London, Methuen, 1987), 252, 255.
32. See Cairns and Richards, 28, and Seamus Deane, 'Civilians and Barbarians', *Ireland's Field Day*, 33, on the colonisers' use of metaphors of husbandry during and after the plantation, in arguing for the necessity to combat Irish wildness by planting and cultivating English civility.
33. See Heaney's poem 'Shore Woman', which takes as its epigraph the Gaelic proverb – 'Man to the hills, woman to the shore', *Wintering Out* (London, Faber and Faber, 1972), 66.

# Index